Copyright © Hansib Publishing Limited, 1994.

First published in 1994 jointly by Hansib Publishing Limited, Third Floor, Tower House, 141-149 Fonthill Road, London N4 3HF England, and Hansib Publishing (Caribbean) Limited, P O Box 2773, St John's, Antigua, Westindies.

Production by Hansib Publishing Limited.
Colour origination by Graphic Ideas Studios, London.
Printed in the United Kingdom by Bath Press Colourbooks, Glasgow.

The information given in this publication on accommodation, restaurants, business services, events and activities have been provided as a guide and are subject to change. Any omissions are entirely unintentional.

British Library Cataloguing in Publication Data.
A catalogue record for this book is available from the British Library.

ISBN 1-870518-29-2

INSIDE FRONT COVER
The Carenage and harbour, St George's

INSIDE BACK COVER
View of St George's and harbour, 1851, taken from Belmont showing the former barracks on Richmond Hill (now the Prison) on the right and Fort George on the left.
Drawn by Capt H A Turner, Royal Artillery
Courtesy: Alice Carlsson

GRENADA
CARRIACOU • PETIT MARTINIQUE

Spice Island of the Caribbean

HANSIB

Grand Anse Beach

Grand Etang Nature Reserve

Gouyave, one of Grenada's leading fishing communities

Sandy Island, off Carriacou

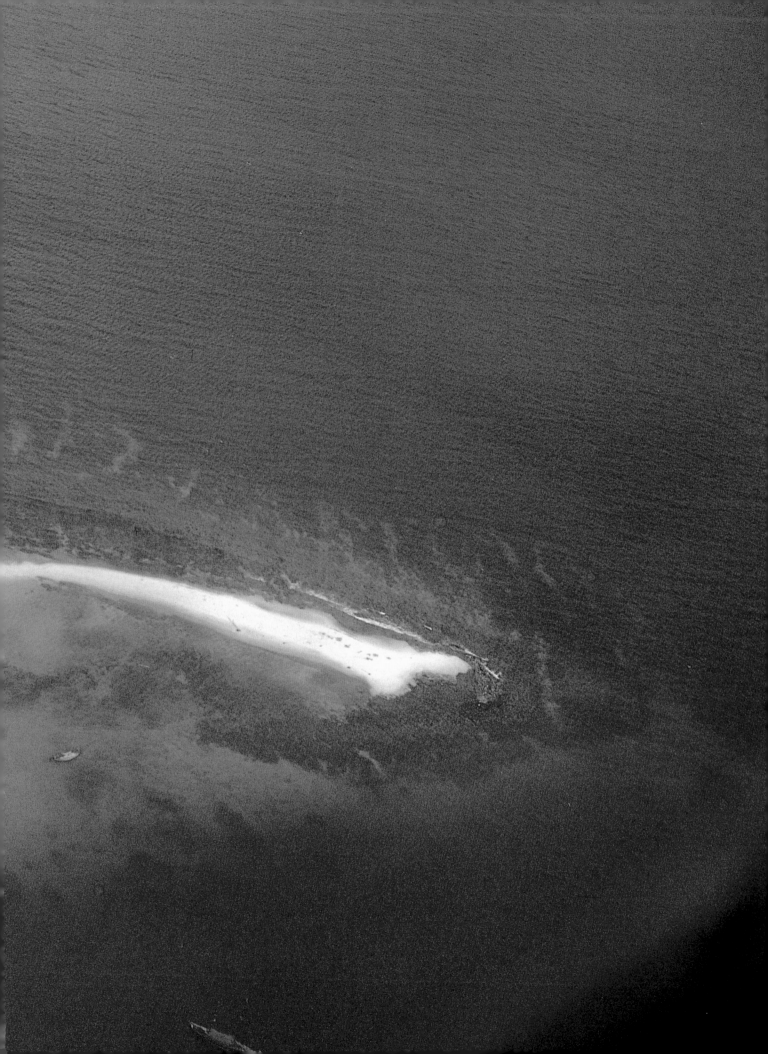

Supporters of this book

The Grenada Board of Tourism and Hansib Publishing Limited thank the following businesses and organisations without whose support this book would not have been possible.

Abbot Grenada Ltd
Frequente Industrial Park,
P O Box 654, St George's,
Grenada. Tel: 809-444 4674
Fax: 809-444 4805

Airlines of Carriacou Ltd
Point Salines International
Airport, Point Salines,
Grenada. Tel: 809-444 3549
Fax: 809-444 2898

Aquarium Restaurant
P O Box 496, Point Salines,
St George's, Grenada.
Tel: 809-444 1410

Arnolds Tours
P O Box 438, 611 Archibald
Avenue, St George's, Grenada.
Tel: 809-440 0531/2213
Fax: 809-440 4118

Caribbean Agro Industries Ltd
P O Box 251, Mount Gay,
St George's, Grenada.
Tel: 809-440 2954/3141
Fax: 809-440-4154

Flamboyant Hotel & Cottages
P O Box 214, Grand Anse
Beach, Grenada.
Tel: 809-444 4247
Fax: 809-444 1234

Embassy of the Republic of China
P.O. Box 36, Archibald Avenue,
St. George's, Grenada.
Tel: 809-440 3054
Fax: 809-440 4177/6622

Funtours Ltd
P O Box 425, Le Marquis
Complex, Grand Anse,
St George's, Grenada.
Tel: 809-444 3167
Fax: 809-444 2840

Geo. F. Huggins & Co. (G'da) Ltd
P O Box 46, Grand Etang Road,
St George's, Grenada.
Tel: 809-440 2031/35
Fax: 809-440 4129

Grenada Bank of Commerce Ltd
P O Box 4, St George's,
Grenada. Tel: 809-440 3521,
Fax: 809-440 4153

Grenada Co-Op Nutmeg Association
P.O. Box 174, Lagoon Road,
St George's, Grenada.
Tel: 809-440 2217
Fax: 809-440 6602

Grenada Sugar Factory
Woodlands, St George's,
Grenada.
Tel: 809-444 5373/5736
Fax: 809-444 2482

Grenada Telecommunications Ltd
P O Box 119, St George's,
Grenada. Tel: 809-440 1000
Fax: 809-440 2123

Horse Shoe Beach Hotel
Lance Aux Epines, St George's,
Grenada. Tel: 809-444 4410
Fax: 809-444 4844

Independence Agencies Ltd
P O Box 218, St George's,
Grenada.
Tel: 809-440 2615/2008
Fax: 809-440-4126

Jonas Browne & Hubbard (G'da) Ltd
P O Box 25, St George's,
Grenada. Tel: 809-440 2087
Fax: 809-440 4008

LIAT (1974) Ltd
The Carenage, St George's,
Grenada. Tel: 809-440 2796

Investment & Agencies Ltd
Kayam's Tyres, The Carenage,
St George's, Grenada.
Tel: 809-440 2312/6500
Fax: 809-440 1251

L L Ramdhanny & Co Ltd
P O Box 382, St George's,
Grenada. Tel: 809-444 4793
Fax: 809-444 2852

McIntyre Brothers Ltd
P O Box 70, St George's,
Grenada. Tel: 809-444 3944
Fax: 809-444 2899

National Insurance Scheme
Melville Street, St George's,
Grenada. Tel: 809-440 3309
Fax: 809-440 6636

National Water & Sewerage Authority
P O Box 392, The Carenage,
St George's, Grenada.
Tel: 809-440 2155
Fax: 809-440 4107

No Problem Apartments
P O Box 280, St George's,
Grenada. Tel: 809-444 4634
Fax: 809 444 2803

New Trends Tours
P O Box 797, St George's,
Grenada. Tel: 809- 444 1236
Fax: 809-444 4836

Q & K Spice Sunsation Ltd
P O Box 856, Le Marquis
Complex, No.22, Grand Anse,
St George's, Grenada.
Tel: 809-444 1656
Fax: 809-444 2836

Rudolf's Restaurant & Bar
The Carenage, St George's,
Grenada. Tel: 809-440 2241

Secret Harbour Hotel
Lance Aux Epines, St George's,
Grenada. Tel: 809-444 4439
Fax: 809-444 4819

Silver Beach Resort
Hillsborough, Carriacou.
Tel: 809-443 7337
Fax: 809-443 7165

Sissons Paints (G'da) Ltd
P O Box 25, St George's,
Grenada.
Tel: 809-444 4157/1457
Fax: 809-444 1676

Spice Island Marine Services Ltd
P O Box 449, Prickly Bay,
Lance Aux Epines, St George's,
Grenada. Tel: 809-444 4257
Fax: 809-444 2816

Tomlin Voss Associates
P O Box 570, True Blue Mall,
St George's, Grenada.
Tel: 809-444 3016/7
Fax: 809-444 2856

Trans-Nemwil Insurance (G'da) Ltd
P O Box 221, St George's,
Grenada.
Tel: 809-440 3099/1585
Fax: 809-440 4113

Vanel's Enterprises Ltd
1A Frequente Industrial Park,
St George's, Grenada.
Tel: 809-444 2052/3
Fax: 809-440 2051

Vena Bullen & Sons
Hillsborough, Carriacou.
Tel: 809-443 7468
Fax: 809-443 8194

W E Julien & Co Ltd
P O Box 76, Young Street,
St George's, Grenada.
Tel: 809-440 2046/9
Fax: 809-440 2301

Contents

Acknowledgements.........................12
Messages......................................14
About the main contributors............15
Foreword......................................16
The National Flag.........................18
The Pledge & National Anthem........20
The National Coat of Arms..............21
About the country..........................22
The Parishes of Grenada.................42
St George *42*, St David *54*, St Andrew *58*, St Patrick *64*,
St Mark *69*, St John *72*

HISTORY
From colony to democracy..............80
National leaders since Independence.........90
Important historical dates and events........100
The first Grenadians......................102
Grenada's "Back-to-Front" Forts.........110
The night "Janet" invaded Grenada...........116
The Saga of the Bianca C................118
Grenada's Non-Standard English...............126

CULTURE
Carnival......................................136
Cannes Brulee *140*, Traditional Mas *142*, Calypso *144*,
Jab-Jab *146*, History Mas *146*, Wild Indians *148*,
Shortknee *148*, Pierrot *150*
Dance...154
Folk and Dance Groups *154*, Traditional Dances *156*
Folk tales...................................158
Carriacou Dance............................162
Quadrille Dance *164*, Big Drum Dance *166*
The Feasts of Carriacou..................170
Local Artists...............................174
Carriacou's seafaring culture..........180

NATURE
Geological history.........................188
Natural vegetation.........................194
Wildlife.....................................200

SPICES
Grenada's spices...........................210
The Nutmeg Story...........................216
There's a secret in the Nutmeg...............222
Recipes using Nutmeg *224*

INDUSTRY AND COMMERCE
An OECS first...............................225
General information........................226
Commercial outline.........................230
Business organisations....................234
Fishery resources..........................242
Trade Agreements...........................248
Incentives..................................250
Business contacts..........................252

FOR THE RECORD
Lord Pitt *253*, Grenada's Miss World *253*

SPORT AND LEISURE
Cricket *254*, Football *254*, Hashing *256*, Triathlon *258*,
Golf *262*, Yachting *264*, Game fishing *272*, Diving *274*

GUIDE
General information *282*, Sights around the country *284*,
Annual events *286*, Accommodation *288*, Eating out *296*,
Things to do *298*, Arriving by yacht *300*, Useful numbers *303*

Acknowledgements

More than anything else, our thanks must go to Grenada, Carriacou and Petit Martinique and to their people for providing the inspiration behind a project such as this, which could only have succeeded with the help, support, faith and enthusiasm of very many individuals and organisations.

It is only fair that I should first mention Wayne Francis, as in many respects this book was his "baby". He was instrumental in raising the matter with me and he has been on board throughout. It was Wayne who arranged my meeting with Prime Minister Nicholas Brathwaite - who immediately took up the idea with enthusiasm, even passion - and with Jude Bernard, the equally receptive former Director of Tourism. I must express similar thanks to Jennifer Francis, a pioneering businesswoman in both Britain and the Caribbean and former Black Businesswoman of the Year in Britain, who immersed herself in support from the earliest days and to Ron Sanders who also supported the project early on. My dear friend Ros Howells, a hyperactive community worker was always there for advice. Wayne , Jennifer and Ros are of Grenadian background themselves and their belief in the project proved a major factor in its successful completion.

An even more crucial role was played by Mario Bullen, the country's present Director of Tourism, who took up his enthusiasm for the project simultaneously with his appointment. It was Mario who facilitated the visit to Hansib's London offices by Grenada's Minister for Tourism, the Hon. Tillman Thomas. Before that meeting ended, both parties had agreed to pursue the project, convinced that it would facilitate Grenada's self-esteem and the promotion of its place in the world. Indeed it must be said that without Mario this book would not have been possible.

A project of this nature needs a reliable and committed team, from the sketching of the broad outline through to the last intricate details. Coordination of these efforts was entrusted to the people responsible for the success of the precursor volumes in this series - the two editions of *Antigua and Barbuda: A Little Bit of Paradise* and *Dominica: Nature Island of the Caribbean*. Special Projects Manager, John Hughes once again displayed a level of enthusiasm that I cannot find words to either describe or appreciate. Equally committed was Hansib Director Shareef Ali. To these two trusted colleagues above all must go the plaudits for this worthy contribution. Other members of the team also deserve a mention, particularly Hansib's Political Editor Keith Bennett, who took a keen interest in the draft manuscript and made a number of helpful suggestions, as well as to Sayrah Burrows, Natasha Persaud, James Jhuman, Ella Barnes, Alan Cross and Adam Licudi. The Grenadian-born photographer, Angus Thompson, took time from his busy schedule to make three trips to Grenada so as to expedite the project.

Thanks must, of course, go to the writers, Alister Hughes and Norma Sinclair and to the other contributors, Christine David, John Benjamin and David Macnaghten who provided not only high quality and authentic information, but also local expertise, insight, background, patriotism, culture, compassion and humour.

But what would a work of this nature be without photographs? Thanks here go to project photographer Angus Thompson, with valuable contributions from Jim Rudin, Julia Emerson, Gary-John Norman, Niki Weidinger, Andrew Bierzynski, Joe K Sylvester, David Macnaghten, Robert L Evans, Heather Bruce, Ruth E Rouse, Maria Hamlet, Winston T Fleary, Paul Slinger, Henry De Allie, D Greasley, G R E Bullen, John Hughes and Shareef Ali. Also thanks to The Grenada National Folk Group, *The Informer*, Grenada Board of Tourism, Grenada National Museum, Carriacou Museum, Rainbow City Festival Committee, Grenada National Parks, Grenada Industrial Development Corporation, the

Government of Grenada, Allsport, Rex Features, Hansib Picture Library and to Alice Carlsson and W Dierterle for the supply of lithographs and sketches.

Among the other individuals, organisations and publications to which we referred to whom I must express my thanks are Edwin Frank, Celine Bullen, Brenda Gibbs, Beverly Renwick, Theresa Francis, Brenda Douglas, Winston T Fleary, Esther Fleary, Shirley Robinson, Jean Pitt, Dr James Pitt, Dana Beck, Ann Marie Marecheau, Theresa La Touche, Sonja Fletcher, Elizabeth Gormon, Werner Nagel, Leo Charles, Dawne Preiswerk-Fletcher, Cassandra Cox Peters, Randolf Mark, Rachael Ramsay, Reynold Francis, Robert L Evans, Shaba (Dexter Edwards), Canute Calliste, Clemencia Alexander, Candace Bartholomew, Cheryl Jarvis, James Benoit, Arnold Cruickshank, Marcia Linton, Sherrie Thomas, Michael Phillips, Carla Briggs, Beverley Reynolds, John De Roche, Mary Bartholomew, Andrew Bierzynski, George Grant and the crew of Rhum Runner, Lin and Norris Nelson of Sunsation Tours, Clement Charles, Nellie Payne, Yolande Joseph (SADO), *Folklore of Carriacou* by Christine David, *Greeting Tourist Guide, Grenada Newsletter, Spicy Grenada, The Grenadian Voice, The Informer, Grenada Guardian, Grenada Today, Discover Grenada. - Carriacou & Petit Martinique, Architectural Heritage of Grenada, Grenada Beacon, The Business Eye, Caribbean Companion* by Brian Dyde, *Trinidad Guardian, The Times* (London), *The Westindian, Grenada's Unforgettable Past* by Randolph Mark, *Winban Newsletter*, Grenada National Trust, *The Carriacou Regatta, Rainbow City Festival, Plan and Policy for a System of National Parks and Protected Areas, Forestry in Grenada, Grenada Environmental Policy*, Grenada Hotel Association, Grenada Chamber of Industry and Commerce, *Grenada Sailing Week Programme, Sailors Guide to the Windward Islands* by Chris Doyle, *More Than You Ever Wanted to Know About Nutmeg* by Merrylee Vernazza, *The Nature of the Islands - Plants and Animals of the Eastern Caribbean* by Virginia Barlow, *Birds of the West Indies* by James Bond, *Flowers of the Caribbean, A Short History of the West Indies* by J H Parry, Phillip Sherlock & Anthony Maingot, *A New System of Slavery* by Hugh Tinker, *History of Slavery* by Susanne Everett, *Grenada: The Struggle Against Destabilisation* by Chris Searle, *Farmers Guide to Cocoa Production, Weekend Nation (Barbados), Grenada Spice Isle Homemakers Cookbook* by Grenada Homemaker's Association, *A Local's Guide to Carriacou, Liat Islander*, the Organisers of Intercol Sports Day and Patrick at Grenadian Sky Ride.

Special thanks must go to Senator Godfrey Ventour and staff at No Problem Apartments, the management and staff at Silver Beach Resort Carriacou, Maitlands Car Rentals, Helenair and Snagg's Water Taxis for their terrific support given to the Hansib team and to BWIA International, Caledonian Airways, British Airways and Geest Industries for transporting copies of this book to Grenada free of charge.

Indeed, a project of this nature needs the support of hundreds, if not thousands, of people. This is particularly so as Grenada, in common with many other small nations, cannot always commit the necessary resources to the external promotion of the country. **This book is also, therefore, a tribute to the patriotism of the Grenadian business community who have shown their commitment to their country and this project by placing sufficient pre-publication orders to ensure its success.**

To all concerned, I send my appreciation and thanks, and ask your forgiveness if you have inadvertently been omitted.

Arif Ali
London, October 1994

Messages

Message from the Prime Minister

It gives me great pleasure to be associated with the publication of this unique book *Grenada - Spice Island of the Caribbean*.

I recall that about three years ago, Mr Arif Ali of Hansib Publishing Limited, having successfully published a similar book for some of our neighbouring OECS countries, approached my government with a proposal to publish what has today become a reality. At the time, my government was too preoccupied with other pressing matters and quite frankly did not have the available resources to pursue the proposal to finality. That is why I am extremely happy to note that the Grenada Board of Tourism, with the active encouragement of the Minister of Tourism, Senator the Honourable Tillman Thomas and its Director, Mr G R E (Mario) Bullen took up the challenge and worked assiduously to make this historic publication a reality.

Let me therefore extend sincere congratulations to all those associated with the publication of *Grenada - Spice Island of the Caribbean*. A perusal of its pages reveals that not only does the book depict every aspect of life of our tri-island state of Grenada, Carriacou and Petit Martinique, but in addition, it includes a portrayal of our history, culture, sports, politics, industry and commerce and above all, tourism. As such, it is a useful instrument for promoting tourism both at home and abroad, not to mention its use as an encyclopaedic reference manual.

My government has demonstrated in innumerable ways it unwavering support for the advancement of the country's tourism industry. In this regard, and bearing in mind that my government has recognised tourism as the main growth sector of the economy both in the immediate future and in the medium term, we will continue to ensure that tourism growth continues along lines that will lead to sustainability and environmental preservation and conservation.

A book of this nature will undoubtedly serve to portray our country and our people in a positive light and encourage people to visit our lovely isles of the sea. My understanding is that the most knowledgeable persons have provided contributions of the highest calibre to this publication, thereby guaranteeing accuracy and authenticity of the information about our country.

It is therefore, with great pleasure that I take this opportunity, on behalf of the government and people of Grenada, to wish you enjoyable reading of this fascinating, illustrative publication about Grenada, Carriacou and Petit Martinique.

Rt Hon Nicholas Brathwaite
Prime Minister
Grenada

Message from the Minister of Tourism

Several months ago when the Grenada Board of Tourism informed me of the approach by Hansib Publishing Limited to produce a comprehensive promotional book about Grenada, Carriacou and Petit Martinique, I welcomed the initiative and advised our Director of Tourism, Mr G R E (Mario) Bullen of the full support of both my ministry and my government for a publication of this nature.

Now that the publication has been completed, it is indeed a great honour for me as Minister of Tourism, Civil Aviation and Social Development to be associated with it and to be given the opportunity to dedicate a message to all whose good fortune it is to peruse a copy of *Grenada - Spice Island of the Caribbean*. It is my sincere hope that it will provide many happy hours, and indeed, years of happy reading and reflection to all those who will continually use it as an invaluable and encyclopaedic reference manual.

In welcoming this opportunity to be associated with this historic publication, let me first of all extend congratulations to all those who conceptualized it and dedicated many hours of arduous work towards its completion. Such an invaluable reference manual was long overdue and I am positive that it will generate a positive impact in the market place.

As you peruse the wealth of information and spectacular photography contained within the pages of this book it is the hope of my ministry and the Grenada Board of Tourism that you will find it to be a perfect memento of your stay among our people, or even be an ideal gift to relatives and friends who are yet to discover the charm, beauty and hospitality of our islands and our people.

My government recognises the importance of a balanced and sustainable tourism industry. This, particularly within the context of the impact this industry will continue to have on the growth of other salient sections of Grenada's economy. My government is therefore confident that the agricultural sector, along with fisheries, forestry, construction and transportation will proportionally expand as the efforts to build Grenada's

tourism continues.

We are fully supportive of the thrust by the Grenada Board of Tourism to attract significant numbers of visitors from all tourism generating markets - Europe, North America, the wider Caribbean and further afield. In fact, involvement as a government to facilitate these efforts are clearly indicated in our readiness to introduce legislation to ensure that the sector is minimally affected by negative influences. The development and expansion of our country's infrastructure and the enhancement of our tourism attractions to ensure visitors satisfaction is also indicative of the importance that my ministry and my government attach to our developing tourist industry.

As Minister of Tourism, I wish to take this opportunity to wish you pleasant reading of this most wonderful publication.

Senator the Honourable
Tillman Thomas
Minister of Tourism, Civil Aviation
and Social Development

Message from the Director of Tourism

This book, *Grenada - Spice Island of the Caribbean* is the first of its kind and it therefore gives me great pleasure to be associated with the first edition of this historic publication.

In September, 1993, shortly after assuming duties as Director of Tourism, I was contacted by Arif Ali of Hansib Publishing Limited who referred me to a proposal submitted two years previously to the Grenada Government for the publication of a book on our tri-island state. This proposal was then pursued by our Minister of Tourism, Senator the Honourable Tillman Thomas and myself during our visit to World Travel Market in November 1993. The Grenada Board of Tourism subsequently endorsed the proposal and in January 1994 contacted Hansib Publishing Limited to proceed with publication of the book and despite various delays the publication has now become a reality.

I would like, on behalf of the Grenada Board of Tourism, to express sincere appreciation to all those companies and individuals who, by their support and encouragement helped to make this unique publication a reality.

A book of this nature serves many purposes. Its 304 pages of editorial and over 500 photographs vividly depict every facet of life of our tri-island state of Grenada, Carriacou and Pétit Martinique, portraying our culture, history, sport, politics, industry and commerce and above all the natural beauty and diversity of our islands. Indeed it is the book's potential for promoting Grenada's tourism both at home and abroad which ensured its endorsement by the Grenada Board of Tourism in the first place. However, *Grenada - Spice Island of the Caribbean* is more than a tourism and pictorial guide. It is also a useful source of information and education for use in our schools, while its comprehensive reference section makes it an invaluable tool for promoting trade, industry and commerce.

G R E (Mario) Bullen
Director of Tourism

About the main contributors

Angus Thompson is a Grenadian living and working in London where his West End studio has been established for over fifteen years. Among his clients are Avis, Revlon, Dunhill and artists (the late) Marvin Gaye, Duran Duran and senior members of government. He specialises in promotional, commercial and advertising photography.

Alister Hughes was born in Grenada in 1919 and his working life has seen him rise from an office clerk to a well-known writer and distinguished journalist. He has received honorary awards and a doctorate in recognition of his dedication and achievements.

Norma Sinclair, a retired bank official who was born and brought up in Grenada, has seen her interest in her country and its people develop to the stage where she became a member of the Grenada National Trust and Historical Society. Also the President of the Society of Friends of the Blind, she has written a guide book on Grenada and is also a writer of short stories.

Christine David is the Principal of Harvey Vale Government School in Carriacou and is a tireless campaigner for the maintenance of, and research into, the rich culture of Carriacou. Her main interests lie in the Big Drum Dance and Tombstone Feast, and she founded the Carriacou Carib Organisation which performs the Big Drum Dance for the general public. She has published two books, *Carriacou Culture* and *Folklore of Carriacou*.

Jim Rudin opened Grenada's first art gallery in 1968. He studied at the New York Institute of Photography and served four years in the US Navy. Following a stint in his father's neon sign business, he studied in New York for a BA degree in art history and literature and subsequently worked in the Rights and Reproductions Department at the New York Museum of Modern Art. Cold winters encouraged him to move to Grenada.

Julia Emerson grew up in northern California, USA, and was educated in both that country and Switzerland. She has worked as a teacher and an administrative assistant, as well as in public relations and photography.

John Benjamin was born in Paraclete, St Andrew and moved to Sauteurs, St Patrick when he was eleven, where he lived for five years. He has a keen interest in the culture of Carnival in Grenada and his childhood recollections of Carnival are particularly noteworthy.

David Macnaghten is a diving instructor and manager of Dive Grenada, based at the Grenada Renaissance Hotel on Grand Anse Beach.

Foreword

Grenada, Carriacou and Petit Martinique - Spice Island of the Caribbean is the fourth in Hansib's series of original and creative guides to the countries and peoples of the Caribbean. As with our two books on Antigua and Barbuda and our book on Dominica, we have aimed to produce a work of lasting value, one that will give pride and pleasure to the country's nationals and promote its image and reputation around the world in the areas of tourism, business, investment, culture, history and politics.

This book, like its predecessors, is not meant as an academic text, but rather as an overview that can serve as the panorama of a nation. I feel that Grenada, in particular, can surely benefit from such a work of national pride, promotion and upliftment. The country's recent history has been a turbulent one. Coup, assassination and invasion are all words that must come to mind as one surveys the recent developmental journey of this beautiful three-island state. But happily such words as reconciliation, development and democracy have also found their place. The tragic and turbulent events of just over a decade ago have no doubt left their mark, but, particularly when one considers the fate of numerous other countries, and how ancient quarrels have festered and, in recent times, erupted with such savage and dreadful consequences in numerous parts of the world, one can only praise Grenada - its people and government - for how well past tragedies have been put to one side as a confident, democratic and increasingly stable country confidently charts its advance in the region and the wider world. Indeed, some of the 'Nelson Mandela-qualities' of forgiveness, tolerance, understanding and compromise that have been writ large in the South African context also find their place in Grenada's current march of progress.

The qualities and maturity displayed by Grenada and its people in emerging from the days of turbulence, division and uncertainty are precisely the qualities needed to further promote tourism and inward investment. They are also realistic and attainable requirements for continued progress and for enhancement and improvement in the quality and standard of life to be enjoyed by all sections of the people. Tourism, of course, can be a precarious and capricious industry and it is, therefore, most gratifying that the government, Tourist Board and people appear united in explaining, safeguarding and investing in the importance of both the natural attributes of sand, sea, sun and their natural environment, as well as the most important resource of any nation, its people. Grenada's people, certainly as much as any other people on earth, enjoy a well-

Publisher's note

To avoid repetition, and to ensure that the diversity of culture and customs are included in this work, the publishers have focussed on the culture and customs from a selection of areas in the country. The fact that Grenada, Carriacou and Petit Martinique are islands has crystalised their separate and unique customs which have survived colonial suppression. Many variations of the same cultural occasions and events exist throughout the country. Any omissions do not imply that traditions perculiar to an area are less noteworthy.

House style

Readers unfamiliar with Hansib's publications may note the use of 'Westindies' (not 'West Indies'). This has been used in all Hansib publications since 1973 in a tribute to the formation of the Caribbean Community (CARICOM) at Chaguaramas, Trinidad, on 4 July 1973 and as an appropriation of the name given by the "discoverers" to assert the region's united, unique and distinctive identity.

deserved reputation for friendliness, courtesy and hospitality.

In producing this book, Hansib hopes to have done something to put the country in the positive and optimistic light that its current circumstances and prospects warrant. It is suitable for home or overseas readers, tourists or investors, historians, students or general readers. I feel confident in stating that it will make a worthy addition to your library or that of a family member or friend.

Forming as it does part of our still-developing Caribbean series, it is the most earnest wish of myself and my colleagues that *Grenada, Carriacou and Petit Martinique - Spice Island of the Caribbean*, together with its companion volumes, both those already published and those still to come, can make a modest contribution to the greater goal of Caribbean integration and Caribbean unity. The unity of the Caribbean and its peoples is a cause that Hansib has always believed in. Recent developments in the international arena - the formation of NAFTA, the North American Free Trade Area; the expansion and consolidation of the European Union (EU); and the emergence of powerful blocs in the Asia-Pacific Region make this timeless goal more relevant than ever. It is a cause for which the citizens of the Caribbean must assume responsibility and to which we at Hansib are pledged to contribute.

Arif Ali
Hansib Publishing
London, October 1994

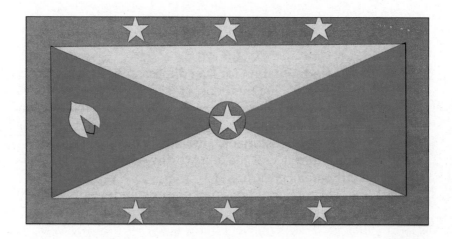

The National Flag

The National Flag of Grenada represents the distillation of a national effort to produce an emblem of a nation that can stand for all time and which incorporates simplicity of form, a pleasing visual quality and, not least, is symbolic of the confidence, hope and aspirations of a courageous people accepting the challenge of nationhood.

The components of the flag have the following significance:

Red: represents the fervour of the people, their courage and vitality - their burning aspiration to be free. The red border is indicative of their dedication to preserve harmony and unity of spirit.

Gold: the colour representative of wisdom also holds significance for Grenadians - a representation of the sun, their islands in the sun, the warmth and friendliness of their people.

Green: symbolises the fertility of the land, the lush vegetation and the islands' agriculture.

The **Seven Gold Stars**: represents the seven parishes and the hopes, aspirations and ideas upon which the nation was founded.

The **Nutmeg**: represents the reputation as the Isle of Spice and its traditional link with the economy.

Flag dimensions

The dimensions of the National Flag shall be in the following proportions:

Flown on land: five to three (5:3)

Flown at sea: two to one (2:1)

The following code should be observed in relation to the flag:

The flag is to be regarded as the sacred emblem of the nation to be paid due reverence and devotion by all its citizens.

The flag should never be allowed to touch the ground or floor nor should it be flown or used for purely decorative purposes on anything that is for temporary use and likely to be discarded, except on state occasions.

The Houses of Parliament, St George's

Etiquette associated with the National Flag

National Flag on display with other flags and emblems

No other flag, colour, standard, ensign or other emblem should be displayed above or to the right of the National Flag, that is the observer's left facing. All other flags flown together with the National Flag of Grenada should be placed to the left of it.

When the flags of two or more nations are displayed together they are to be flown from separate staffs of the same height and all the flags should be, as far as possible, of the same size. The flag of one nation should not be displayed above that of another.

When the National Flag is flown in a group with local flags, standards, ensigns, or emblems, such as those belonging to our city, boroughs, institutions, societies, organisations etc., it should be at the centre and at the highest point in the group.

When the National Flag and any other flag or flags are displayed from crossed staffs against a wall, the National Flag should be on the right with its staff placed in front of any other staff.

The Grenadian Flag should never be smaller than any other flag flown at the same time. When the flag becomes worn and must be replaced it should be burnt and not used for any other purpose than that for which it was designed.

No other flag should be placed above or to the right of the Grenadian Flag, except at foreign embassies, consulates and missions.

Except at foreign embassies, consulates and missions - no foreign flag may be flown publicly, unless the Flag of Grenada is also flown.

All merchant ships of Grenadian registration should fly the flag.

The flag when carried in procession with another flag or flags should be on the marching right, or, if there is a line of flags, in front of the centre of that line.

The flag should not be draped over vehicles of any sort except on military, police and state occasions.

The flag should be flown in or near every polling station on election day.

The National Flag should not be dipped to any person or thing.

The National Flag should not be used for purpose of adornment or advertising without the prior permission of the appropriate government authority. It should not be printed or reproduced on articles of clothing or furniture without permission as stated above.

The flag should not have placed on it or attached to it any mark, insignia, letter, word, figure, design, picture or drawing.

The flag should not be used as a receptacle for receiving, holding, carrying or delivering anything.

The flag should not be tied in a bowknot or rosette or used as drapings.

The flag should not be displayed, used or stored in a manner as would permit it to be easily torn, soiled or damaged.

The flag should not be allowed to touch anything beneath it.

Flying the National Flag at night

The National Flag should not be flown after sunset, except inside a building. However, on important ceremonial occasions, the flag may be displayed in the open after sunset when it should be floodlit if possible.

The flag should be flown at half-mast as a sign of official mourning when so declared by the Prime Minister's Office for a period determined by this office.

The flag, when flown at half-mast, should be first hoisted to the peak for an instant and then lowered slowly to the half-mast position. It should be again raised to the peak before it is lowered.

During the ceremony of hoisting or lowering the flag or when the flag, is passing in a parade or in a review, all persons present should face the flag and stand at attention. Persons in uniform should salute. Men should remove their hats.

When the National Flag is flown with other flags it must be the first to go up and the last to come down. It must never be lowered while other flags are flying or are being hoisted.

The flag should be flown on all government and municipal buildings and offices, on or near the main administrative building, but it is recommended that if possible each day it should be lowered at sundown and raised at 8.00 am.

The flag should be flown on all government-aided schools when the school is in session.

At the beginning and end of each term there should be a special flag raising and lowering ceremony so organised that performance in the ceremony should be regarded as a special privilege.

It would be appropriate for any school to have a special flag raising ceremony on the anniversary of independence. All youth camps, clubs and institutions for young people should fit similar ceremonies into their schedules.

The flag may be flown on private buildings on all national and state occasions and should always be flown on any private building on the occasion of official visits by the governor-general, and the prime minister.

The flag should be flown at the official residence of the prime minister when he is in residence.

The flag should be flown on the governor-general's and prime minister's cars.

All government-owned ships, defence craft and light-houses should fly the flag. All government-owned aircraft and motor vehicles should bear a representation of the flag.

The Pledge

Grenadians who attended school during the first three decades of this century repeated this pledge as part of their daily assembly exercise:

"I pledge allegiance to my flag and to the Empire for which it stands; with Justice and Liberty for all".

This practice was discontinued in the 1940s. However, when Grenada attained Associated Statehood Status in 1967, the practice of having school children repeat a pledge was revived and a new pledge replaced the old one for the Statehood Day Celebrations:

"I pledge allegiance to my flag and to the country for which it stands, with Liberty, Justice and Equality for all. I pledge also that I shall defend and uphold the Honour, Dignity and Laws and Institutions of my country".

The young citizens here recognise and pledge their allegiance to their country above all else, which, through its constitution, guarantees them certain inalienable rights.

They recognise also their responsibility to defend this constitution if they are to enjoy those rights and privileges.

The National Anthem

Hail Grenada, land of ours
We pledge ourselves to thee
Heads, hearts and hands in unity
To reach our destiny
Ever conscious of God
Being proud of our heritage
May we with faith and courage
Aspire, build, advance
As one people, one family
God bless our nation

The National Coat of Arms

The Coat-of-Arms, like the National Flag, represents the distillation of a national effort to produce armorial bearings for an independent Grenada, incorporating important historical and indigenous features of Grenada, Carriacou and Petit Martinique, in a design approved by the College of Arms.

A Coat-of-Arms, also called an Achievement of Arms, comprises:

1. The Livery Coat or Colour on a Shield
2. Charges or Devices on the Shield
3. The Helm of special design
4. The Mantle which covers the Helm
5. The Wreath to hold the Mantle in place
6. The Crest
7. Supporters
8. The Motto

The National colours of Red, Gold and Green, which comprise the National Flag are used on the shield with the same symbolism attached to them.

The ship Santa Maria at the centre point of the shield and Gold Cross represent Grenada's sighting by Christopher Columbus, and our continuing link with yachting and tourism.

The Gold Cross itself is significant of God consciousness which underlines the national effort.

The Lion in the first quarter of the shield, and repeated in the fourth, symbolises strength, and the unswerving determination to face the challenges of nationhood with courage and resourcefulness.

The Madonna Lily resting between the horns of the Crescent, (inspired by Murillo's famous painting of the Immaculate Conception) indicates that Grenada has, since its sighting by Columbus, been dedicated to Mary of the Immaculate Conception and in whose honour the island was named Conception Island; the shield itself rests in a valley between two mountains, representing the spectacularly picturesque topography of the islands.

The Grand Etang Lake is also represented amid luxuriant green vegetation in the foreground of which is placed a sprig of cocoa, with a ripe pod balanced by a sprig of nutmeg also showing the ripe fruit. Growing from the vegetation on the left side of the shield is a stalk of maize flowering and bearing three ears of ripened cobs and on the right a banana tree bearing a full bunch. These fruits all represent Grenada's traditional link with an agricultural economy; the cradle of their heritage.

The Helm is a royal helm, a gold helmet facing front and having seven gold bars across the visor, the interior lined purple. A star symbolic of our hopes, aspirations and ideals is placed to the forefront. The crest is made up of seven roses, representative of the seven parishes and set between two sprays of bouganvillea, the national flower.

The supporters are, on the left, a Tattoo or Armadillo and on the right, the Grenada Dove, representative of the fauna of the islands.

Grenada's motto, "Ever conscious of God, we aspire, build and advance as one people", is itself sufficiently eloquent on the subject of those high ideals and principles upon which the nation is founded.

The Coat-of-Arms or Seal, adopted at Independence, replaced the one introduced in April 1903, with the Latin motto: "Clarior e Tenebris". The seal appears on all official documents generally in black and white or, on more important occasions, in colour.

About Grenada, Carriacou and Petit Martinique

By Norma Sinclair

Grenada, Carriacou and Petit Martinique. Three beautiful tropical islands in a chain of islands that forms a graceful curve between the continents of North and South America. The Caribbean Sea laps the shores on the western side of the islands and the dramatic Atlantic swells break on the eastern coasts.

The islands are of volcanic origin and extinct explosion craters can still be seen in many parts of Grenada. This accounts for its natural beauty, numerous hills and valleys and lush tropical vegetation. Elfin woodland and tree-ferns adorn the peaks, the highest of which, Mount St Catherine, rises to a height of 2,756 feet above sea level. The annual dry season does not affect the evergreen tropical rainforest which appears lower down the slopes. Below this however, all trees and other vegetation have to withstand a dry season which lasts approximately from January to May each year when there is very little rainfall on the islands. The rivers run low, the waterfalls diminish noticeably in volume and the vegetation on the hills and in the valleys dries up and turns brown. The little rain that falls at this time is known locally as 'dry season rain'. It barely wets the surface of the earth, and avid gardeners have a hard time keeping their more delicate plants alive. However, the bougainvillea, Grenada's national flower, blooms beautifully in these months as do other flowers and shrubs that can withstand this harsh treatment by nature.

The wet season lasts essentially from June to December. Heavy showers and even an occasional thunder storm may occur at this time. This torrential rainfall gives rise to another local expression - 'it's raining a bucket a drop'. The rivers sometimes overflow their banks and the waterfalls are beautiful to behold. The farmers are happy, the land is happy, and the people can enjoy their favourite pastime of river bathing.

In the Caribbean, generally, this is the season of violent storms and hurricanes. Hurricane watches are in effect from August to October. However, Grenada is fortunate in that it lies just outside the hurricane belt so the country has escaped the worst of these devastating tropical storms. In the recorded history of the island only hurricane "Janet" reached Grenada, in September 1955, although a few severe tropical storms have been experienced since then.

The highest rainfall naturally occurs in the hilly areas along the central range of hills which runs north to south. The coastal areas are somewhat drier, with the southern end of the island being the most arid. This area is not very good for agriculture, but it is studded with the most magnificent beaches - a perfect setting for visitors looking for sun, sand and sea.

Bouganvillea - the national flower of Grenada

OPPOSITE
Map of Grenada, Carriacou and Petit Martinique
Courtesy: Government of Grenada

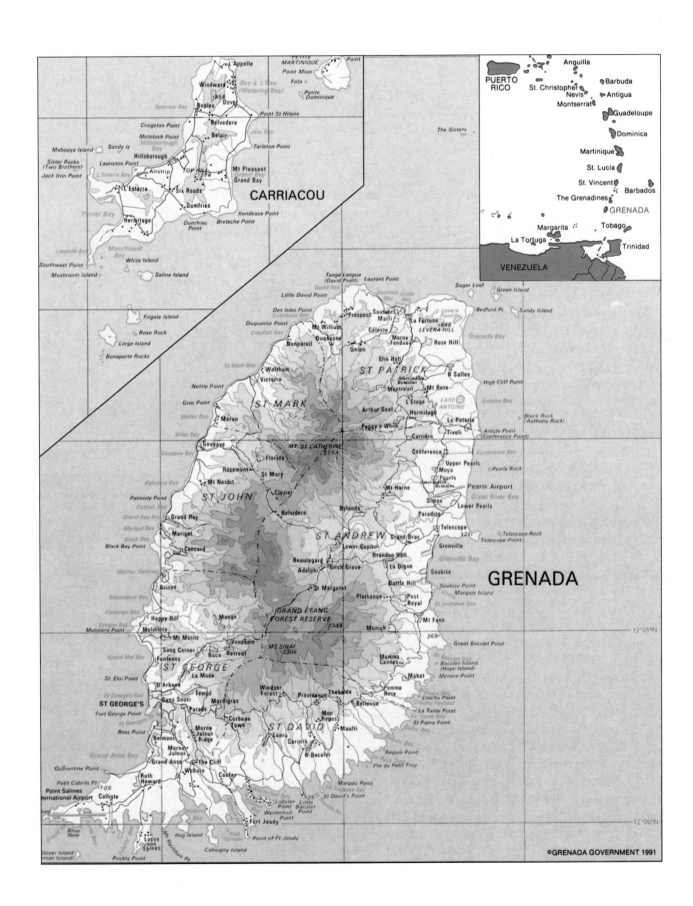

CARRIACOU

GRENADA

ST GEORGE'S

PUERTO RICO
VENEZUELA

Anguilla
Barbuda
St. Christopher
Nevis
Antigua
Montserrat
Guadeloupe
Dominica
Martinique
St. Lucia
St. Vincent
Barbados
The Grenadines
GRENADA
Margarita
La Tortuga
Tobago
Trinidad

©GRENADA GOVERNMENT 1991

The islands of the Grenadines are usually drier. Carriacou and Petit Martinique, although not experiencing much rainfall, can also boast of beautiful beaches and coral reefs in unbelievably clear waters that are just waiting to be discovered by the snorkeller.

There are a number of shipwrecks around the islands that provide an enduring source of fascination and adventure for scuba divers.

The tri-island state has an area of 344 sq km with a population of 95,000. It is the southernmost in a group known as the Windward Islands. St Vincent and the Grenadines, St Lucia and Dominica are the other three. This collection of islands, in turn, forms part of the Lesser Antilles in the Caribbean archipelago. A submarine ridge stretching between Grenada and St Vincent produces a host of tiny islands, each with inviting sandy beaches and safe, clean waters. Flying high above these islands on a clear day affords a view that will never be forgotten. It could be the Neverland of Peter Pan, beautiful and unspoilt.

The temperature averages about 30 degrees centigrade but can rise as high as 35 degrees centigrade during the day in the hotter months (August to November), falling as low as 18 degrees centigrade in the mountainous areas at night in the cooler months (December to March). However, the North-East trade winds tend to keep the temperature and humidity at a comfortable level even on the hottest day.

Coral reefs abound around the islands, affording divers a unique opportunity to enjoy the underwater world with clear visibility sometimes to a depth of about 200 feet. The white sand beaches are formed from pulverised coral "rock" and tiny fragments of mollusc shells. There are a number of black sand beaches as well, where the sand is of a finer, softer quality. This is due to a large extent, to the presence of silica and illmenite in small amounts, the colour being provided by oxides of iron and manganese. Prior to the construction of the new airport, one of the tourist attractions was a narrow strip of land leading to a small hill at the tip of the peninsular on which stood an old lighthouse. One beach contained dazzling white sand and on the other beach, the sand was a beautiful, silky black. A four-and-a-half metre roadway separated the two beaches. Turtles were known to come ashore on the black sand to lay their eggs.

Twilight is virtually non-existent in this part of the world and there is a difference of about two hours in the amount of daylight experienced through the year. In June there would be some 13 hours of daylight, whereas in December this would decrease to around 11 hours. The sun dips into the ocean, there is a short period of dusk and within an hour,

Windward Islands
The Windward Islands comprise of: Grenada, Carriacou and Petit Martinique; Dominica; St Lucia; St Vincent and the Grenadines

OPPOSITE
Grand Anse Beach stretches over two miles and is protected by coral reefs

24

night has fallen. The sunsets, however, are often spectacular.

There are no dangerous animals, no poisonous snakes or insects. Numerous bays and harbours provide a safe anchorage during storms and the yachting world takes full advantage of this natural facility. On a practical note, there is a good communications system offering worldwide direct dialling, telegraphic, telex and facsimile services. Electricity is supplied at a rating of 220/240 volts, 50 cycles AC. The water supply system provides good quality, treated water. As regards health care, there are two hospitals in Grenada and one in Carriacou, both adequately staffed. There are also a number of doctors and dentists working privately. Among the offshore islands that dot the coastline, a number are privately owned. Glover Island can be seen just off the southern end of Point Salines airport as planes come in to land.

The principal island crops are cocoa, nutmeg and bananas which provide the bulk of export trade. The nutmeg and its lacy red membrane, called mace, are both highly prized in the international pharmaceutical industry as well as being essential spices for adding to cakes, puddings, meats and vegetables. A popular drink is rum punch, made with lime juice, rum, syrup and ice. Nutmeg is grated on the top, and there you have the nectar of the Gods!

The fruit of the cacao (cocoa) tree is an oval shaped pod with a reddish brown or yellow colour. The seeds are covered with a soft white substance which is pleasant to the taste. The pods are cut open and the seeds extracted, washed, dried on huge trays in the sun, or electrically in large bins, then bagged for export where it is processed into cocoa powder, chocolate and cocoa butter. Grenada's cocoa is of a particularly high quality, and is often used as a blending cocoa with other, poorer varieties. About 38 per cent of agricultural export earnings come from cocoa.

Bananas, another major export crop, came into their own after the hurricane of 1955 denuded the nutmeg and cocoa plantations, and a source of quick export earnings was needed while these plantations were re-established. It may interest the reader to know how this fruit grows and develops. It begins life as tiny fingers close together, facing downwards on the stalk. Gradually these fingers get bigger, then begin to separate and curl upwards completely defying the pull of gravity. The full fruit all curve upwards around the stalk. This is known as a 'stem' of bananas. A cut of 12-14 bananas from the stem is known as a 'hand' of bananas.

"Isle of Spice" as Grenada is often called, also produces cinnamon, cloves, allspice, pimento and turmeric (known locally as saffron) which

Black coral
George Pascal, a fully licensed coral vendor in Market Square, makes by hand all the work he sells. The pendants and braclets are filed or bent into shape by slowly heating them

OPPOSITE
Grenada's telecommunication system is a leader in the Caribbean, with worldwide dialling available to all residential and business customers and from payphones and card phones

are processed and exported by the Minor Spices Society. Other spices available at the local supermarkets are peppers of different varieties, bay leaf, vanilla, sapote, ginger and tonka bean, all used for flavouring innumerable dishes.

Another important ingredient in the well-being of the nation is the use of local leaves and herbs for curing various ailments - in local parlance, "bush medicine". Leaves from a number of plants are brewed into teas, which are recommended to help cure stomach-aches, insomnia, colds, influenza, constipation, diarrhoea and many other symptoms of ill health.

Carriacou

Carriacou, the most populated island of the Grenadines, is home to about 7,000 people and has an area of 13 square miles.

The Grenadines comprise a chain of beautiful small islands, islets and uninhabited rocks that form a link between the larger islands of Grenada and St Vincent. This is really a yachting paradise. Crystal clear waters, safe anchorages, perfect sailing weather year round and it's ideal for snorkelling in most areas among the reefs.

Administrative responsibility and sovereignty of this chain was determined by drawing an imaginary line through the Grenadines. It was agreed that the islands north of the line would be under the control of the St Vincent Government and those to the south would be administered by Grenada. This imaginary line does not accurately follow a line of latitude. It cuts through the northern tips of Carriacou and Petit Martinique. Consequently, standing at Rapid Point in Carriacou (locally called Gun Point because of the cannon placed there) one is actually in St Vincent territory!

There are over 80 miles of roadway in Carriacou, originally built by the French to enable them to transport their artillery speedily from one place to another in their constant fights against the British. More often than not, there was no naval support so their military fortifications had to be well manned and easily accessible. These fortifications have all but disappeared. However, one fort overlooking the main town of Hillsborough has been turned into a waterworks and the cannon from the site were relocated to Hospital Hill from where there is a magnificent panoramic view of Hillsborough Bay and some of the Grenadines.

On the east coast the bays are sheltered by an almost continuous reef, making it a safe anchorage from the rough Atlantic swells. A shipbuilding

Bananas were introduced in Grenada as a source of quick income after hurricane "Janet" wiped out the nutmeg plantations

The Dumfries Lime factory, east of Hillsborough, was built in the early nineteenth century, and production of lime juice boomed for a few years. No longer in use, it could be restored for its architectural value and crafted brickwork

Derivation

The name Carriacou itself is supposed to come from the Carib word for the island. In the 17th and 18th century records it was spelt *Kayryouacou* (Land of reefs).

OPPOSITE
The busy Hillsborough jetty

industry is carried on at Windward, on the northeast coast, by the descendants of Glaswegian shipwrights. Many local schooners that ply between Grenada and Carriacou and even farther afield, are built here.

Apart from a regular schooner service, there are daily flights from Grenada to Carriacou. A day tour can be arranged with a visit to some offshore islets. Those with more time can book into a comfortable hotel and spend days exploring the wonders of the beautiful Grenadines.

Fishing, with some agriculture and livestock-rearing for home consumption, form the mainstay of the island's economy, and tourism is now coming into its own. The spiny lobster (*langouste*) is plentiful here and is found on the menu at any restaurant in Hillsborough.

Tree-oysters grow on mangroves in the lagoon adjoining Tyrrel Bay. The harvested oysters are sold to local restaurants and to visiting yachtsmen, who prefer this sheltered bay to the more exposed bay at Hillsborough.

The residents of Carriacou are a proud and independent people. As with the Glaswegian descendants, the African descendants can often trace their ancestry back to the African tribe to which they belonged. The Big Drum Dance is a traditional African dance that remains popular with a form of it being enacted for tourists. However, it was originally performed only on special occasions - at planting time, the launching of a boat, or at a tombstone feast, when a tombstone was erected on the grave of a relative.

Unlike Grenada, Carnival in Carriacou is celebrated just before the start of the Lenten Season in February each year, as determined by the church calendar. This two-day festival was originally observed only in Catholic countries, as a means of expurgating the sins of the flesh before the start of the forty-day Lenten Season with its strict observances.

Nowadays, it is spread over a week and more to encompass a kiddies Carnival and a Queen Show, when a Carnival Queen is picked from the many contestants to reign over the Carnival celebrations. A calypso monarch is crowned and a King and Queen of the Bands is also chosen. On the two days before Lent begins there is a parade of the costumed bands, and much dancing in the streets. The tunes of the most popular calypsoes accompany the revellers as they make their way through the streets behind the steelbands, feverishly beating out the rhythms that entice the listeners to tap their feet, to jig, then to join in the jump-up behind the pulsating stream of merrymakers. It is an unforgettable experience.

The traditional English custom of dancing the Maypole is still a part of the May Day celebrations in Carriacou. Coloured streamers attached to

The first census

The first census on Carriacou was in 1750, when the population was 199 made up of 92 whites, 92 "negroes", and 15 "mulattoes". In 1776 the island had a population of 86 whites and 3,153 slaves. Free "negroes" and "mulattoes" were not counted. Of the island's 47 estates, 22 were English or Scottish owned with a total of 2,027 slaves. The 21 French owned estates had a total of 866 slaves. The remaining four belonged to free "negroes" or "mulattoes" who had 138 slaves.

ABOVE
St Mary's Catholic Church, Hillsborough

OPPOSITE
View of Hillsborough Bay from Hospital Hill

OVERLEAF
Hillsborough Bay

the central pole are held by the dancers, who weave in and out as they plait the pretty ribbons around the pole.

In the State of Grenada, the first Monday of August is Caricom Day. The following day is also a holiday and on these two days a regatta is held in Carriacou. There are workboat and yacht races, water skiing, various other water and land sports, as well as cultural shows and street parties.

This festival has been in existence for over twenty-five years and is very popular within the local yachting community. The food is plentiful and the drink is good, including Jack Iron - a very potent Caribbean rum. This is the only known alcoholic drink in which the ice sinks to the bottom of the glass rather than floating. The calypso singers are on form and the music usually at fever pitch. There is dancing in the streets as the sleepy little town of Hillsborough comes alive for a brief annual season.

Just before Christmas, a Parang Festival is held. This is when guitars and quatros are brought out and played by talented islanders. Stalls are set up in the streets to sell all sorts of food and drink. There is dancing and singing as the lively music entices everyone to enjoy themselves.

A son of the Carriacou soil who has made a name for himself in the world of art is Canute Calliste. His form of national art is extremely popular, creating a lot of interest among the many visitors as well as art lovers generally.

Carriacou is an island of many interests and much enjoyment. There is also a very impressive museum, displaying Amerindian artefacts and local 'finds' from the era of French and the British occupation. It is also possible to buy a tape of the Big Drum Dance music, which is truly exciting to listen to and a magnificent memento of a visit to Carriacou.

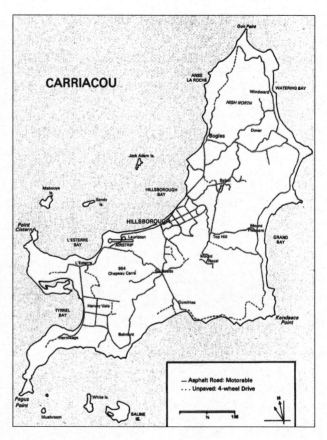

ABOVE
Map of Carriacou
Courtesy: Carriacou Tours and Travel Service

OPPOSITE
The Caribbee Inn at Prospect, a small country-house and nature reserve

OVERLEAF
View of Petit Martinique from Carriacou

Petit Martinique

This small volcanic cone of just 486 acres has a population of about nine hundred, fairly evenly divided between males and females. The windward coastline is covered with rocks, but on the leeward side there are some excellent beaches.

Like its sister island Carriacou, Petit Martinique was settled by the French and the names of the inhabitants attest to this history.

Over the years small shacks have given way to more substantial concrete houses as the living standard of the population has improved. Many of the roads are now paved; the island has electricity and a telephone service. There are no rivers on Petit Martinique and each house has a storage tank for rainwater collected from the roofs.

A small medical centre is visited once a week by the government doctor resident in Carriacou. The police force stationed at Carriacou under the leadership of an assistant superintendent of police also pay regular visits to this tiny isle. A post office, a school and a Catholic church cater to the needs of the population. Outdoor services are held by members of other religious denominations.

Petit Martinique is known for the large number of goats and sheep that roam freely up and down the hill which rises almost in the centre of the island. Each owner places his special mark on the ear of the animal to prevent disputes over ownership.

Most of the men opt for a life at sea and are known to be hardy seamen. Fishing is the main source of revenue and experienced boat builders are found here as well. Corn and peas are planted for local consumption but almost everything else has to be imported.

Decades ago, smuggling developed as a simple way to obtain needed items. The fishermen would travel north to St Maarten, a freeport, where they would sell their catch, purchase what they needed, and return home. No customs officer or similar official was stationed on the island and the few inhabitants survived as best they could. The purchase of un-customed goods eventually spread to the sister island of Carriacou, and a lucrative smuggling trade became firmly established. Many a Grenadian household knew where to go for their stock of Christmas liquor. This would include good French brandies, wines, liqueurs and even champagne. No wedding was held without the best champagne available, and purchased duty-free! In the 1930s a new district officer, posted to Carriacou, decided to try and stamp out this illicit trade. On an official visit to Petit Martinique, he found

a huge hole dug in the sand with a wooden cross at one end bearing the words: "The Grave of - - - - - " naming the commissioner. Not a very pleasant welcome, but he got the message. The trade has continued apace, despite many subsequent attempts to curb it.

Cricket and rounders are the main sports. There is a women's cricket team and they play regularly against teams from the neighbouring Grenadine islands.

Carnival is celebrated on the two days before the start of the Lenten Season. Costumed revellers take to the streets and there is much music, dancing and general merriment.

At Easter, the inhabitants of Petit Martinique hold a two-day regatta. Competitors from the neighbouring Grenadine islands take part in the boat races. The greasy pole competition is always a popular attraction. A well-greased pole is hung over the water with a prize attached to the far end. Men gingerly balance on the pole, much like a tightrope walker, as they try to reach the prize. Most of them end up falling into the water, much to the delight of the onlookers who spur them on with shouts and hand-clapping. Donkey races also form part of this festival.

A visit to Petit Martinique

Petit Martinique is less than three miles from Carriacou and can only be reached by boat. Pictured above is Cuthbert Snagg (left) and colleague, offering trips to Petit Martinique and all around the Grenadines from Hillsborough Bay

Seeta Humphries, Augustina Bethal and the owner of Petit Martinique's 'Standing Wave', Elisabeth Bethal

OPPOSITE
Catholic Church, Petit Martinique

OVERLEAF
Yachtsmen preparing for the Petit Martinique Regatta

The Parishes of Grenada

By Norma Sinclair

There are six parishes on the island of Grenada, each with its own fascinating charm, special traditions and festivals. A drive through any parish will open up some of its history, reveal its heartbeat in the warmth and friendliness of its people, and bare its beauty for all to see.

St George

This parish of approximately 32,000 people occupies the southeastern end of the island and is a place of haunting beauty, magnificent beaches, translucent waters and ideal year round weather.

Grenada's capital city, St George's, lies in this parish. It is regarded as the most picturesque city in the Caribbean and is divided by a central ridge which separates the Bay Town overlooking the outer harbour from the Carenage, or inner harbour, and the lagoon - a quiet body of water just south of the Carenage. Fort George was built here by the French in 1706 to protect the harbour and the town that gradually sprang up on the hills surrounding this beautiful site. The fort and its buildings are now used as the police headquarters, barracks and training school for new recruits.

At the farthest point on this hill, at the back of the fort, is the general hospital occupying for the most part what used to be the original military barracks. This is a modern facility with experienced medical practitioners, nurses and other hospital staff.

In former times, following the European settlement of the island, ships were careened (put on their side) in the inner harbour, hence the name 'Carenage' (pronounced Ca-reh-nagh) given to this area. A road follows the sweeping curve of the bay, linking the port where cruise liners and cargo vessels dock with the major business houses in the city. There are a variety of restaurants around here and a number of interesting tourist shops and roadside vendors selling the aromatic spices for which the island is famous.

Some old cannons have been sunk vertically into the ground on the sea side of the Carenage to serve as bollards for vessels using the harbour.

The Grenada Yacht Club is located on a small promontory overlooking both the lagoon and the Carenage. Basic yachting services are available at berths in this lagoon which is a very safe anchorage in stormy weather.

St George's is a beautiful city, with its houses rising in tiers up the surrounding hillsides, giving the impression of a vast amphitheatre.

Six forts were built on the hills encircling the city. Only two remain as a reminder of Grenada's strife-filled past, when the British and French were battling for control of the island.

The port of St George's
For those arriving by sea, St George's is the major port, with berths for two ocean-going cruisers 400-500 feet long and 30 feet deep. There is a 250 feet schooner pier. Entrance to the harbour is through a buoy-marked channel 600 feet wide and 45 feet deep

The Carenage
A volcanic explosion crater created this natural harbour. European settlers of the island careened (put on their side) their ships here, hence the name 'Carenage'.

*OPPOSITE & OVERLEAF
St George's is regarded as the most picturesque city in the Caribbean*

At one end of the city, the Sendall Tunnel connects the Carenage area to the Esplanade, Bay Town.

Fifty years ago, this frontal portion of Bay Town looking westward, was a quiet, peaceful place of shady trees, benches, concrete walkways and a small water fountain; a place where the inhabitants of the city could relax and enjoy themselves. Today, the Esplanade is lined with mini-buses that travel to various parts of the country. A medical centre has been set up here, as have several small shops and eating places.

In the centre of Bay Town, amid the hustle and bustle of traffic, is the Market Square, a central point for buying and selling produce, for meeting old friends, making new ones, and exchanging titbits of gossip from time to time.

All manner of fruits and vegetables in season can be purchased here, attractively arranged in large trays to catch the shopper's eye. Coconut water is drunk straight from the freshly-opened nut; black pudding (blood sausage) is seen frying over a coal pot, and delicious, freshly made salt fish cakes are available. One of these salt fish placed in a bun of leavened bread is the perfect way to start the day.

The Market Square has always been the place for buying and selling produce, and at one point in Grenada's history it was also used for public executions as well as a market for buying and selling slaves. The rebels captured after the overthrow of the Fedon rebellion in 1795/6 were hanged on this site.

A bus terminal now occupies a portion of the Market Square. This adds to the bustle and general light-hearted pandemonium that is an everyday experience here: minibus drivers shouting to each other and to prospective customers as they try to compete for fares; market vendors loudly offering their wares, which, apart from fruit, vegetables and spices would include cane baskets, bamboo brooms and straw items like hats, bags and sun visors. Church Street runs along the central ridge between the Carenage and Bay Town. Here stand the Catholic, Anglican and Presbyterian churches. These contain pretty stained-glass panels and in the Anglican church some interesting memorial plaques can be seen. The Scots Kirk as the Presbyterian Church is known, was built with the assistance of the Freemasons.

Water taxis ply the Carenage from one end to the other, and are also available for trips to Grand Anse beach - a two-mile stretch of spectacular white sand beach with crystal clear waters cosily tucked into a bay. A coral reef guards the entrance, thus making it safe for swimming and snorkelling.

The Sendall Tunnel
Named after Governor Sir Walter Sendall, the tunnel was completed in 1895 to join the two parts the city.

The Market Square
Established in 1791, the square is central to the life of the nation. Today, it provides the visitor with a colourful selection of fruits, vegetables and an incredible variety of spices and their by-products - jams, jellies, sauces, drinks and ornamental handicrafts.

OPPOSITE
A cruise liner arrives and anchors off St George's

OVERLEAF
Market Square, St George's

Several major hotels and top restaurants are located in the Grand Anse area, as are a number of holiday cottages and apartments.

Further south is Point Salines International Airport and a coastline studded with bays, peninsulas and small offshore islands, each with its own beauty and charm.

Homes are gradually being built on each peninsular as the demand for living accommodation increases. The more affluent members of society have moved into these areas, as have many European and North American immigrants. True Blue, L'Anse aux Epines Peninsula, Fort Jeudy and Westerhall Point were dry areas growing sugar cane and raising sheep and cattle. All these have been gradually transformed into residential areas with beautiful homes, many having beach front lots, swimming pools or both. There are two marinas at L'Anse aux Epines offering excellent services to visiting yachts, as well as catering to the holiday-maker wishing to charter a yacht for a day, a week or even longer.

Back to the city and driving eastward, we can visit Richmond Hill and Fort Frederick, the last of the old forts that has been restored. The view of St George's from here is just magnificent, stretching far beyond to encompass the southern peninsulas of Quarantine Station (once used as a hospital for soldiers who had contracted smallpox in the nineteenth century) and Point Saline. On the ridge just below the fort is the prison compound, which was originally built as a military hospital. Looking eastward over the hills and valleys surrounding this magnificent vantage point, the panorama is truly spectacular.

The tunnels at this fort are sealed off now, but it is common belief that the forts surrounding the city were once connected by subterranean tunnels. Certainly tunnels have been blocked at each fort and it takes little imagination to believe the rest.

Further east, into the district of St Paul's we come to the Bay Gardens. These well-tended gardens have excellent specimens of tropical flowers, trees and fruit. For a small fee, visitors are shown around the gardens and can see specimens of Grenada's major crops as well as spice trees like the bay, cinnamon and clove.

Leaving the city and travelling north, we come first to Queen's Park. This is the key venue for important outdoor functions, as it is the largest flat open space near to the city. All major sporting events are played here; parades are held and carnival bands and other contests are judged here. In the early part of the century, this was also the venue for horse-racing.

Further along, at a right-hand fork in the road and travelling uphill

Queen's Park
Used for national and international sports events including cricket, football and athletics. It is also used for political rallies, pageant and Carnival

A policeman directs traffic at the top of Young Street

OPPOSITE
A schools athletics meet held at Queen's Park

50

we arrive at Mount Moritz. Descendants of English settlers in Barbados moved here in the 19th century when they found themselves without employment because of the change in the economy brought about by the Emancipation of the slaves in 1834. They were conveyed throughout the Caribbean by the Anglican Church and those brought to Grenada formed a community at Mount Moritz.

Another interesting landmark in this parish is Annandale Falls, nestled in the central range of hills south of the Grand Etang Lake. The area around the falls has been neatly landscaped and there is a rest room close by with changing and washroom facilities. The pool at the base is large and deep enough for swimming, and the water is cool and refreshing.

The parish of St George is best geared towards accommodation and entertainment for visitors to the island. The major hotels are all located here and their nightly entertainment is varied. Also, there is the Marryshow Folk Theatre in Tyrrel Street in the city where concerts and good local plays are performed from time to time. There is a very popular moonlight cruise on a twin-deck catamaran complete with barbecue, drinks and music for dancing. The view of the harbour and the city at night is breathtaking.

A nine-hole golf course is situated near St George's, as are several tennis courts and health clubs, many of which are available to visitors.

The waters surrounding the islands teem with coral reefs and beautiful underwater sights. Diving, sailing, fishing and other water sports are always available.

An annual Billfishing Tournament is held in January. This attracts local, regional and international sports fishermen. Records are often broken and excellent sportsmanship is displayed in the good-natured bantering that is so much a part of this sport.

A Triathlon also takes place at this time with both males and females competing in a swim-cycle-run race; an endurance test that attracts many local and foreign competitors.

Grenada's annual Sailing Festival is also held in January. Regional and international yachts compete with the locals for attractive prizes. The weather at this time of the year is just perfect for sailing and many enthusiasts make these competitions a 'must'.

A very important day in the island's history is February 7. On that day in 1974 the country achieved independence from Britain. It is celebrated in each parish with church services. A large parade of local forces and representation from schools island-wide, takes place at Queen's Park.

The largest festival celebrated in Grenada is Carnival, which is held

Modern hotels and apartments such as the Flamboyant Hotel and Cottages (top) and Gem Holiday Beach Resort offer a wide choice of holiday options

*OPPOSITE
Annandale Falls*

52

on the second weekend of August each year. The largest concentration of revellers is centred in St George's. A Queen is chosen to reign over the celebrations, and contests take place to choose the best calypso, the best steelband, the best costumed band as well as a King and Queen of the bands. Carnival is two days of fun and dancing in the streets.

St David

The parish of St David is on the southeastern end of the island, and is home to a population of approximately 11,000. The coastline is littered with small bays and inlets, many with pocket-size sandy beaches, just perfect for a quiet picnic and a swim.

This is basically an agricultural parish growing the traditional crops of cocoa, nutmegs, bananas and spices together with a large portion of the sugar cane which thrives in the drier atmosphere of this southern parish. It is interesting to note that this is the only parish in Grenada without a major town although there are several small villages and settlements. A police station, post office and some churches are all centrally located. The Catholic Church is predominantly situated on a bluff high enough to be seen many miles away in the south.

On the border between St George parish and St David is the last known habitat of the Grenada Dove, a rare and beautiful species of dove endemic to the island. Its existence is now being threatened but it is hoped that the necessary safeguards will be put in place in time to save this lovely bird from extinction.

Just past the boundary with the parish of St George is Westerhall Estate. Originally a sugar plantation, its small factory is used now for the distillation and processing of rum. The huge old water wheel is still evident, but is no longer in operation. At the turn of the century, the river running at the back of the factory was diverted and used to turn this large wheel. This in turn, started the machinery used for grinding the sugar cane to extract the juice which was then processed into sugar and rum. This relic of the past stands as a silent reminder of the time when sugar reigned supreme on the island.

Westerhall Point, a small peninsular and once an unused part of the estate, was sold to developers in the mid-twentieth century. It is now a private residential development with many of the beautiful homes having their own private beach fronts. The landscaping has been tastefully executed and the private roads and grounds are well-maintained. Originally, this development

The Grenada Dove
Not just any dove - the Grenada Dove *(leptotila wellsi)* is found only in Grenada. Numbering less than one hundred, this unique bird is under threat of extinction from hunting and destruction of its habitat. Awareness campaigns in Grenada to save the dove are well under way. They promote the care of Grenada's Parks and Forest Reserves and the reporting of illegal hunting.

ABOVE
Entrance to the Westerhall Estate Rum Distillery

OPPOSITE
Westerhall Point

was home mainly to retired people from Europe and North America, but over the years, for various reasons, ownership has changed hands, and now many well-to-do local residents also own property here.

Further along the route, we arrive at the La Sagesse Nature Centre which is housed in a building constructed by the late Lord Brownlow, equerry to the Duke of Windsor when he abdicated the British throne in 1936 to marry the American-born Mrs Simpson. Lord Brownlow seldom visited his tropical retreat and eventually his property was purchased by the Government in the 1970s. There is now a small restaurant at the beach front, and changing facilities are available should one care for a dip in the ocean. The water though, is very shallow for quite a distance out to sea, and therefore not particularly ideal for swimming. However, snorkelling along the coral reefs is an interesting and exciting experience.

This area was the site for one of the first settlements in Grenada but hardly anything is left now to pinpoint the original site of Megrin, as it was called.

At the Nature Centre, arrangements can be made for hikes through the wooded estate or for visits to a mangrove estuary - a bird watcher's paradise. The balance of the estate has been divided into five-acre model farms run by experienced Grenadian farmers. The Republic of China on Taiwan and the French Government both have ongoing projects in the area in an attempt to improve the agricultural irrigation systems and to introduce new and different varieties of vegetables to the Grenadian farmer.

Just off La Sagesse Point, in the year 1900, a ship was wrecked when trying to enter the harbour. The date was November 1, All Saints Day, a holy day in the church calendar. Grenadians have always been religious and it was the practice then to light candles on the graves in memory of their loved ones. Hundreds of candles would be lit as the living met and conversed by the graves of their dear departed. Electricity had not yet come to the island, and the myriad of lighted candles was an impressive sight.

The S S Orinoco, on her way to St George's, mistook the candle lights for those of the city and, turning towards them, came to grief on the rocks. The wreck is in rough waters, and only experienced divers ever brave the elements to make this dive. The Atlantic swells break on this coastline and consequently the sea is more lively than that experienced on the western side of the island.

After a long, gradual climb, you arrive at the post office and the police station serving the district. Not far away is Requin Bay which was once a

Westerhall Rum Distillery

Located along the Southern Main Road north of the Westerhall Bay on the Westerhall Estate.

The distillery has been updated but there are still vestiges of the old processes similar to those used at the River Antoine Distillery. The water wheel used in the late 19th and early 20th century is still present and could be put back into operation. The distillery no longer grinds its own cane, but purchases the molasses used in the rum distilling process. Unlike River Antoine, the distillery uses chemicals and additives to hasten the process of fermentation and therefore has a higher production capacity.

ABOVE
La Sagesse Nature Centre

OPPOSITE
La Sagesse Beach

busy port in St David. Cocoa and nutmegs were shipped from this port and much of the material used in building the Catholic Church there came through Requin Bay, particularly the tiles and the church statues. This port is no longer in use, with almost everything imported to Grenada passing through St George's harbour.

Cricket and football are popular local pastimes. In the country areas children can be seen using a bit of coconut palm as a bat as they practice cricket in the hope of one day making the Westindies team.

At Marlmount, an old estate house has been turned into a restaurant catering to all tastes with local dishes being a speciality. Carnival in August is the major celebration in St David with costumed folk dancing and singing in the streets. Those joining bands, however, journey to St George's to take part in the celebrations there.

St Andrew

The parish with the longest coastline, St Andrew has a population of approximately 23,000. There are many well established estates here, consequently it is the largest producer of Grenada's main export crops - cocoa, nutmegs and bananas, as well as spices, vegetables, coconuts, fruit and flowers.

Rainbow City is the name affectionately chosen by residents to call their lovely old town of Grenville. It is situated at the eastern end of the parish, nestled around a wide bay which, were it not for a series of coral reefs which make shipping manoeuvres a bit tricky, would be a much busier port especially for the shipping of produce from this highly agricultural parish. This often has to be trucked to St George's where the deep-water harbour is much more accessible to ocean going vessels.

The French, when in possession of the island, called this Grenville harbour "La Baye" and the name has continued to be used to designate the area in and around the town.

Grenville was originally built on a site just south of its present location, in the Fedon rebellion of 1795/96 it was the first town to be sacked by the rebels. After the rebellion, the town was rebuilt on its present site. Many interesting old buildings are in evidence here, for example the Anglican Church, the police station, the government revenue and post offices and the courthouse behind which the market is located.

On Saturdays, the Market Square is a hive of activity. Beef from freshly slaughtered animals is on sale, as well as fish, live crabs, all

Fedon's rebellion

The French, by the Treaty of Versailles in 1783, returned Grenada to the British. In the years that followed those French who remained in Grenada, suffered immense loss of liberties and religious persecution under British rule, although not equal to the cruelty experienced by the slaves.

On March 3, 1795, with support from the French Revolutionaries in Martinique and joined by slaves and 'free coloureds', the French rebelled, and under the leadership of Julien Fedon a Grenadian of African and French descent and the owner of Belvidere Estate, attacked the British. Apart from the capital St George's the rebels took virtually all of Grenada, razing Grenville town in the ensuing battles. Many people were killed.

Fedon established his head-quarters on a mountaintop stronghold and fought courageous battles against great odds. These 'rebels' were considered freedom fighters by the slaves throughout the Caribbean. The French, however, saw the rebellion as an opportunity to regain a colony.

The extent and success of the revolt sent shock waves around the British Empire and despite numerous attempts to retake the island, Fedon's rebels remained in control for fourteen months.

It took one of the largest land forces ever used in a military operation by the British in the Caribbean to defeat the rebels. The British eventually overran Fedon's Camp. The surviving 'freedom fighters' were executed by public hanging in the Market Square in St George's. Julien Fedon was never captured and he disappeared.

OPPOSITE
St Andrew has the longest coastline of all the parishes

manner of vegetables and fruit in season, coconuts, flowers and items made of plaited grass.

The village of Marquis lies just south of the town of Grenville. Grand Marquis was the name given to the entire parish during the period of French jurisdiction but this was changed to St Andrew when the British took over. In this little fishing community, the industrious villagers also process and plait a special kind of pandanus grass which is eventually fashioned into attractive hats, bags and mats that are sold island-wide. These products are popular with both residents and visitors.

The Marquis river empties into the bay near here. None of Grenada's rivers are very large and to some people, they might be considered little more than streams. Higher up this river, in an area known as Mount Carmel, there are two pretty waterfalls. A 15 minute trek will take you from the main road to the higher falls, which are the highest in Grenada. The lower falls are further away with a more precipitous approach. These are not very high, and much wider than the upper falls. Young boys enjoy sliding over them into the natural pool below. It is a perfect swimming place where the water is cool and pleasant, even on the hottest day.

The first airport in Grenada was situated at Pearls, just north of Grenville. This fell into disuse after Point Salines International Airport in the south of the island was opened in 1984. The buildings at Pearls have been refashioned into site offices for various projects underway in that part of the island. This area is rich in Amerindian artefacts and now and again archaeological digs are arranged, usually through the Grenada National Trust and Historical Society which has its headquarters at the Museum in St George's.

There are some attractive beaches around Pearls - wonderful picnic spots - but the seas are rough and the tides strong, so only experienced swimmers should brave the waves.

Another interesting place to visit is the Cocoa Fermentary at Carlton Junction. Here the cocoa is purchased from the farmers, processed and made ready for export.

The largest nutmeg station on the island is situated in Grenville, and visitors are welcome to tour it any time to see where the nutmegs and mace are purchased, separated, dried and prepared for shipment. The smell of aromatic spices is all around. Boulogne and Mirabeau are two Government-run agricultural research stations in St Andrew where plants and flowers of all varieties are sold to the public. Boulogne is used mainly as a cocoa propagating station and a nursery for decorative

The site of Pearl's Airport
Pearl's Airport, in St Andrew, Grenada's first airport, was in use from 1943 to 1984, until it was replaced by Point Salines International Airport. This site was one of the greatest Arawak Amerindian settlements in the Caribbean. The area has now been declared an archaeological site of great international importance. Excavation and removal of artefacts without governmental permission is illegal and any such finds become the property of the government of Grenada.

Marquis Falls
Marquis Falls, also known as Mount Carmel Falls, is the highest waterfall in Grenada, located in a setting of outstanding natural beauty two miles south of Grenville. The falls are already popular with locals and increasing numbers of tourists and are currently under development. Improvements include creating easier access, adding signposts, setting up picnic areas, the establishment of a Visitor's Centre and the training of guides.

OPPOSITE
Marquis Falls

The Rainbow City Festival

Every August, Grenville is host to the Rainbow City Festival, which is a forum for local arts, crafts and entertainment which include games, competitions and concerts. Pictured are the Schools Competition Programme (top and bottom left), the opening night Cultural Show (top right) and display booths in the Market Square (bottom right)

Renovating Grenville Old Church

A fundraising campaign is under way to renovate this old Catholic church (right) and turn it into a cultural centre to include a museum, library and art gallery. Nadia Benjamin and Yolande Joseph (top) get ready for the clean-up. The Hon. Tillman Thomas, Senator and Minister of Tourism (bottom) attending the launch of the fund-raising drive

plants. At Mirabeau the concentration is on economic plants and research into vegetable pest control.

In the second week in August, Carnival is celebrated island-wide, but the largest celebration in St Andrew is the Rainbow City Festival of Arts which takes place during the first weekend in August each year. Booths are erected in Grenville to display the talents of the local residents in various forms of arts and crafts as well as the domestic arts of preserving, pickling, jam and jelly-making and the preparation of confectionery.

Entertainment is available through the entire week, in the form of concerts, competitions, exhibitions, games and music. Residents and visitors turn out in full force to enjoy themselves.

This is a parish full of history. Pilot Hill and Battle Hill are both good vantage points for the town of Grenville. Remnants of old fortifications can be seen on each hill as well as at Post Royal, another battleground. The views from each of these hills are fantastic, overlooking, as they do, much of the countryside and extending far out into the ocean.

St Patrick

The most northerly parish in Grenada, St Patrick has a population of about 10,000. Many beautiful old homes and some estate houses can still be seen there, some are well-kept originals and others have been restored to a replica of their former glory.

Most of the main agricultural crops are grown in St Patrick, as well as lots of citrus and ground provisions - yams, tannias and sweet potatoes. Some estates however, have been given over to development schemes.

The principal town of Sauteurs got its name from an historical event that took place in the mid-seventeenth century. At that time, the French were fighting the Carib inhabitants for possession of the island. The Carib warriors facing defeat, ran to the cliff overlooking Sauteurs Bay and leapt to their deaths rather than surrender. The victors named the town that grew up in this area "Bourg des Sauteurs" - "The town of the Leapers". The Catholic Church now stands on that site. It is possible to walk to the edge of the precipice and look down at the rocks and angry waters below and imagine the tragic event that took place over three hundred years ago.

There's a small candle making industry in the building next to the church. The wax is melted on open fires outside and brought inside to fill the moulds. Everything is done manually, visitors if they wish can be shown around.

Sauteurs is an old town, built in the days when the horse and buggy

Hibiscus, at their best when just opening at sunrise

Carib's leap

Also known as Leaper's Hill, located at the hilltop and cliff-face directly north of Sauteurs, the most northerly town on the island, where St Patrick's Catholic Church, school and cemetery are located. To the northern part of the promontory is a cliff face, descending 100 feet vertically into the sea.

Grenada's inhabitants before the French and English colonisation were the Amerindian Carib race. In 1651, after much struggle for control of the island, the Caribs were driven by the French to the north of the island. Their last stand was at this precipice named by the French, "le morne de Sauteurs" or 'leapers hill' in memory of the leap of the Caribs. It was reported that about forty Caribs leapt to their deaths over this cliff rather than surrender to the French.

OPPOSITE
Old windmill in the district of Mount Rose, St Patrick

OVERLEAF
Carib's Leap and Sauteurs Bay

were the only means of transport. There are still steps specially constructed to ease the ascent and descent from carriages which were in use until the early part of this century. Old tethering rings are still attached to the wall in the grounds of the Anglican Church to which the horses were tied while their owners worshipped in the beautiful old church.

In the early 1900s, the only means of communication with the capital was by boat. A small jetty was built in Sauteurs Bay and produce was brought to this point for shipment to St George's. At that time, an influential citizen erected a drinking fountain and a horses' trough in the town so that man and beast could be refreshed after the long haul from the estates. He built it in memory of his father and it is still standing, although it is no longer in use.

There is a small batik factory in the town that is worth visiting. Some young women have been taught the art of batik and they produce many attractive designs for dresses, wraps, scarves, cushion covers and bags.

East of Sauteurs is the district of Levera. A secondary road leads to Levera Bay from where three offshore islands can be seen. The nearest is Levera Island, commonly known as 'Sugar Loaf' because of its shape. Further out is Green Island, then Sandy Island. Birds are plentiful on these privately owned islands which are not normally accessible to visitors. Levera Pond on the mainland however, is an ornithologist's delight where kingfishers, waterfowl and several other species of bird can be seen.

Lake Antoine, the explosion crater of an extinct volcano, is another area where birds gather to feed, to nest and generally to make themselves known with their loud squawking noises.

Levera Beach is a beautiful site for picnics and a portion of the adjoining estate has been developed into a national park. On weekends and holidays visitors and locals intermingle as they enjoy a day at the beach.

About 200 years ago, a breakwater and a small jetty were built here to aid shipping produce from the estates. A fort was erected at Bedford Point, overlooking the bay to protect this operation. The remains of the fort are still visible, but the old cannon have been removed. Some of the islands between Grenada and Carriacou can be seen from this point.

Further south is another popular beach - Bathway. Here, a small reef shelters the bathing area from the worst of the Atlantic swells and makes it a safe place for children to swim. Just west of Bathway beach is the Levera Development Site. Some Canadians have winter homes here and a few locals, some returning from abroad, have erected large modern homes in the area.

Mount Rich Amerindian remains

Located along the St Patrick's river valley in the village of Mount Rich, the Amerindian remains are primarily stone carvings on rocks on the valley floor. These carvings have been attributed to Caribs as the work depicts their typical features and lifestyle. They can be easily seen on the top and sides of this very large stone on the river bank where six carvings, headpieces, pottery, implements and tools (spears, bows and axes) used in their hunting and fishing are found. Several small stones in the vicinity have different carved features but they are not clearly discernible since they are covered by weeds and mosses.

The remains are easily accessible since they are located alongside the main road from Sauteurs close to the Mount Rich village. A community group has planted flowers along the access footpath and installed a sign reading "Carib Remains-Enter".

A small cottage industry making dolls out of corn straw, was started nearby. Visitors are shown around and introduced to the young people who have been taught to produce these fascinating dolls.

At Mount Rich, Amerindian petroglyphs have been discovered on a large stone in the St Patrick's river. This is probably an area full of Grenada's past history where future archaeologists may be able to uncover much interesting information.

Two old estate homes have been opened to the public serving lunches and dinners for hotel guests or other parties. Reservations are necessary as these are both popular stopover points for tour operators.

Morne Fendue, a beautiful stone structure, was built in the early part of this century. The mortar used for bonding the stone was a mixture of molasses and limestone, both easily available in Grenada at that time.

Mount Rodney, another beautiful old family home complete with fretworked eaves, provides a terrific view of some of the islands of the Grenadines. Many interesting trees and shrubs grow on the hillsides around the house completing a spectacular backdrop to a lovely setting.

The Feast of St Patrick, a religious celebration, usually falls about the third week in March. The town of Sauteurs comes alive with an exposition of arts, crafts and agricultural produce. There are cultural performances, lots of music and dancing. Of course, a variety food and drink is available.

St Mark

St Mark is the smallest parish, with about 3,800 people who live mainly by fishing and working on the surrounding estates. The main crops of cocoa, bananas and nutmegs are grown here, as well as other spices, fruit and ground provisions. There is a good fishing industry and the town of Victoria has one of the six cold storage market places for fish on the island.

In this parish, Mount St Catherine rises to a height of 2,756 feet above sea level and is the highest peak on the island. From its summit all the parishes of Grenada are visible. Guides are readily available for the eager mountaineer but the ascent is precipitous and should be left to experienced climbers.

Grenada experienced severe volcanic activity in the past and although its volcanoes are now all extinct, there are still hot mineral springs in certain parts of the island. On the slopes of Mount St Catherine, above Tufton Hall Estate, some of these hot springs can be visited. There is a Forest Reserve in this central range of hills that encompass a portion of each parish that is very important to the ecosystem.

Sulphurous springs
The sulphurous mineral springs at River Sallee, St Patrick. Local people use the waters for the healing effects that they are claimed to possess. Candles are often lit and placed around the springs as part of this ritual

St Patrick's Day Fiesta
The St Patrick's Day Fiesta, at Sauteurs, is becoming a very successful annual event which attracts thousands of people during the two weeks of celebrations. Police bands, steelbands, calypso and sound systems compete for the attention of the revellers. Side attractions such as agriculture and cultural shows and food vendors add to the vibrant atmosphere.

OVERLEAF
Sugar Loaf and Green Island,
Levera National Park

At Tufton Hall Estate itself, a small project centre was established some years ago by the Catholic Church. Called the Tufton Hall Adventure Project (TAP) it was aimed at helping young boys to become useful members of society. The boys were clothed and housed and taught agricultural skills. Sale of the crops grown helped to cover the expenses of the boys' care.

Victoria is the main town in St Mark. This area was called Grand Pauvre (*great poverty*) when the French ruled the island. The town is little more than a large seaside village of industrious and friendly people. Old buildings and small shacks are gradually being replaced by more modern structures which brighten the face of this small town.

Kite-flying from a roof in Victoria

There's a small mop-making industry in the town - a joint venture of the Society of Friends of the Blind and the Grenada National Council of the Disabled. One disabled and two blind persons are employed here, producing well made mops that are sold island-wide.

St Mark's Day Fiesta is celebrated during a week at the end of April each year. Local arts and crafts are on display, as well as home-made jams and jellies, sweets, pickles and drinks. Concerts and other cultural performances are staged.

The annual harvest celebrations take place in Victoria on Whit Monday. All the produce grown in the area is exhibited and blessed by the clergy of various denominations. After the church services, food and drink is on sale and local people enjoy meeting and socialising.

Every parish in Grenada has a coastline and consequently fishing is a major industry. On June 29, the Feast of St Peter and St Paul, is celebrated island-wide as Fisherman's Birthday. The festivities are spread over a week so that each parish can have its own special activities.

Each year the celebrations begin at Waltham, a small village about a mile north of Victoria, with priests blessing the boats, the nets and the fishermen. Naturally, there is much merrymaking in the streets as the people of the parish give thanks for the sea's bounty.

St John

About 8,700 persons live in the parish of St John, located on the west coast of Grenada, adjoining the parishes of St Mark to the north, St George to the south and St Andrew to the east.

Near to the boundary with St Andrew is Fedon's Camp, high up in the hills in the central range. It's a steep climb, but for eager hikers it's well

OPPOSITE
View from Belmont near Victoria towards Mount St Catherine

72

worth it as they are rewarded with a fantastic view of the surrounding countryside.

Belvidere Estate, up in the hills is an interesting place to visit. A rather bumpy road runs through the estate, connecting with a main road in St Andrew. Almost everything grown in Grenada can be seen in these hills. The three major crops - cocoa, nutmegs and bananas - are all in evidence, as is the breadfruit, brought from the Far East to the Caribbean by Captain Bligh, of 'Mutiny on the Bounty' fame.

The breadfruit was brought to Grenada as a source of cheap food for the plantation slaves, but today, its popularity rivals the potato, and it is much preferred in many households.

The Dougaldston Estate is another interesting place. Here, cocoa trees, banana plants, cinnamon and clove trees are in evidence and visitors can see the spices in various stages of processing and preparation for the market.

Racks for drying nutmegs at the Dougaldston Estate, Gouyave. The racks are designed to be wheeled under cover should it rain

The main town in this parish is Gouyave. When the British took possession of the island they tried to rename it 'Charlotte Town' but the residents would have none of this, and 'Gouyave' stuck. Old maps show both names but the map-makers have finally conceded defeat and modern maps show the town as 'Gouyave'. This is one of Grenada's six main fishing areas, with cold storage facilities available for the day's catch. St John, like St George, is famous for the yellow fin tuna which can weigh between 100 and 160 pounds. Much of the catch is exported to the United States. The Lance, a beach just north of the town, is where the fishing boats are beached after the day's catch has been landed. The boats are all colourfully painted and it is a beautiful sight to see them all together.

At the Nutmeg Processing Station in Gouyave, the two spices, nutmegs and mace, are separated, dried and made ready for shipment. Guides are available to show visitors around, pointing out the various stages of processing. The smell of this delicious spice permeates the entire building.

Sacks of nutmegs ready for shipment at the Nutmeg Processing Station in Gouyave

There are pleasant eating places in Gouyave serving very tasty local dishes. The surroundings may be a bit rustic, but the food is good. Further south at Palmiste, there's NEWLO. The New Life Organisation is a Vocational Skills Training Centre brought into being by four church groups in Grenada to help provide educational support for 16-23 year-olds. Over the years a number of skills have been taught, with trainee carpenters and masons building additional classrooms and furniture for the centre. There is also a small craft shop selling items made on the premises.

On the hill behind the NEWLO buildings an artificial lake was formed

OPPOSITE
A fisherman off Gouyave

by damming the river. It is a lovely cool spot, ideal for a quiet picnic. At Mount Nesbit there is a small batik factory where Thomas Sylvester runs a successful operation in the ground floor of his home. He creates all the interesting designs and has trained his workers in the art of waxing and dyeing the materials. The designs are all freehand and consequently each piece is unique. Beach wraps, scarves, bags and other products are on sale and he has markets for everything he produces.

Concord Falls are in this parish. There are actually three falls. The first one has been developed complete with changing rooms, washrooms and a small bar serving drinks and light snacks. The swimming area is not very large, but the pleasant, cool water makes it a perfect way to relax on a hot day.

The other two falls require a bit of mountaineering but they are in much more pristine settings for those who enjoy nature in the raw. The changing rooms and washrooms are behind the nearest bush but the swimming beneath the falls is an invigorating experience.

Back to the main road and travel west to arrive at Black Bay. The sand here is a glistening black, fine and soft underfoot. The sea water is clear and cool. On the road to the beach there's an old water wheel, once used for driving the machinery that squeezed the juice from the sugar cane. It has long been out of use but still stands as one more relic of Grenada's past history when sugar was the mainstay of the island's economy.

The highlight of the year for this parish is the Fisherman's Birthday celebrations which are held on the Feast Day of St Peter and St Paul - June 29. The fishermen, their boats and nets are all blessed by the clergy of different denominations and this is followed by boat races.

Stalls are set up along the streets to sell food and drink to the revellers who turn out to enjoy the day. There's singing and dancing and various other entertainments, including popular steelband music. Good-natured celebrations continue far into the night.

Roadside memorial
In 1991, on the Western Main Road on the way to Concord, a sudden landslide caused a huge rock to fall and crush a passing school bus - killing thirteen children and the driver. The memorial, laid by the Prime Minister, the Rt Hon Nicholas Brathwaite, and donated by Otways Funeral Home reads: *"Dedicated to the memory of those who lost their lives in the tragic accident on January 16, 1991. May they have eternal rest."*

ABOVE & OVERLEAF
Fisherman's Birthday, Gouyave

OPPOSITE
Concord Falls

HISTORY
From colony to democracy
By Alister Hughes

In 1498, six years after his first round trip, trans-atlantic cruise to the Caribbean, Christopher Columbus made a third return visit to the area, this time favouring a southerly approach to the mysterious, unnamed 'continental' coastline known later as the Spanish Main. After a clockwise near circumnavigation of Trinidad, the Italian explorer sailed north out of Trinidad's inland sea known as the Gulf of Paria, passing through the island-studded Dragon's Mouth Channel separating Trinidad from the mainland.

Journals kept by Columbus have been lost, but contemporary records compiled from them say that the day after leaving Trinidad's mountains well astern, low on the southern horizon, he sighted Grenada from a distance and named it "Concepcion". He never set foot on the island and was unaware that it was then inhabited by an Amerindian people. These early inhabitants were subsistence agriculturists who had migrated to Grenada from the South American mainland about the first century AD. Archaeological analysis indicates that, some six centuries later, another tribe of Amerindians, the Arawaks, arrived in Grenada from the mainland.

About the time Columbus was opening up the 'New World' to Europe, the powerful Caribs swept through the Lesser Antilles. They conquered the Arawaks, established several settlements on Grenada and, after Columbus passed by, remained undisturbed for over a century before European colonisation encroached on their lives. Early explorers rendered the Amerindian name for the island as 'Camerhogne'.

Following two unsuccessful attempts at colonisation, 200 Frenchmen from Martinique settled in Grenada in 1650. Within a year, the Carib inhabitants began to kill Frenchmen found hunting in the forest. This brought a violent reaction from the French who successfully called for reinforcements from the colony of Martinique. The Caribs retreated to a precipitous hill in the north of the island where they sought refuge. After a long search, the French discovered their refuge and took them by surprise. Most of the Carib Indians committed suicide by leaping into the sea below. In several raids until 1654, the French all but completely exterminated the Caribs. A few elements of the Amerindian culture survive today. These include some words of Amerindian origin, pottery and other burial site

Sketch of a steam ship in St George's harbour, from 'The Illustrated London News', February 21, 1846
Courtesy: Alice Carlsson

Historical artefacts
The Carriacou Historical Society have a museum in Hillsborough, Carriacou, with a small collection of Amerindian and European artefacts.

Emancipation

In the Caribbean, *Emancipation* is the term used solely in association with the abolition of slavery, which began in the British Westindies in 1834 and ended in Cuba in 1878. It is one of the most significant events in Westindian history and involved the passing of Acts in six European parliaments over a period of more than 40 years before it was completed.

Apprenticeship

This was the period of four years following Emancipation in the British Westindies, during which time all 'ex-slaves' over the age of six were obliged to work, without pay, for their former owners for three-quarters of each working week.

Indentured labour

A 'new system of slavery' under which people from Europe, Africa and Asia were contracted for a fixed period to work on estates in the Westindies. It began in the seventeenth century with the introduction of English, Irish and other European indentured 'servants', who worked for three to seven years for no wages with the expectation of a grant of land at the end. Such people were impossible to obtain after the middle of the eighteenth century.

The main demand for indentured labour occurred after Emancipation, in 1834, and large numbers of Chinese and Indians, together with large numbers of Madeirans and West Africans, were brought to the Caribbean throughout the nineteenth and into the twentieth centuries.

remains, and petroglyphs in the Mount Rich area. Leapers Hill and the town of Sauteurs are named after the tragic events that brought an end to the Carib nation in Grenada.

The first successful European settlement of Grenada was a private development venture which was sold to the French West Indian Company in 1665. Nine years later, in 1674, the Company was dissolved and the island came under the French Crown. It remained a French colony until 1762, when it surrendered to a British squadron without firing a shot. The Treaty of Paris, signed in the following year, confirmed the British possession, and the first British Colonial Government of Grenada was created by royal proclamation of George III.

In 1771 a fire completely destroyed St George's, which was then a town of wooden buildings. Four years later, the greater part of the town was again destroyed by fire, as a result of which the Legislature enacted laws prohibiting construction of buildings which were not of brick or stones and covered with tiles. Those laws had a fundamental effect on the rebuilding of the town and are responsible for the unique architectural character of modern St George's.

The 1775/6 War of American Independence also led to Britain's involvement in a war with France in 1778, which had repercussions for Grenada. A French fleet sailed to the Caribbean after engaging British vessels along the American coast. For several months, the fleet was blockaded at Martinique by the British Navy. Breaking out in 1779, the French sailed south to St Vincent where the British capitulated. The fleet then moved on to Grenada and captured the island from the British by a clever manoeuvre, after a brief but fierce fight.

Grenada changed hands again when it was returned to Britain in 1783 by the Treaty of Versailles. The Colony of Grenada was then defined as ".... the island of Grenada and such of the islands commonly called the Grenadines to the southward of Carriacou, including that island, and lying between the same and Grenada", a delimitation still in force today.

During the French occupation, British settlers had been treated very badly, and this was not forgotten when the island was restored to British rule. Laws repressive to the French were enacted; Frenchmen were excluded from the Legislature and were persecuted because of their religion.

But the French in Grenada had their revenge. After the French Revolution of 1789, they rose up in rebellion against the British, instigated and armed by their countrymen in Martinique. Led by Julien Fedon, a Grenadian of African and French blood who owned the Belvidere Estate

which was then the largest estate in Grenada, this revolt began in March 1795 and was not crushed until 14 months later. Joined by slaves and 'free coloured', Fedon took possession of all of the island except St George's. In 1796 a very large British force was sent to Grenada under the command of Sir Ralph Abercromby, who overcame the rebel forces by capturing their stronghold located on a flat-topped peak in the central mountain range (now called Fedon's Camp). Sir Ralph went on to capture Trinidad from the Spanish. Fedon himself was never captured.

In spite of this unrest, the colonists in Grenada prospered. It had become a 'free port' in 1767, a status conferred by Imperial Acts on several British islands in the Caribbean. Under this system, Britain allowed small vessels from neighbouring foreign colonies into certain ports of the British Westindies with the privilege of importing and exporting specified types of goods. Grenada benefited from this trade for about 30 years. Nevertheless, during this time, the principal interest of the British was agriculture, as it had been with the French colonists.

The first French settlers in 1650 planted tobacco and by 1700 were producing indigo and livestock. In 1702 sugar cane was introduced from South America, and cane cultivation gradually took over from indigo in the early eighteenth century. Sugar cane cultivation being labour intensive, could only be profitable through the introduction of cheap labour into the country. The colonists seized upon slave labour as their saviour, thus the slave trade was developed. Until the abolition of slavery in 1834, sugar cane was by far the most profitable crop cultivated on almost all low-lying land in the country. In 1714, cocoa, coffee and cotton were introduced and, after 1783, under British administration, exports of these crops were expanded. Fustic (dye wood), slaves, hides and wood were also added to the list of exports.

Trade in fustic declined drastically early in the nineteenth century, production of indigo had been abandoned by 1846 and exports of tobacco petered out in the late 1890s. Coffee lingered until the first quarter of the twentieth century, and cotton, its production eventually confined to the sister island of Carriacou, was exported for the last time in 1981 - although there is some discussion of reviving the industry as part of a larger regional strategy.

Maltese, Portuguese and liberated slaves from Africa were imported in 1839 to provide another cheap labour force to replace the Emancipated slaves, but this experiment failed. Additionally, the price of sugar began to show a marked decrease because planters had to compete on the European market with the sugar still produced by slave labour in Spanish

Washing in a river with 'wattle and daub' houses in the background, around 1890. 'Wattle and daub' was a method of simple house construction involving the interlacing of rods and twigs (wattle) which are then plastered (daub) with either mud or clay. This method of house building existed in the Caribbean up until the middle of the twentieth century.
Courtesy: Jim Rudin

St. Georges, Grenada.

TOP
A panoramic view of St George's, 1885
Courtesy: Grenada National Museum

ABOVE
View of St George's looking towards Fort George, taken around 1900
Courtesy: Paul Slinger

FAR RIGHT
The Carenage, St George's, thought to be around the mid-to-late 19th century
Courtesy: Grenada National Museum

RIGHT
The Carenage today

colonies. By 1856, many sugar estates in Grenada had been abandoned.

Immigration of indentured labourers from India to work on the estates began in 1857. This new source of near-slave labour permitted several sugar estates to be reclaimed, the gradual transference of agricultural interest from sugar to cocoa, which began with Emancipation, continued. The emancipated slaves and indentured labourers took readily to this crop; a quantity of land could be easily had in the interior, and the cultivation of cocoa offered an independent existence and reasonable profits for a minimum of labour. This quest for vast profits led to the clearing of a large part of the remaining upland rainforest.

Nutmegs (which earned Grenada the name 'Isle of Spice') were introduced about 1843 as a curiosity by sugar planters returning from the Far East. Less than a decade later, when disease seriously depleted the Indonesian nutmeg plantations, Grenadian agriculturists started planting nutmegs seriously as an economic crop, but it was a slow process and there were no exports until 1881. Today, together with bananas (which became an economic crop in the mid-1950s) and cocoa, nutmeg forms the backbone of the island's agricultural economy.

The promotion of Grenada's excellent potential as a tourist destination was first undertaken in 1938 when the government appointed a 'Tourist Committee', but real development of this sector of the economy did not begin until the early 1950s after World War II. Since then, tourism has developed to the stage where it is key to the national wellbeing.

Constitutionally, Grenada had an elected House of Assembly after the island was captured from the French in 1763. Except for a brief period from 1779 - 1783, that House continued to sit until 1876 when the House voted itself out of existence. From that date, until 1924, Grenada was a Crown Colony governed from London. It was the efforts of one of the island's national heroes, Theophilus Albert Marryshow, which set the country again on the road of constitutional advancement. As a result of Marryshow's agitation, elections for a Legislative Council were held in 1924 under a limited franchise.

In the years following, there was gradual constitutional improvement until, in 1951, adult franchise was introduced. This was also a time of great civil unrest. The liberalising of the franchise coincided with the birth of trade union activity, and both political and economic issues created strife between the 'plantocracy' and the working masses.

In 1967, Grenada became a State in Association with Britain. This arrangement for the first time gave Grenadians complete internal self-

Theophilus Albert Marryshow, (1885-1958), remembered as 'The Father of the Nation'. After leaving school he entered journalism, starting as a newsboy, and became editor of the *St George's Chronicle* by the time he was 26. In 1915 he helped found *The West Indian* in which, as editor, he campaigned for representative government and federation of the British Westindies. He is pictured here in 1955.
Courtesy: Grenada National Museum

OPPOSITE
(Top) Government House, 1890 and (bottom) Market Square, St George's, early 1900s
Photos courtesy: Jim Rudin

BELOW
Government House today

government, while Britain administered the portfolios of Defence and Foreign Affairs. But this constitutional advance heralded another period of civil unrest.

Against this background, and in an atmosphere of continuing unrest, Grenada achieved independence on February 7, 1974. During this period, the left-wing New Jewel Movement (NJM) was born, led by young intellectuals who contested and won seats in the 1976 General Elections. In March 1979, however, NJM abandoned democratic parliamentary procedure for revolution. In an almost bloodless coup, NJM seized and held the government for four-and-a-half-years. In October 1983 a power struggle within the party resulted in the assassination of the revolutionary Prime Minister Maurice Bishop with members of his Cabinet and in the deaths of a still unknown number of other Grenadians.

Days after these traumatic events, military intervention by the United States and Caribbean forces recovered the island from the Revolutionary Military Council which had seized power from Bishop and his colleagues and, after a period of rule by an interim government, parliamentary democracy was restored with general elections being held in December 1984.

The year 1990, marking the three hundred and fortieth year since the first colonisation of the island, found the country with a flourishing democracy (seven political parties), freedom of speech (six newspapers), a good record of human rights (attested to by Amnesty International in 1988) and an improving economy. There is some, although limited, evidence of a growing realisation by government and the public of the need for environmental management and control. Provided that the lessons of historical experience are heeded, that wise political and economic management prevail and that sustainable use of the nation's resources can be achieved, the citizens of the "Isle of Spice" seem to enjoy excellent prospects for continuing improvement in the quality of their lives.

West Indian Regiment

A unit of the British Army, manned by Westindians under British officers, which existed from 1795 to 1927. Consisting at first of two battalions, created from irregular bodies of black troops raised in South Carolina and St Vincent, by 1800 it was composed of 12 battalions stationed throughout the Caribbean.

Plaque to commemorate the US/Caribbean military intervention of October 1983

OPPOSITE
(Top) The 3rd Grenadian contingent of the British West Indian Regiment prepared to embark on a troop transport vessel to join the Allied Forces on the other side of the Atlantic in 1914 under the command of Major David L Slinger.
(Bottom) The regiment on the Carenage, 1914
Photos courtesy: Paul Slinger

LEFT: **Nominated and Elected Members of the Legislated Council, Grenada, 1951**
Standing back row (L - R): A N Hughes, Dennis Henry, R O Williams, R K Douglas, L C J Thomas, Joseph Gibbs, Gordon L Gun-Munro and Allan Williams
Seated front row (L - R): A L Dopwell, T A Marryshow, Bernard Gibbs (Colonial Administrator), Edward Beecham-Bethan (Governor), C F Henville (Attorney General), F B Patterson and E M Gairy
Courtesy: Grenada National Museum

National leaders since Independence

By Alister Hughes

Prime Minister Sir Eric Gairy (1974 - 1979)

The task of leading Grenada into Independence on February 7, 1974 fell to Prime Minister Sir Eric Matthew Gairy, who had entered political life after pioneering the country's trade union movement.

Sir Eric Gairy

Sir Eric was born on February 18, 1922 and received a primary school education. Leaving school, he was employed as a primary school teacher for three years before migrating to Trinidad where he worked for two years as a clerk/typist.

He then moved to, and, for six years, worked in the Dutch controlled island of Aruba before returning to Grenada in 1949 when he founded the Grenada Mental & Manual Workers Union (GMMWU).

In the following year, Grenada was thrown into violent civil strife as a result of an island-wide strike called by GMMWU. Prior to this, such trade unions as had existed in Grenada were not militant. GMMWU broke with this tradition and, the strike having brought considerable gains to the workers, Sir Eric was placed firmly in the leadership of labour in the island.

The year 1951 saw Grenada's first General Elections on the basis of adult suffrage. Sir Eric contested those elections under the banner of the Grenada United Labour Party (GULP), which he had founded, and captured five of the then eight seats in the Legislature.

GULP was the first organised political party in the island and, in the General Elections of 1954, four seats went to that party while independents won the other four.

It was not until the General Elections of 1957 that other political parties entered the hustings, and it was during the campaign for those elections that Sir Eric committed an election offence which lost him his franchise.

Re-elected in a by-election when the franchise was regained, Sir Eric went on to lead GULP to victory in the 1961 General Elections. Following this, however, a Commission of Inquiry found his administration guilty of questionable governmental expenditure.

Grenada was then still a colony and Britain suspended the Constitution, governing the island for a short while from London before calling new elections at which GULP was defeated.

Sir Eric regained the Government in the 1967 General Elections which were held under a new Constitution giving the Government full internal self government. GULP was again victorious with a landslide win in the 1972 General Elections, but this period was marked by extreme lawlessness and violence.

A Commission of Inquiry examining Sir Eric's administration did not submit a favourable report but, though with a reduced majority, GULP captured the Government again in the 1976 General Elections.

Sir Eric was deposed by the 1979 New Jewel Movement revolution. He was visiting the United States when the overthrow took place and did not return to Grenada until January 1984, after the military intervention by United States and Caribbean forces.

Sir Eric was not a candidate in the 1984 General Elections and GULP was decisively beaten. In the 1990 General Elections, he contested his usual seat in the constituency of South St George and, for the first time in his political career, suffered a personal electoral defeat.

In the Queen's New Year Honours of 1977, Sir Eric was elevated to membership of the Privy Council and, later that year, in the Queen's Birthday Honours, was made a Knight Bachelor.

Prime Minister Maurice Bishop (1979 - 1983)

Prime Minister Maurice Bishop did not assume leadership of the Government of Grenada through the ballot box but by proclamation.

Bishop was leader of the New Jewel Movement revolution of March 13, 1979, and Peoples Law Number 11 of March 29, 1979 proclaims that "the People's Revolutionary Government is pleased to appoint and hereby appoints Maurice Rupert Bishop to be Prime Minister of Grenada....."

At that time, Bishop, born in Aruba on May 29, 1944, was 35 years old. His parents, Rupert and Alimenta Bishop, both native Grenadians, had moved back to the island in 1950 and placed their six-year-old son at the Wesley Hall Primary School.

A year later, he was moved to the St George's Roman Catholic Primary School where he won one of the few scholarships then offered to attend a secondary school. That was in 1956 and, on that scholarship, he went, in January 1957, to the Roman Catholic Presentation College.

In his final years of secondary education, Bishop decided he would study law and, when he left Presentation College in 1963, he worked just a few months at the Registry in Grenada before leaving for England.

Entering Gray's Inn immediately, Bishop simultaneously gained a degree at London University's Holborn College of Law. He then began postgraduate work at King's College, in the field of Grenada's constitutional development, but left to take up employment in the British Civil Service as a surtax examiner.

In 1969, he returned to the Inns of Court and successfully completed

Maurice Bishop

his Bar Finals examination, returning to Grenada in March 1970, where he went into private practice.

Responding to the situation in Grenada in 1973, Bishop formed a political group called the "Movement For Assemblies of the People" (MAP), and, in the same year, merged MAP with another political group established and led by his colleague, Unison Whiteman.

Whiteman's group had the name "Joint Action For Education Welfare & Liberation" (JEWEL), and the organisation resulting from the merger was called the "New Jewel Movement" (NJM).

It was on the NJM ticket (in alliance with two other political parties) that Bishop was elected to the House of Representatives in 1976, winning the seat for the constituency of St George's South-East .

Appointed to be Leader of the Opposition, he held that post for some three years until March 13, 1979 when he successfully led an armed, and almost bloodless, take-over of the Government.

Because of a power struggle within the People's Revolutionary Government, Prime Minister Bishop was placed under house arrest on October 13th 1983. Six days later, on October 19, a large crowd freed him and accompanied him to Fort George (then Fort Rupert).

The forces opposing the Prime Minister then sent a detachment of the People's Revolutionary Army to attack the fort, which resulted in the deaths of a still unknown number of Grenadians. Prime Minister Bishop was captured and, together with ten of his supporters, was assassinated.

Prime Minister Herbert Blaize (1984 - 1989)

Prime Minister Herbert Augustus Blaize made his political debut in 1954, when he contested the Carriacou & Petit Martinique constituency unsuccessfully as an independent, and first took his seat in the Legislature when he won that constituency in 1957 as a member of the Grenada National Party (GNP).

Some two years later he took over the political leadership of the GNP, was Minister of Trade and Production from 1957 to 1959 and Chief Minister from 1960 to 1961.

The GNP lost the 1961 elections and Blaize became Leader of the Opposition but, after the Constitution was suspended by Britain in 1962 (following a Commission of Inquiry into the then Administration) the GNP had an outright win in the elections of that year and he held the position of Chief Minister until 1967.

Herbert Blaize

During that term of office, Blaize obtained for Grenada the Constitution of a "State in Association with Britain". Under it, in March 1967, complete internal control was vested in the Grenada Government, while Defence and Foreign Affairs remained in British hands.

Blaize's title under the new Constitution was "Premier" but he reverted to being Leader of the Opposition when the GNP lost the General Elections of August 1967.

The GNP lost the General Elections again in both 1972 and 1976. In the latter year, the party teamed up, under the banner of "The People's Alliance", with two other parties, the New Jewel Movement (NJM) and the United Peoples Party, and, following that election, Blaize relinquished, to Maurice Bishop of the NJM, the position of Leader of the Opposition.

Blaize was educated at the Hillsborough Government School in Carriacou and at the Grenada Boys' Secondary School (GBSS). Following his retirement as Leader of the Opposition, he took the opportunity for further study and, self-taught, qualified as a solicitor.

The NJM revolution of 1979-1983 saw the GNP in abeyance but, following the military intervention of October 1983, Blaize was the moving force in forging the New National Party (NNP) out of the GNP and two newly formed parties, the Grenada Democratic Movement and the National Democratic Party.

Under Blaize's leadership, the NNP was successful in the 1984 General Elections, winning 14 of the 15 seats in the House of Representatives. These elections marked also the seventh consecutive time Blaize had won the seat for Carriacou & Petit Martinique.

Blaize's last session in the House, which was terminated by his death on December 19, 1989, was marked by controversy within the Government, resulting in defections which reduced the NNP majority to nine against an opposition of six.

At a convention in January 1989, Prime Minister Blaize lost the NNP political leadership. With growing friction within the party, he withdrew from the NNP and, with a group of members loyal to him, launched The National Party (TNP) on August 31, 1989.

At TNP's first convention on December 17, 1989, two days before his death, Blaize was officially elected the party's Political Leader.

Blaize was born in Carriacou on February 26, 1918.

At the Grenada Boys' Secondary School, he proved to be an excellent student and, in 1937, his final year at GBSS, was the runner-up in the examination for the Island Scholarship awarded by the Government.

Leaving school, he was a civil servant in the Treasury and Administration Departments of Government until he migrated to Aruba in 1944 where he worked with the Largo Oil Transport Company as a stenographer/secretary and section head in the office service of that company. Blaize returned to Grenada in 1952.

Prime Minister Ben Jones (1989 -1990)

The mantle of leadership of the Government of Grenada fell on the shoulders of the Honourable Ben Joseph Jones when his long-time friend and political colleague, Prime Minister Herbert Blaize, died in December 1989.

Ben Jones

Appointed by the Governor General to succeed Prime Minister Blaize, Prime Minister Jones had less than 100 days before the Constitution demanded that General Elections be held. At his discretion, those elections were fixed for March 13, 1990 and, although his political party, The National Party (TNP), did not retain the Government, he won again the seat for the constituency of St Andrew South West.

Prime Minister Jones was born on August 5, 1924 in Carriere, a small village in the parish of St Andrew. Educated at the Belair Presbyterian Primary School, he left school in 1943 and, after short stints in the commercial and agricultural fields, enlisted, for the duration of World War II, in the Windward Islands Battalion of the South Caribbean Force.

For a short time after being demobilised, Jones was employed in agriculture again before migrating to the Dutch-ruled island of Aruba where he worked for nine years with the United States oil refinery, Largo.

Hoping to fulfil his ambition to become a barrister, Jones migrated to the United Kingdom in 1956. Having only a primary school education at this stage, further basic study was required before that ambition could be realised and, to achieve this, he entered the Chiswick Polytechnic.

Advised by the Polytechnic officials that it would take him seven years to upgrade his primary education to the level required to study law, Jones entered a self-imposed, intensive study routine which achieved the seven year goal in eighteen school-months.

Then, entering Gray's Inn, he began his study of law. At the same time, he enrolled as an external student at London University, adding to this a correspondence course in law, and, successful in his examinations, was called to the Bar on February 6, 1962.

There followed two years experience with a firm of solicitors in London, after which Jones returned to Grenada and accepted a post of magistrate which he held for about a year before returning to private practice.

In anticipation of Grenada's new constitution of "A State In Association With Britain", which came into effect in March 1967, he was invited by Premier Herbert Blaize to establish and head, as Senior Assistant Secretary, a Ministry of Foreign Affairs. This Jones did, but relinquished the post to contest the General Elections of August 1967 under the banner of the Grenada National Party.

He was defeated at the polls but Herbert Blaize, as Leader of the Opposition, nominated him to a seat in the Senate. Jones did not contest the General Elections of 1976 but, following those elections, was nominated again as an Opposition member of the Senate, a post he held until the revolution of 1979.

In the 1984 General Elections, Jones successfully contested the seat for St Andrew South West and, in the ruling Grenada National Party Government of Prime Minister Herbert Blaize held, at various times, the Ministries of Legal Affairs, External Affairs, Agriculture, Tourism and Forestry & Lands. He has also held the post of Attorney General.

Jones was one of the group which broke away from the GNP with Prime Minister Blaize to launch TNP, and he was Deputy Political Leader of that new party.

Following the General Elections of 1990, Jones, while retaining his membership of TNP, threw in his lot with the National Democratic Congress and was given the Ministry of Agriculture, Forestry, Lands and Fisheries.

The relationship, however, was not a comfortable one and, in January 1991, Jones resigned from the Government and returned to private practice.

Prime Minister Nicholas Brathwaite (1990 -   )

The Honourable Nicholas Alexander Brathwaite, Grenada's current Prime Minister, headed the Interim Government appointed by Governor General Sir Paul Scoon following the military intervention by United States and Caribbean Forces in 1983.

At that time, Brathwaite, stationed in Guyana, was Regional Director of the Commonwealth Youth Programme, an appointment he had held since 1974. He relinquished that post to fill the position of Chairman of the Interim Government, supervising preparations for the General Elections which led the island back to parliamentary democracy in the aftermath of the revolution of 1979-1983.

Born on July 8, 1928, Brathwaite, a native of Grenada's sister island of

Nicholas Brathwaite

Carriacou, was educated at Mount Pleasant Government School in Carriacou and at the Grenada Boys' Secondary School.

His education continued at the Teachers' Training College in Trinidad and at the Mona campus of the University of the West Indies in Jamaica.

Except for a break from 1951 to 1957, when he was an oil refinery operator in the Dutch-ruled island of Curacao, his work experience over the 30 year period 1945 to 1974 was dedicated to the education field.

Starting as a primary school teacher, he rose to be Principal of a primary school, advanced to be a tutor at the Grenada Teachers' College and, in 1968, became Principal of that College.

In the following year, he was appointed Grenada's Chief Education Officer, a position he held until 1974 when he became the Regional Director of the Commonwealth Youth Programme.

The Interim Government was dissolved after the General Elections of December 1984 and, from then until 1986, Brathwaite performed the duties of Executive Adviser to Prime Minister Herbert Blaize.

Brathwaite's elected political career can be said to have began in January 1989 when he was elected President of the National Democratic Congress. Under that banner he won the Carriacou seat in the General Elections of March 13, 1990 and, on March 16, 1990, was appointed Prime Minister.

His public service record includes serving as President of the Carriacou branch of the Grenada Union of Teachers, President of the Grenada Civil Service Association and President of the Grenada Cricket Umpires Association.

In July 1991, he was appointed a Member of the Privy Council.

On September 5, 1994, Brathwaite resigned as leader of the National Democratic Congress.

Governor General Sir Leo DeGale (1974 - 1978)

Grenada's first Governor General, appointed when the island became independent on February 7, 1974, was the late Sir Leo Victor DeGale.

Born on December 28, 1921, Sir Leo was a qualified land surveyor and held diplomas in accountancy and business administration. His early education was received at the Grenada Boys' Secondary School (GBSS) and he afterwards attended Sir George Williams University in Montreal, Canada.

During World War II, Sir Leo served from 1940 to 1945 as a gunner with the First Survey Regiment of the Royal Canadian Artillery, following which he returned to Grenada and was co-founder of the auditing firm of

Modern Political Parties

MBPM - Maurice Bishop Patriotic Movement
GULP - Grenada United Labour Party
NNP - New National Party
NDC - National Democratic Congress
TNP - The National Party

DeGale & Rapier from which he retired in 1964.

From 1951 to 1954, Sir Leo held a commission in the Grenada Volunteer Constabulary and his public record includes service as President of the Catholic Men's Society, Member of the West India Committee, and Member of the West Indies Associated States Judicial and Legal Services Commission.

Sir Leo served also as Chairman of the Grenada Banana Co-operative Society and Chairman of the Board of Governors of the GBSS.

Queen Elizabeth II honoured Sir Leo twice, the first time being in 1969 when he was made a Commander of the Most Excellent Order of the British Empire (CBE). On the second occasion, in 1974, he was elevated to be a Knight Grand Cross of the Most Distinguished Order of St Michael and St George (GCMG).

His term of office as Governor General ended in 1978 and, soon after the revolution of 1979, he took up residence in Bristol, England. Sir Leo died on March 23, 1986.

Governor General Sir Paul Scoon (1978 - 1992)

Sir Paul Scoon served as Grenada's Governor General during a difficult period of tremendous turmoil in the country. Sworn in, on October 4, 1978, as the island's second Governor General, he found himself, within six months, faced with the reality of the New Jewel Movement (NJM) revolution.

The revolutionaries suspended the Constitution and the office of Governor General was placed in a precarious position for over four years.

Following the military intervention by the United States and Caribbean Forces in October 1983, Sir Paul, as the Representative of Her Majesty the Queen - who remained as Head of State, even after independence - assumed control of the business of the State, ensuring a return to parliamentary democracy by appointing an Interim Government which arranged for General Elections to be held under a reinstated Constitution.

Born on July 4, 1935, Sir Paul was educated at the St John's Anglican School and at the Grenada Boys' Secondary School. He studied as an external student of London University acquiring a Bachelor of Arts degree and, later, attended the Institute of Education at Leeds University. He also holds a Master of Education degree from the University of Toronto.

Sir Paul taught at the GBSS before serving as Chief Education Officer, and later as Permanent Secretary in the Prime Minister's office, before being appointed Cabinet Secretary, the top post in the Grenada Civil Service.

In 1973, he was seconded to the post of Deputy Director of the

Sir Paul Scoon

97

Commonwealth Foundation in London, which he relinquished in 1978 to become Grenada's Governor General.

In the field of public service, Sir Paul has served on the Grenada Library Committee, on the Board of Governors of the Grenada Teachers' College, on the Governing Body of the GBSS, on the Prison Visiting Committee, on the Board of Education and on the Management Council of the Civil Service Association.

He is co-founder and former President of the Secondary School Teachers Association, and was a member of the Board of Governors of the Centre for International Briefing at Farnham Castle in Britain.

Rotary Foundation of Rotary International named Sir Paul a Paul Harris Fellow in 1984, and he was honoured by the Queen on three occasions: In 1970 when he was made an Officer of the Most Excellent Order of the British Empire (OBE); in 1979 when he was made a Knight Grand Cross of the Most Distinguished Order of St Michael and St George (GCMG); and in 1985 when he was made a Knight Grand Cross of the Royal Victorian Order (GCVO).

He retired from the post of Governor General on July 31, 1992.

Governor General Sir Reginald Palmer (1992 -)

Sir Reginald Oswald Palmer, Grenada's present Governor General, born on February 15, 1923, was sworn in as the Queen's Representative on August 6, 1992.

Sir Reginald Palmer

Educated at the Beaulieu Roman Catholic School and the St George's Roman Catholic Boys' School, Sir Reginald was a pupil teacher for a short while before moving, in 1943, to the Government Teachers' Training College in Trinidad where he spent two years and was awarded the Trained Teachers Certificate.

Dedicated to the field of education, Sir Reginald was an assistant teacher at the St George's Roman Catholic Boys' School from 1945 to 1956. During that period, he acquired the London Matriculation Certificate and, in 1956, was made the Head Teacher of that school.

In 1963, Sir Reginald entered the University of Birmingham in England and, following a two year programme, was awarded a certificate relative to a Course of Studies in Education for Heads of Schools and Administrators.

Sir Reginald was appointed a tutor at the Grenada Teachers' College in 1968 and, two years later, entered the University of Calgary in Canada. He returned to Grenada in 1971 with a Bachelor of Education degree, and, the following year was promoted to the post of Assistant Education Officer.

There was further promotion in 1973 when he was made Principal of the Grenada Teachers' College, a post he held for only one year before being made Chief Education Officer.

Sir Reginald retired from the public service in 1980 and, entering the private sector, served for two terms as President of the Grenada Employers' Federation.

In addition to membership of several Catholic organisations, he has been, at various times, a member of the Governing Body of the Grenada Boys' Secondary School, of the Public Service Commission, Grenada Education Advisory Council, Grenada Civic Awareness Organisation, the Labour Advisory Board, the Drug Avoidance Committee and the Local Advisory Council of the University of the West Indies School of Continuing Studies.

Sir Reginald is a foundation member of the Catholic Teachers' Association, the Caribbean Association of Catholic Teachers and the Grenada Teachers' Social Security and Welfare Association, and was Secretary to the last mentioned body from 1951 to 1969.

In the Grenada Union of Teachers, Sir Reginald advanced from assistant secretary to secretary, through to vice president and finally held the post of President. He has also represented this union on the Board of Education.

Sir Reginald is a Director of the New Life Organisation, the Richmond Fellowship of Grenada and the Grenada Bank of Commerce.

In 1973, his services to education were recognised when he was made a Member of the Most Excellent Order of the British Empire (MBE) and, in 1972, when he became Governor General, he was made a Knight Grand Cross of the Most Distinguished Order of St Michael and St George (GCMG).

Important historical dates and events

1 - 500 AD	The Arawaks (Saladoids).
500 - 1000	The Arawaks (Barrancoids).
1000 - 1650	The Caribs settled Grenada.
1498	Columbus sights Grenada, names it "Concepcion".
1609	Attempted settlement by British settlers who started Megrin Town at La Sagesse.
1638	Attempted settlement by the French.
1650	Grenada's successful settlement by the French under du Parquet. First town Port Louis built.
1651	War between French and Caribs.
1700	Grenada visited by Fr. Pere Labat who recommended that the town should be moved.
1705	New town called Port Royale built.
1706	Fort George built.
1763	The island ceded to the British by the Treaty of Paris.
1771	Town consisting of wooden houses destroyed by fire.
1775	Town again destroyed by fire.
1776	Grenada became a separate political unit with Tobago after being a single colony with Dominica, St Vincent and Tobago.
1779	Grenada recaptured by the French who started the construction of Fort Matthew, Fort Frederick, Fort Adolphus and Fort Lucas.
1783	Island restored to British rule by Treaty of Versailles.
1791	The forts at Richmond Hill completed. Market Squares established in St George's, Gouyave, Victoria, Sauteurs, Grenville and Hillsborough in Carriacou.
1792	A third of St George's again destroyed by fire. An Election Act was passed which required all members of the Legislature to subscribe to the Test Act which resulted in the virtual exclusion of all Catholics from the Legislature.
1795/96	Fedon's Rebellion.

1818	Catholic Cathedral built.
1820	The Methodist Church in St George's built.
1826	Renovation of Anglican Church, rebuilt in Georgian manner.
1833	Grenada included in the Government of the Windward Islands, comprising Barbados, Grenada, St Vincent, Tobago and dependencies.
1834	Abolition of slavery.
1877	Grenada proclaimed a Crown Colony.
1880	The military hospital at Richmond Hill converted to a prison.
1894	Sendall Tunnel completed.
1903	A land settlement scheme started in Carriacou.
1925	Whaling station built on Glovers Island.
1955	Hurricane Janet struck Grenada.
1958 - 62	The West Indies Federation.
1961	Cruise liner 'Bianca C' sank off Point Salines.
1967	Grenada granted Associated Statehood.
1974	Independence from Britain.
1979	The Grenada Revolution and the assumption of power by the People's Revolutionary Government (PRG).
1983	Prime Minister Maurice Bishop assassinated. US/Caribbean military intervention.
1989	Death of Prime Minister H A Blaize
1991	Bicentenary of the Public Market Squares. Completion of the fort at Richmond Hill.
1992	Bicentennial of the great St George's fire.
1994	20th Anniversary of Independence. Prime Minister Nicholas Brathwaite resigns as leader of the National Democratic Congress (NDC).

The first Grenadians

By Alister Hughes

The Arawak houses (top) were round, with steep conical roofs. Carib houses (bottom) were usually oblong.

Don't waste your time. Don't bother to look for it in the history books. They won't tell you anything because it happened long before Caribbean history began to be recorded. And that's why nobody knows for sure. You can make a good guess however, that, plus or minus a century or two, the first Grenadians came to the island about two thousand years ago.

Whatever the exact date, archaeological research indicates that these first Grenadians were Amerindians of the Arawak people. They originated in South America and there is an interesting theory concerning their settlement in Grenada.

The Arawaks were excellent seamen and skilfully navigated the coastal waters of the mainland. Those waters are known for their strong winds and tides, and the theory is that some of these seamen were accidentally swept out to sea, ending up hundreds of miles away on a Grenada beach.

Like so many of today's visitors, they found the beach and, indeed, the whole island, attractive and spread the news. Others followed, paddling their dug-out canoes northward from Trinidad. They established their first village at the south end of Grenada, close to Point Salines International Airport, and called the island Camahogne.

These Arawaks, a quiet, peaceful people, were agriculturists. They cultivated cassava, maize, sweet potato and other crops. They expanded through the island setting up many other towns and villages, but their tranquil life was to be brutally disrupted.

About 700 AD, disaster struck. Grenada was invaded by another Amerindian tribe, the martial Caribs, and the Arawaks didn't have a chance. The invaders swept through the entire island and no Arawak man was spared. All were killed. Then, all Arawak women and children were rounded up to become the Caribs' wives and slaves.

The descendants of these Arawak/Carib Amerindians made up the Grenadian population when Columbus sighted Grenada on August 15, 1498. But he did not see them. He sailed past the island and these first Grenadians remained undisturbed until 1609.

In that year, a party of Englishmen tried to set up a colony and theirs' is an unhappy story. The Caribs gave them a hard time. Many were killed and, because of Carib resistance, it was impossible to establish plantations, the purpose of the settlement. The life of these pioneers was laced with terror and, within a year, those few who survived were forced to abandon the venture.

The Amerindians

There is no evidence at this time of the presence of the Siboney people on Grenada - the first people believed to inhabit areas of the Caribbean about four thousand years ago.

Both the Arawaks and the Caribs, for which there is evidence, constructed simple houses of thatched roofs, wooden posts at the corners, sides made from wattle or plaited reed, a window or two and a door.

Some of the dwellings of the Arawaks were rounded or bell shaped and capable of housing several families. These houses were called *caneye*. The Arawak Chief, on the other hand had a rectangular house called a *bohio*, which sometimes was larger than an ordinary caneye.

The Caribs basically designed rectangular houses for their homes with wooden posts at the corners. However, in some territories, sizes varied from a single family house to several families occupying a house. The most important house was the *carbet* which was the main meeting place. It was capable of holding over a hundred persons, and in most cases were oblong buildings.

Arawak artefact, dated 500-1000 AD
Courtesy: Jim Rudin

About 30 years later, another attempt at colonisation was made when a party of Frenchmen tried to land. But the Caribs had lost none of their traditional fierceness. They attacked the would-be colonisers so aggressively that the Frenchmen were glad to be able to beat a hasty retreat.

The Caribs were indeed a tough bunch. They were a well-built, olive-skinned people with a certain brave swing in their walk. High cheek bones were a characteristic, with almond shaped eyes and long black hair.

Some records claim they were cannibals. It is claimed that, after defeat of their enemies, the victorious Caribs would: "...eat part of the prisoners of war while they were in triumph, which they rather did out of malice, chewing only one mouthful and spitting it out again ...."

There were many positive sides to these people. They were ingenious hunters and invented a unique way of catching wild ducks. A calabash (gourd) with eyeholes was fitted over the hunter's head and he entered the water up to his neck and waited patiently. Unwary birds, not knowing the danger lurking beneath the drifting calabash, were seized by the legs, dragged underwater and drowned.

One of the problems of those days was the preservation of meat and the Caribs solved this in a manner still used today.

From the root of the cassava plant, these Grenadian ancestors processed a preservative liquid they called 'casareep'. They discovered that, cooked in casareep, meat will last indefinitely. Fresh supplies may be added, the only requirement being that the pot be heated to boiling point every day.

This kitchen technology has been handed down from generation to generation, and casareep can now be bought in the supermarkets. A dish of meat cooked in casareep with added pepper and other ingredients is the well-known Grenadian 'pepper-pot', and there are legends of family pepper-pots, started decades ago, being passed on to younger generations as heirlooms.

These first inhabitants still controlled Grenada in 1650 when 200 Frenchmen arrived from Martinique. This time, the Caribs were tricked into selling the island and the Frenchmen bought it at a bargain price. They paid for it with a few knives and hatchets and with a quantity of glass beads. And, for good measure, they threw in a couple of bottles of brandy for the Carib Chief.

But this deal didn't stick. Whatever alerted the Caribs to the unfairness of the business they had done, they changed their minds within a year and wanted to recover their island. So, they started a campaign of resistance

Cannibalism

There is no evidence of the practice of cannibalism. It was typical of the times that rumours of cannibalism were put out by the Europeans to justify the cruelty inflicted on the Amerindians and other people in the region. These rumours also helped to scare away potential settlers from certain islands.

Casareep

Casareep is a preservative liquid made from grated cassava and flavoured with cloves, cinnamon and sugar.

against the settlers. Any Frenchman found in the woods was killed and it became dangerous to travel into the countryside. Matters went from bad to worse and the French realised that, if they were to continue to develop their plantations, they had to do something.

That 'something' turned out to be a full-scale war against the Caribs. Boarding several boats in St George's harbour, a contingent of about 100 Frenchmen sailed up the west coast and attacked the Carib's strongest fortified village which was perched at the top of a steep mountain.

The location of that village had been well chosen. It had only one approach, and the Caribs did not wait for the French to find it. They met their attackers as they approached the beach at the foot of the mountain and fought fiercely to prevent a landing. But their poisoned arrows were no match for French firearms and they were forced to retreat.

Even then they did not give up. Large boulders and tree trunks were rolled down on the advancing French. This failed to stop them, however, and the village was captured with horrific slaughter of the Caribs.

This did not put an end to hostilities and both sides continued to prepare for a decisive showdown. The French sent to Martinique for reinforcements while the Caribs, regrouping on the east side of the island, were strengthened by large numbers of Caribs who poured in from St Vincent.

The crisis came when the Caribs, considering themselves to have grown to a sufficiently large number, resolved to take on their French enemies. They decided they had become strong enough to capture the town and fort which stood on a narrow neck of land then separating the inner harbour from what is now the yacht marina.

Eight hundred Caribs took on this challenge. Armed with their poisoned arrows and clubs, they stormed the approaches to the fort. The result was a total disaster.

Waiting until the attacking Caribs were almost up to the stockade around the fort, the French opened fire with their cannon and small arms, releasing a death-dealing shower of chain and grape shot, together with bullets from their small arms.

The dead and dying lay everywhere. The ground before the fort was soaked in blood and it was then that the French counter-attacked. Poisoned arrows and clubs had no chance against French firearms in a pitched battle and the outcome was inevitable. The small remnant of the attackers was compelled to flee into the woods with the French in hot pursuit.

As far as the French were concerned, this had to be an action resulting in total extermination. They had had enough of Carib resistance. They

ABOVE
Carib arrows and clubs were ineffective against the cannon and guns of the Europeans

OVERLEAF
Carib's Leap, a 100 feet high cliff in Sauteurs, from which, in 1651, Carib warriors threw themselves rather than surrender to the French

wanted to make sure they had the island to themselves and they chased the fleeing Caribs all the way to the northern tip of the island until they cornered them on a towering headland overlooking the sea.

Of the original 800 attackers of the fort, only some 40 now remained but, for them, surrender was out of the question. Death was preferable to their fate at the hands of the French. So, as the French closed in on them creeping through the bushes, guns at the ready, this story came to a tragic end. The Caribs flung themselves over the cliff and died in the swirling waters below.

The French soon found, however, that their troubles were not yet over. The dramatic death of the forty fugitives did not mark the end of the war. There were still Caribs on the island and they longed for their revenge. They now knew better than to plan another attack on the fort, but Grenada sat on a powder keg of hostility which needed only a spark to set off the explosion.

That hostility existed throughout the islands of the Eastern Caribbean and a series of horrendous incidents inflicted on the Caribs precipitated the inevitable confrontation.

First, a Frenchman, acting on unfounded suspicion, flogged a Carib. Another, having had too much to drink, picked a quarrel with a Carib chief and would have killed him if his pistol had not misfired. The final straw came when a number of Caribs were tricked on board a vessel in an attempt to carry them off as slaves.

This was too much for the Caribs to bear. Everywhere, they vowed death to the Europeans and, in Grenada, a general assembly decreed that every Frenchman was to be killed. But there would be no frontal onslaught this time. The lesson had been learned. Instead, there would be guerrilla warfare.

In these circumstances, the Caribs had a distinct advantage, and this tactic may have had eventual success. However, the French were not prepared to continue to live under these conditions. They would not sit and be picked off one by one. They decided to take drastic action.

Leaving the fort quietly under cover of darkness, a strong force surprised the east coast Carib village at daybreak and launched a vicious attack. Regardless of age or sex, they mutilated every Carib they found. Vegetable gardens were uprooted, huts were razed to the ground, canoes were seized and packs of bloodthirsty Europeans hunted the woods, ravines and mountains liquidating any survivors of the previous massacre.

This bloody event marked the end of resistance by Caribs living in

Grenada but did not mark the end of French troubles. Infuriated by the massacre, Caribs from St Vincent and other islands made surprise raids on outlying areas of the island. They killed every white person they found and did as much damage as they could.

Again, the French resolved that draconian action was needed. Two ships were equipped and commissioned to take on the Carib guerrillas and this move proved decisive. In a series of skirmishes, the Caribs were so severely mauled they were forced to abandon the raids and, at last, surrrender and subject themselves to the will of the Europeans.

When the well known Catholic priest, Pere Labat, visited Grenada in 1700, there were still Caribs on the island. Labat was concerned to find a few of them squatting on church lands in the St Mark district, but they no longer posed a threat to the colonial occupiers. Today in Grenada, however, except for a quota of the melange of blood now flowing in Grenadian veins, there is no longer any living evidence of the Caribs.

But there is archaeological evidence of their presence. There are several petroglyphs, the most important of which is at Mount Rich in St Patrick. Here, a huge boulder is covered with rock carvings. Some show clear a relationship to fertility symbolism but the mystery of others is still to be unravelled.

There are also many sites, complete with kitchen middens, waiting to be scientifically excavated. Some work has been done already, but there is no complete island-wide plan to unlock the information waiting to be unearthed. A definitive, all-inclusive exploration of these ancient Carib dwelling places is still to be done.

When that day comes, if archaeological finds excavated in South America and in other Caribbean islands may be taken as an indication, fascinating material will be recovered.

There will be curious beads, beautiful ornaments, incense burners and other vessels used in religious ceremonies. There will also be unusual cooking utensils and ingenious shell tools, all material which will tell the tale of an ancient existence difficult to visualise today.

Displayed, this material will be not only an education for today's generation, but a fitting memorial to the first Grenadians.

Artefacts

In the future, recovered material will tell the tale of an ancient existence. This will not only be an education for today's generation, but will be a fitting memorial to the first Grenadians.

OPPOSITE
Visited by many, this Carib Stone is situated on the shoreline near Victoria. On the huge boulder is carved a face, a typical mark of the Carib presence

Grenada's "Back-to-Front" Forts

By Alister Hughes

These ancient fortifications have existed for almost three hundred years. They crown the dominating hilltops east of St George's and are important monuments to Grenada's colourful past. Strategically, they could not have been better placed to repel an attack on the town, but there is something very unusual about them.

By all appearances, the engineers who built these forts had lost their sense of direction. They made no provision for the guns of the four forts to face the harbour entrance, and one is left to wonder what their purpose was. Believe it or not, none of the cannon could be aimed at attackers approaching the island by sea from the west.

Check it out yourself. You'll find all the guns face to the north or east. That is, inland. Their muzzles stood ready to pour round shot and grape or whatsoever, not at attacking warships, but into the wooded hills of the interior. Yes, these forts have their backs to the sea. Surprising as it seems, they appear to have been deliberately designed to defend against attack from the plantations of the colonists.

To discover the facts behind this strange situation, one must go back a couple of centuries. Back to the days when Caribbean islands were very valuable possessions. The islands agricultural produce made millionaires out of traders in London, Paris, Amsterdam and Madrid. This, certainly, was wealth worth fighting for. European nations were fully aware of this and the English, French, Dutch and Spanish struggled fiercely to possess them.

Much of the fighting took the form of naval battles. When territory was captured or new lands colonised, however, national territorial interests had to be safeguarded and forts were the obvious answer to this problem.

In Grenada, the first fort to be erected was prefabricated and brought in by the French who came from Martinique in 1650. The French were the first successful colonists and they set up their town and fort on a narrow strip of land which then separated the inner harbour from what is now the yacht marina.

Compared with fortifications which were to be built in later years, including the strange 'back-to-front' forts, that first fort was a primitive affair. It was just a large wooden building surrounded by a stockade and was armed with only two cannon. Nevertheless, it served its purpose and was to be the salvation of the colonists.

Trouble began when the deal the French made with the original inhabitants, the Caribs, turned sour. Grenada was ruled at that time by the Carib Chief, Kaieroune, and the French 'tricked' the island from him for a few knives and hatchets. For good measure, they also gave the Carib

Fort Frederick, on Richmond Hill, overlooking St George's

a bucket or two of glass beads and generously threw in two bottles of brandy for the Chief himself.

But, it was not long before Kaieroune realised he had been short changed and, seeking to recover the island, he instituted guerrilla tactics against the settlers. Any French found hunting in the hills were killed. The Caribs were armed only with basic weapons, but in their desire to drive the French into the sea, they became bolder and made daring attacks on the town.

The wooden fort then became a sanctuary. Nobody could wander far from the town without risking death, and life became very difficult. It was almost impossible to work the sugar and indigo plantations they had established and it was not until the French launched an all-out, island-wide, slaughtering drive against the Caribs that their existence on the island became relatively safe.

Of course, while their wooden fort could keep Kaieroune and his Caribs at bay, it was no protection against pirates. Nor could it withstand an attack by any Spanish, English or Dutch warship. Nevertheless, it survived for about 50 years and was not replaced by another fort until the settlers moved their town to the other side of the harbour where St George's now stands.

A new and improved fort was built on the site of present-day Fort George but, when the influential and knowledgeable French Catholic priest, Pere Labat, visited the island in 1700 he was quite unimpressed with it.

Labat knew a lot about forts and, when he returned to his base in Guadeloupe, he wrote a detailed report of his Grenada visit. And he pulled no punches. His comments were caustic and probably exerted a great deal of influence on the circumstances of those later forts which face the 'wrong' way.

Fort Frederick

Said Labat, the new fort was in an excellent position to defend the harbour but he did not think much of its construction. That, however, was not his most important criticism. From a military point of view, he said, the fort had a serious strategic problem. Just to the north of it was much higher ground.

And then Labat made a statement which, in the light of future developments, was nothing short of prophetic. If that higher ground ever fell into the hands of an enemy, he said, the fort would not have a ghost of a chance of defending itself.

Whether or not it was Labat's report which influenced them, the French on Grenada, soon after his visit, decided to get themselves a proper fort. They commissioned the official public works man in Paris, Engineer-General

View from Fort George

Fort George

Town plan, 1706, showing Fort George

OVERLEAF
Cannon facing 'the wrong way' at Fort George

of the American Islands and Terra Firma, Monsieur de Callus, to do the job and, using the same site on the western side of the harbour mouth, he designed a really good fort and completed its construction in 1706.

This fort, originally called Fort Royale by the French, still stands today as Fort George, the oldest structure on the island. It is superbly located to guard the entrance to the inner harbour but, no matter how good a job de Callus did, it still had the problem Labat saw. There was undefended high ground to the north from which an enemy could easily dominate it.

The settlers, too, recognised the problem. And, they did something about it. They fortified that higher ground. It is not certain when this was done, but they constructed what they thought was an adequate fort to protect the flank of the main defences at the harbour entrance.

Then they relaxed. Events were to prove, however, that these fortifications were less than adequate and their design and construction are the next step in the story of the forts which face the 'wrong' way.

Perhaps the French in Grenada became too complacent, but their long, unbroken spell of colonisation came to an end in 1762, when, without a fight, they lost the island to the British. In the following year, Grenada was officially ceded to Britain by the Treaty of Paris, and the final chapter in the saga of the 'back-to-front' forts had begun.

The peace did not last long. In 1778, as a result of the American War of Independence which began in 1775, Britain became involved, once more, in a war with France. The French fleet in the Caribbean was then under the command of the Comte d'Estaing and, on July 2, 1779, he arrived off the west coast of Grenada with 25 ships of the line, ten frigates, and 10,000 soldiers.

Once there, the wily d'Estaing executed a brilliant manoeuvre which completely outfoxed the British and had much to do with the 'back-to-front' forts which were built later. D'Estaing did not attack St George's from the sea. Instead, he landed a strong force a few miles up the coast, marched inland and, making a turning movement, attacked from the east - from the interior.

When the French fortified the high ground to the north, the work had been done with the thought of repelling invaders from the sea. The fortifications had little or no defence against a force coming from the interior. D'Estaing exploited this fact and, when his soldiers attacked from that direction, they overran the high ground with comparative ease.

And it was then that Labat's fears of eight decades before were realised. The British, looking up to the attackers in possession of the high ground to the north, had no choice but to surrender and the French took over the island.

But they did not leave it there. They learned from the sharp lesson d'Estaing taught the British. It was not enough that the high ground to the north of the main fort had to be fortified. The town and its existing forts had to be protected against an attack from the interior. D'Estaing had proved that it was essential that other forts be built on the high ground east of St George's.

That's when the 'back-to-front' forts were constructed. Only, they were not really back-to-front. They were intentionally built to face inland and to provide a defence against anybody who tried to attack from that direction.

Four years later, in 1783, when Grenada was returned to the British under the Treaty of Versailles, the French had not yet completed the four forts they had started. But the British also remembered d'Estaing's lesson. They realised the vital importance of these fortifications and finished the job.

Two of the forts were called Frederick and Adolphus, respectively after the second and tenth sons of George III, then Britain's monarch. One was named Matthew in honour of Edward Matthew, Grenada's Lieutenent-Governor at that time, and the fourth carried the name Lucas, after William Lucas, a prominent Grenadian from whom the French had acquired the lands on which these forts stand.

But it was nearly all wasted effort. These forts never saw action. Not that the wars were over. For some 30 years after the Treaty of Versailles, Britain was at war with several European nations. In 1793 with France, in 1795 with Holland, in 1796 with Spain, and in 1801 with Sweden. Then, in 1812, with the United States of America.

Except for Fedon's rebellion in 1795 which did not involve the forts, however, all this passed Grenada by. There were no attacks on the island. The forts lay peacefully on guard and, when the fighting was all over, they gradually lost their importance as instruments of war.

Today, the 'back-to-front' forts still straddle the hilltops east of St George's, standing majestically as the centre-piece, the hub, of a magnificent panorama. And their ramparts provide a convenient photographic platform. Here, from this vantage point, it is easy to capture the quaintness of St George's. The uniqueness of the beautiful landlocked harbour and, in the distance, the tranquillity of the mountains.

Meanwhile, the empty gun ports still look expectantly eastward in the 'wrong' direction. They face the island's picturesque interior and wait patiently for the attack that will never come.

The night "Janet" invaded Grenada

By Alister Hughes
Courtesy of the *Grenada Newsletter*, September 30, 1989

A "killer" hurricane (named) "Janet" swept in from the Atlantic on September 22, 1955. For several days the forecast had said there was bad weather out there to the east, but few people took it seriously. In those days, Grenada's tourist literature said the island was "outside the hurricane belt". In fact, no living Grenadian resident on the island had experienced a hurricane; there was nobody to describe the coming terror.

During the afternoon of the 22nd, it became markedly more overcast and, by dusk, the wind, which had been light all day, began to increase in velocity. But, even then, Grenadians didn't worry much. The forecast said Barbados and St Vincent would take the brunt of the blow and Grenada expected only to be brushed lightly by the tail end.

But "Janet" surprised everybody. After striking Barbados, she abandoned her northwest direction and veered southwards towards Grenada, the eye of the hurricane passing between the northern tip of Grenada and the sister island of Carriacou, 20 miles offshore.

The final build-up to this onslaught began shortly after nightfall. Torrential rains poured down, and the island was plunged into darkness as the electricity supply failed. Exceeding 130 miles per hour, the wind increased to a roaring intensity while vivid flashes of lightning rent the sky to the accompaniment of loud peals of thunder.

"Janet" reached her peak before midnight as the eye passed through, but there was no sleep for anyone until well into morning. Then, with the dawn, Grenadians woke to scenes of devastation beyond their wildest nightmares.

In St George's, the 850 feet long pier and customs warehouses had disappeared. It lay at the bottom of the harbour, together with millions of dollars worth of merchandise. Hurled by the roaring waters, bags of flour, boxes of foodstuff, cases of general cargo and bales of assorted merchandise lay strewn in untidy heaps on the Carenage roadway encircling the inner harbour.

St George's is a solidly built city, but it did not escape damage. As compared with other parts of the State, however, that damage was negligible. In the parishes of St John and St Mark, the loss was much greater. The parish of St Patrick and the islands of Carriacou and Petit Martinique took the heaviest blow.

The eye of the hurricane passed very close to those areas, and they experienced the full fury of "Janet". The destruction was tremendous, and the death toll was highest here. "Janet" killed 114 persons in Grenada, and, of

Hurricane

The name, from the Carib word *hurracan*, used in the Caribbean, Central America and the USA for a tropical revolving storm of sustained winds of over 73 miles an hour. Also known as a 'Westindian cyclone'. The storms are intense depressions that usually form in the middle of the North Atlantic and can have a diameter of up to 500 miles. The winds blow in a spiral movement inwards. The centre, or 'eye', of the storm is relatively calm and moves along at approximately ten miles an hour.

Courtesy: Brian Dyde, *Caribbean Companion*

HURRICANE DAMAGE IN B. HONDURAS

TOWN DEVASTATED
FROM OUR CORRESPONDENT
BELIZE, BRITISH HONDURAS,
SEPT. 28

After threatening British Honduras during a tense night, hurricane Janet finally hit the north coast of British Honduras and unconfirmed reports say that six persons were killed and 90 per cent. of the houses of the northern coast town of Corozal were destroyed. The population is about 2,500.

Communications were disrupted between the capital and northern British Honduras. A platoon of local militia has been dispatched to Corozal. The district commissioner of Corozal has sent an appeal for food and clothing. In Belize floods rose during the night nearly 2ft. and minor damage was caused to a few houses.

RELIEF FUND OPENED

APPEAL BY GOVERNOR OF TRINIDAD
FROM OUR CORRESPONDENT
PORT OF SPAIN, SEPT. 28

The Governor of Trinidad, Sir Edward Beetham, to-night announced the establishment of a Hurricane Janet appeal fund, to be administered by a board of which he would be chairman. He said that he hoped there would be an immediate and generous response not only in the West Indies but much farther afield.

Over 20,000 people were homeless in Barbados, and the damage to property there was frightening, the Governor said. Almost the whole of Grenada and Carriacou was devastated; almost all crops were destroyed and three out of five houses destroyed or seriously damaged in most areas.

The Trinidad Government has contributed $150,000 to the fund.

The Governor of the Windward Islands, Mr. C. M. Deverell, left Grenada yesterday for Carriacou in the United States destroyer Henley. Another United States destroyer, the Putnam, brought food and medical supplies and water purification equipment to Grenada.

MANY DEAD IN YUCATAN

MEXICO CITY, Sept. 28.—Hurricane Janet swept across the Yucatan peninsula to-day. A presidential spokesman said the number of people believed killed was 200, and that the toll of injured might run to " several thousand."

The weather bureau at Tegucigalpa, Honduras, reported to-night that the hurricane had entered the Gulf of Campeche and was moving towards southern Mexico's eastern coast between Vera Cruz and Tuxpan.—Associated Press.

TURKISH AMBASSADOR'S

these, 32 were in St Patrick, 25 in Carriacou and two in Petit Martinique.

Throughout the State, thousands were homeless. Communications were knocked out and schools, churches and community centres were razed. Several persons were buried alive as landslides covered their homes under several feet of mud and debris. Others died as structures collapsed and still others were swept out to sea by the flood waters of raging rivers.

Seventy-five per cent of the nutmeg plantations were destroyed, cocoa and coconut fields took a tremendous beating and the new banana plantations were completely wiped out.

More than three decades have passed since hurricane "Janet", and the memory has grown dim. There is now a new generation without hurricane experience and lurking in their minds may be hope that Grenada "is outside the hurricane belt".

Hurricane "Janet" first struck Barbados, and moved on to St Vincent and the Grenadines. It reached Grenada, the eye passing over the island's northern tip, then moved west to Central America, still causing damage six days after devastating Grenada and Carriacou. The report (left) is taken from The Times, London, Thursday September 29, 1955

117

The Saga of the Bianca C

By Alister Hughes
Courtesy of *The Greeting* tourist guide, Winter 1993/4

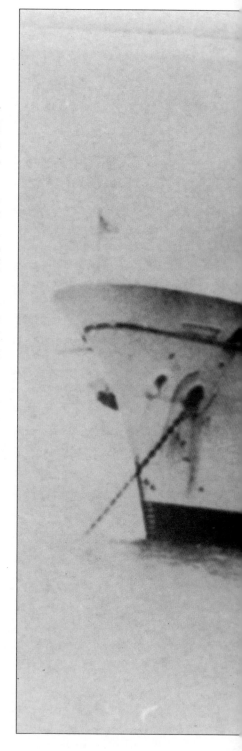

She lies on the seabed in relatively shallow water. She's the luxury liner Bianca C, the largest and, perhaps, most interesting submerged wreck in the Caribbean. Her 600-foot length nestles close to Grenada's southwestern coast, and there's a fascinating story as to how this once-beautiful ship got there.

It began more than 30 years ago when, on a quiet Sunday morning, the mournful wail of a ship's foghorn shattered the calm. Bianca C lay at anchor in the outer harbour, and everything about the ship seemed normal.

Very elegant-looking, this cruise liner was a familiar sight to Grenadians, and her persistent, complaining foghorn was totally out of keeping with the peaceful picture she presented.

At the Grenada Yacht Club on the eastern side of the town, yachtsmen were gathered for a morning of dinghy racing. Attracted by the wail of the foghorn, they noticed something else. An unfamiliar flag signal was flying from the cruise liner's yardarm. Quickly deciphered, it conveyed an alarming message. Bianca C was on fire and required assistance immediately.

Reaction was prompt as members hurried to mobilise the Club's resources. The harbour authorities were informed, and every available boat was manned. An urgent call for help was relayed to all vessels in the harbour ... and so was launched a unique community effort that saved many lives.

The date was October 22, 1961, and, that morning, the 18,000-ton Bianca C, a frequent caller at the island, had completed a visit with nearly 400 passengers and a crew of some 300. She had also taken on a small contingent of Grenadian immigrants bound for the United Kingdom.

Owned by the Italian Costa Steamship Line, Bianca C was under the command of Captain Francisco Crevaco, a short, stocky mariner of 40 years' experience. Captain Crevaco was on the bridge that morning and had given orders for Bianca C to prepare to sail.

Before the anchor could be lifted and the ship put under way, a terrific explosion destroyed the engine room. That started a raging fire. The ship's fire-fighting equipment was unable to cope with it, and spreading flames threatened to engulf the entire ship.

Sabotage was not suspected. It has been speculated that explosives were smuggled on board and that these were accidentally ignited. Another theory is that one of the ship's engines blew up when an attempt was made to start it.

Whatever the cause, the explosion killed one crew member on the spot. Suffering from severe burns, the Second Mate died at Grenada's General Hospital two days later. A third badly burned crew member, flown

The Bianca C, burning in the entrance to St George's harbour before being towed to her final resting place. Sadly, three crew members died, but, the speed of the rescue by the people of Grenada saved a great many lives
Courtesy: K Sylvester

to Caracas, Venezuela, for urgent medical attention, also died.

Rallied by Yacht Club personnel, a Dunkirk-type flotilla hastened to assist the stricken ship. Included were classy ocean-going yachts, some smaller day-sailers, and rough-and-ready fishing boats of all sizes. There were power boats, sailing boats, tiny dinghies and 50-ton inter-island trading schooners. Even a few rowing boats were there.

In an heroic and determined effort to rescue the passengers and crew from the flaming ship before fire consumed them, this motley armada, ignoring the considerable danger of the moment, moved quickly to the outer harbour.

By the time the first rescue craft got to Bianca C, the fire had spread and intensified. Rumbling explosions echoed from the bowels of the ship, hurling burning debris into the air. And thick, black smoke billowed from the forward end of the liner.

There was no time to lose. The ship's crew had directed frightened passengers to the relative safety of the stern and, from that point, an orderly evacuation took place. Women and children first, followed by the men, scrambled down rope ladders, swaying perilously, and huddled in the few lifeboats the crew had been able to launch.

The flotilla of assorted Grenadian craft joined the rescue effort immediately, and the skipper of one of these boats remembers the pathetic state of the distressed passengers:

"They were in various stages of dress and undress," he says. "Most were scantily clad, some had on no more than a pair of pyjamas, and they were all obviously in shock."

The rescue boats moved promptly alongside Bianca C and began to accept the scared passengers as they nervously descended the swinging rope ladders. The ship's lifeboats were taken in tow by the larger power boats, and all rescue craft, loaded to capacity, quickly ferried their human cargo to the shore before hustling back for another pitiful load.

Throughout the operation, loud explosions continued to tear through the hull of the burning ship, serving as constant reminders of the need for haste. There was no time to lose as, at any time, Bianca C might be blown

The ship that sank twice

The Bianca C, the largest wreck in the Caribbean, which sank in Grenada in 1961, was first sunk in a French harbour soon after being built, by the retreating German army in 1944 during World War II. The ship lay on the seabed for two years before being raised, refurbished and put into service for the first time.

The 'Trinidad Guardian' newspaper, October 24, 1961

La tragica fine della "Bianca C"

An Italian newspaper reports "the tragic end of the Bianca C"

apart, enveloping all around her in flames.

Eventually, all passengers were evacuated safely with no more than a few minor injuries. And, with the exception of Captain Crevaco and a few of his officers, all the crew had also been taken off. The captain and his officers had been on the bridge of Bianca C, but the spreading fire forced them to retreat toward the bow. This almost resulted in disaster as, when the time came for them to be taken off, fire had cut off their route to the evacuation point at the stern. Fortunately, a rope ladder was found and they, too, scrambled to safety.

This heroic rescue operation took some two hours to complete and, according to the skipper of another rescue boat, had it taken longer, there certainly would have been great loss of life.

"After everyone had been evacuated," he said, "we cruised around for a while, at a safe distance, listening to rumbling explosions from inside the ship. We watched as her plates began to glow a bright cherry red, paint peeled off her sides in great chunks, and anyone on board at that time could not have lived."

On the waterfront in the inner harbour, an impromptu but efficient organisation had been hastily thrown together to deal with the crisis. Ambulances took the injured to the General Hospital. And a corps of volunteers, manning a fleet of taxis and private cars, took passengers and crew to a special camp set up by the government.

With more than 600 people to care for, accommodation was at a premium and, when the camp overflowed, the community came to the rescue. All doors were open to the unfortunates. Wherever beds were available, the volunteers shuttled the survivors to accommodation at hotels, guest houses, and private homes.

Other sectors of the community then got into the act. Free of cost, grocers supplied meat and canned goods. Farmers sent in truckload after truckload of fresh fruit and vegetables. Local cooks manned the camp kitchen until the ship's cooks could take over and, through the Red Cross, merchants donated clothing, toilet items, and other necessary personal effects to each of the survivors.

On the following day Bianca C was still burning and was obviously settling deeper in the water. Fearful the ship would sink and block the harbour channel, the administrator, James Lloyd, was eager to have her moved. But this raised controversy.

Captain Crevaco absolutely refused to give permission for his ship to be towed away. He wanted the fire damage verified first, he said. Manning one of the Bianca C lifeboats, he sat, with some of his officers, in the outer harbour, hour after hour, a sad and dejected figure, keeping faithful watch over his beloved ship - determined no one was going to move her.

At the administrator's request, a British warship, the frigate HMS Londonderry arrived, discussions were held and, eventually, a compromise was reached. It was agreed the vessel would be inspected. Following that, the Londonderry would get Bianca C out of the shipping channel as soon as possible and beach her on a reef near the southern tip of the island.

It was dangerous to board the ship but, as far as was possible, an inspection was carried out and, before dawn on the Tuesday, sailors from the British warship were on the job.

At this time, the ship was still smoking, but there were no leaping flames. However, sections of her hull glowed a dull red, and, in some areas, the water boiled around her.

At first, all went well and according to plan. Demolition experts from the frigate blasted off the ship's anchor chains and she was taken in tow. The ship swung into line and, wallowing sluggishly in the wake of the Londonderry, Bianca C was on the way to her final resting place.

Soon after the Londonderry began to tow, it was clear this was not going to be an easy task. A strong cross wind blew across the outer harbour and, to make matters worse, the rudder of the burning ship was jammed. Navigation was tricky and Bianca C began drifting towards Grand Anse Beach.

With difficulty, the Londonderry got the hulk of Bianca C heading in the right direction again. Then, it happened. Within a few hundred yards of the designated reef, a strong gust of wind swung the ship around and the towing cable broke. The ship lost momentum, drifted off course, and that marked the beginning of the end.

Before Londonderry could run another cable, Bianca C was seen to hesitate momentarily. Then amid shooting gusts of hissing steam, she slipped under the surface, stern-first, into some 20 fathoms of water. The time was noon, exactly.

Unfortunately, that wasn't the end of the story. And what followed was not in keeping with the spirit of brotherhood the incident had generated before. This aftermath left a bitter taste. The passage of time has removed the sting and the hurt does not remain but, it is still worth a telling.

After the loss of his ship, Captain Crevaco, with his passengers and crew, spent about a week as guests of the people of Grenada. Two ships arrived to take them away and a central player in organising their safe repatriation was a Grenadian, W E Julien.

He was managing director of the company which represented the Costa Steamship Line, and the Italian government, recognising the services he had rendered in the disaster, conferred on him the honour of Cavalier of the Order of Merit.

At the same time, the Costa Steamship Line presented a token of their appreciation to the people of Grenada. It was a life-size bronze replica of the statue, 'Christ of the Deep', the original of which was said to have been sunk in the Bay of Naples as a symbol of God's care for all who sail the high seas.

The statue was sent to the administrator, and he asked the City Council to choose a site for it. He asked the council also to have it erected and submit a bill. That seemed simple enough, but it brought an unhappy quarrel between the City Council and the ship's agents.

The council decided the statue should be erected at the water's edge on the eastern arm of St George's harbour. The agents didn't like it there. They wanted it placed on the town's western seafront. Since the council had been charged with the job, however, their choice prevailed. But the agents were to have the last word.

After the statue had been erected at some considerable cost, the council sent the bill to the administrator. He forwarded it to the Costa Steamship Line in Genoa, Italy, for payment, and they sent it to their agents in Grenada for verification. And that's where the bitterness started.

The agents said emphatically the bill should not be paid. The City Council had to shoulder the cost and the mayor, aldermen and councillors were not amused. There were heated words on both sides and, for a while, the statue became a sore point.

But the passage of time has blunted that. Today, this replica of Christ

The Cavalier of the Order of Merit, awarded to W E Julien in recognition of his services during the disaster

Thank You Nice People Of Grenada

The Owners of the "BIANCA C" through me would like to say again.

THANK YOU

to the Government and kind people of Grenada. It is only in distress one appreciates that the true Christian Spirit is still very strong, and the brotherhood of man stands first and above all else,

We shall always remember you:

Mario Costa (Sgd)
On Behalf of the Owners

The Costa Steamship Line thanked the people of Grenada in the 'WestIndian' newspaper, October 29, 1961

123

of the Deep, has been moved from its original location at the harbour entrance and now stands on the Carenage at the head of the harbour.

With arms outstretched, it represents the gratitude of the Costa Steamship Line. And it is a reminder of Grenadians' generous response to the needs of the distressed passengers and crew of the ill-fated Bianca C.

Today, the wreck has shifted a little and lies in about 170 feet of water. It is said to be slowly sliding into a deep trough. The top decks are some 100 feet below the surface, which makes the ship relatively easy to reach, and she has become a valuable addition to Grenada's many attractions.

The island's tourist authorities have announced that the wreck is to be declared a marine national park. This will preserve it and guard against vandalism. Bianca C will remain an interesting and exhilarating challenge for the experienced diver, but, be warned. The area is swept by strong, unpredictable currents. If you want to experience this thrill, don't try it on your own. Get in touch with one of Grenada's scuba operations.

Whether or not you are a dive enthusiast, you should visit the statue on the Carenage in St George's. As you contemplate the arms of Christ of the Deep outstretched in blessing over the calm waters of the harbour, you'll certainly be touched by the disastrous tragedy this monument commemorates.

You'll thrill to the memory of the dangerous rescue mission which saved so many lives. And you'll have a true sense of the torrent of hospitality which flowed so generously from the Grenadian people to the distressed passengers and crew of the Bianca C.

Christ of the Deep

(Opposite) As a token of their appreciation, the owners of Bianca C, presented the people of Grenada with a life-size bronze replica of the statue, 'Christ of the Deep', the original of which was said to have been sunk in the Bay of Naples as a symbol of God's care for all who sail the high seas. The statue was erected at the water's edge on the Carenage to welcome seafarers.
(Below) The plaque on the statue

Grenada's Non-Standard English

By Alister Hughes

According to the guide books, English is the national language of Grenada. Certainly, English is the official language. That's what you'll hear spoken in the hotels and shops. You'll have no problem communicating with the islanders, but don't let anybody tell you that English is the native tongue of Grenadians.

Take a ride in any Grenadian minibus and discover the truth. Or visit one of the island's marketplaces. From a linguistic point of view, that's where Grenadians "let their hair down". What you'll hear spoken in these places is based on standard English, but the Grenadian vocabulary is liberally strewn with a host of picturesque, expressive words and phrases which will take you on an exciting linguistic adventure.

This version of the English language did not evolve by accident. Centuries of European colonisation have shaped the way we Grenadians express ourselves today. Trade with the Spanish Main in the eighteenth century had its influence and pockets of Old English still remain.

More recently, contact with North America added to the vocabulary, while African slaves and indentured Indian workers put their indelible stamp on the Grenadian tongue.

Until you get the hang of it, expect to be puzzled. But, not to worry. Many Grenadians are unaware of the origins of the words they use, but they are very willing to explain meanings. They'll help you out and you certainly would have needed assistance if you had seen a press report of a case in the magistrate's court some time ago.

At that time a man was charged with wounding someone in the foot, "six inches above the knee". That's quite impossible by normal standards because, as everyone knows, the foot is not above the knee. It is that part of the leg below the ankle.

But, this seemingly ridiculous charge didn't surprise the magistrate at all. In Grenada, you see, the foot is the whole limb from the hip to the toes. Hand, too, is the whole limb from the shoulder to the fingers.

And, here's the surprise. Three hundred years ago, when Britain was carving out her Empire, English colonists in the Caribbean used the words "hand" and "foot" with exactly the same meanings as these words have in Grenadian English now.

Going back to the beginning, the process of creating a Grenadian vocabulary started nearly 350 years ago when the French tricked the Caribs and obtained this island for some trinkets and a two bottles of brandy.

They, and their successors, remained in unbroken possession of the island for over a century and the only European language heard here during that period was, of course, French.

Little wonder then that French is the most powerful single external influence on Grenadian English, and this has laid a solid setting for the linguistic gems we find in use today.

Indeed, the Francophone foundation was reinforced by an interesting development in the island's history.

The British first took possession of Grenada in 1763. British settlers moved in and the English language made its debut. But that didn't last long. Sixteen years later the French recaptured the island and the next four years were tough ones for the new British settlers.

The conquering French Government was extremely hostile towards them. The use of the English language was frowned on and great stress was laid on being 'French'. The Francophone foundation was greatly reinforced and this lasted until 1783 when the Treaty of Versailles gave Grenada back to Britain.

Now the hostility was reversed, the emphasis switched to being 'English' and that emphasis has been in effect now for over two centuries. In spite of this length of time, however, the Grenadian vocabulary testifies to the powerful influence of the first European settlers who placed an unmistakable French seal on English-speaking Grenadian tongues.

Nowhere is that seal more noticeable than in the island's folklore which features an important character, namely the spirit of a woman who died in childbirth.

On rainy nights, if one should hear the voice of a child crying outside in the dark, the worst possible thing one could do is to open the door to investigate. That is to invite certain disaster. Lurking out there is a dreadful supernatural being which has a French Creole name, **Mama Maladie**, the mother of diseases, and should you make the mistake of letting her into your house, you and your family will be visited by most horrible illnesses.

Grenada has, also, the dreaded **Lig-ah-rou**, a word

which is a corruption of the French Creole for a werewolf, *loup-garou* . But the Grenadian Lig-ah-rou is far more terrifying than its French cousin. The Grenadian version has the ability to fly and, unless precautions are taken, he (or she) can enter your home through a keyhole in order to suck the blood of its victim.

Fortunately, there is a defence. If a handful of sand is placed on your doorstep at night, the Lig-ah-rou must count every grain before he can get in to you. This will take many hours until daylight and, since Lig-ah-roos must be away by dawn, you remain protected.

But the sand defence has a drawback. If it is used, the Lig-ah-rou's identity remains unknown. The best way to discover who this monster is, is by exploiting one characteristic of the Lig-ah-rou - that the Lig-ah-rou cannot fly unless he takes off his skin.

This is where you take action. The Lig-ah-rou's favourite hiding place for the skin is under a turned down mortar in the kitchen and the plan is to find that skin and rub it liberally with salt. This will make it terribly uncomfortable for the Lig-ah-rou when the skin is put back on, and to identify the monster, you have only to keep an eye out for anyone who is constantly scratching and squirming with a skin that's obviously burning them.

In the island's mythology, there is also a frightening, female figure which is the dread of all husbands who may be tempted to stay out late at night. This female wears a long dress to hide the fact that one of her feet is normal while the other is a cloven hoof. She has a beautiful, voluptuous figure and wears a wide-brimmed floppy hat which hides her face.

Undoubtedly, this legend was created by lonely wives, and the story goes that, late at night, some half-drunk, wayward husband, on his way home, is propositioned by this seductive lady.

Hand in hand, and with encouraging words, she leads him to a lonely spot on the edge of a precipice. There, while the husband anticipates an amorous embrace, she lifts the brim of her hat to disclose a skull face. Literally frightened to death, the unfortunate man falls over the precipice and is killed.

The Grenadian name of that female apparition is **La-jab-less** and it is easy to see there the French word *la diablesse*, a "female-devil".

If that wayward husband was considered to be somewhat foolish or bemused, Grenadians would say he was **too-tool-bay**, that word coming from the French, *totalement bete*, a totally stupid creature .

But the word is not always used in so derogatory a context. Considering the foolish way in which we are all likely to behave when we are in love, it is quite common to say that some boy is too-tool-bay over his girlfriend.

On the other hand, **quel-bay** is always derogatory. It refers to someone who is mentally slow and it has overtones of the person being repressed. Quel-bay probably derives from the French, *Quelle bete!*, an exclamation of, "What a fool !"

Another interesting word with a somewhat similar meaning is **ba-so-dee**. One may describe someone as being ba-so-dee or unbalanced either figuratively, if that person is somewhat mentally vague, or actually, if they are dizzy from a blow on the head.

Ba-so-dee comes, of course, from the French Creole, *pas solide*, not stable.

Grenada's annual Carnival festival is another fertile source of French-based non-standard English. As any Grenadian will tell you, the first part of the first day of Carnival is called **jou-vay**. All Grenadians use the word and it has become so commonplace that few recognise in it a corruption of the French Creole words, *jour ouvert*, the dawning, or the opening of the day.

And, one of the principal masquerading figures you will see at jou-vay is certain to be the **jab-jab**. Dressed in a loin cloth only, covered with black grease, with two horns on his head and with a tail, this character is easily recognised as a devil, and jab-jab is readily seen as originating from the French Creole word for a devil, *diable*.

The jab-jab sometimes wears a home-made wig of flowing white "hair" made from the fibre of a plant which grows in profusion in the east coast villages of Marquis and Soubise, and here is more unmistakable evidence of the French footprint on Grenadian tongues.

The English botanical name of that plant is the agave and the French name for the agave is *la pite*, a word very similar to **la-pit**, the word Grenadians use for the material from which the jab-jab makes his wig.

One feature of Carnival which has disappeared is the stick fight, but that bloody, brutal sport has left words which are still current. The stick fight ritual was that, when the drums started, the bravest fighter went to the centre of the ring. There, he danced around and assumed defiant postures of bravado, daring the other fighters to attack him.

As the fighter danced, he had his stick poised for attack. That stick, wood or club, his weapon, was called his **bois** (stick), a direct use of French Creole and, as he danced, he was said to **kar-ray**. The pronunciation of that word and what it stands for has a close resemblance to the French, *se carrer*, meaning to strut or to pose, and kar-ray is still used, figuratively, of anyone assuming a defiant posture.

Indirectly, the stick fight has given us another word Grenadians still use, figuratively. It was the standard boast of the stick fighter that he would batter an opponent until that opponent shouted, or more colloquially, bawled, **am-way**. Today, beset by difficult circumstances, the Grenadian will say, "This is more than I can take, I must bawl am-way."

Whether in the context of a stick fight or figuratively, am-way is a call of distress, and is a corruption of the words a Frenchman might use when in difficulty, *A moi*, that is, "come to me" or "help!"

The field of agriculture is also rich with special Grenadian words. For instance, you'll seldom hear reference to a bunch of coconuts. Most times, it is a **grap** of coconuts. This is the straight use of the French Creole word for a bunch, *grappe*, and grap is also used figuratively for anything in quantity. A rich man is said to have money "by the grap", or a woman to have "a grap of clothes in her wardrobe".

There is a weed in Grenada which is special in that the seeds of the plant are in an unusual place. They are on the underside of the leaf and Grenadians call this weed **gwen-amber-fwail**. Like many other non-standard words he may use, the average Grenadian has no idea what this word means, but it is the direct use of the French Creole phrase, *graine a bas feuille*, meaning seeds under the leaf.

You'll soon find out that, in Grenada, mangoes come in all shapes, colours, sizes and flavours. Some are nice, others are hardly worth eating while still others are excellent, and there is a Grenadian phrase which proclaims the ultimate in approval of a good mango or, for that matter, any other fruit.

For someone to say of a mango, **ah fus it sweet**, is high praise. The derivation of this Grenadian word is from the French, *a force*, which means extremely, and in any situation where an extreme is indicated, the use of **ah fus** is appropriate. For instance, for great emphasis, you could say of the holiday atmosphere of Grenada, "Ah fus it nice !"

Perhaps the most interesting name in the field of plant life in Grenada refers to a poisonous weed. Animals avoid this weed as long as it is growing in the soil but, if it is cut with other fodder, cows, goats and sheep are unable to detect it and suffer the consequences.

This weed is certain death for a sheep or a goat. It will make a larger animal very ill and this poisonous plant reflects something of the history of the French Court.

Soon after the French first colonised Grenada in 1650, it was discovered in Paris that a French marchioness had been involved in an attempt to poison her rich husband and his relatives so she could inherit the family wealth.

This lady had formed what the history books call "an improper attachment" to a young cavalry officer who was an expert in the art of poisoning.

Together, they had killed the marchioness' father-in-law, two brothers-in-law and a sister-in-law but, at that stage, the murders were discovered and the marchioness was tried and executed.

This scandal would have been well known to the French settlers and, when they discovered the poisonous weed, it was natural that it should have been linked in their minds with the murdering marchioness. She was the Marchioness of Brinvilliers, and the French settlers gave the poisonous weed her name.

In other parts of the Caribbean, this weed is still called "brin-ve-a", but in Grenada the word has been corrupted to **bon ve-a**.

French is not the only source feeding the Grenadian vocabulary. Many non-standard words in use today came in slave ships from Africa, and one such word is from the Twi language, spoken in areas of what is now Ghana. That word is **ko-ko-bay** and it is preserved in an old Grenadian proverb which says "If you have ko-ko-bay you can't get yaws."

Both in Grenada and Africa, ko-ko-bay means leprosy. "Yaws" is

the standard English word for a contagious skin disease (frambisia) and, when the proverb is used, it indicates that things couldn't get any worse with the speaker. In other words, figuratively, if you have leprosy, why worry about a little skin disease?

Another African word, **kata**, to cover and protect, has been absorbed directly into Grenadian English. Grenadian women cover and protect their scalps with a pad of straw or cloth when they carry loads on their heads and this pad is called a kata.

The derivation of **jook**, to prick or pierce, another widely used Grenadian word, is uncertain but it probably came from jukka, to poke, a word from the vocabulary of the West African Fulani people.

Jook is found in many combinations. To step on a nail is to get a nail-jook. To jook ants-nest is to stir up trouble, and spoiling fish (detecting whether it is still edible) which generates a pricking sensation in the mouth is said to be jooking-tongue.

There is a part of the human body which Grenadians call the **boo-shet**. This section of the anatomy is known to be somewhere in the vicinity of the chest, but its exact location is unclear. What is clear is that if one attempts to lift too heavy a load, the boo-shet may "fall".

Undoubtedly, boo-shet is derived from the French *brachet*, the breastbone, but what is interesting is the prescribed remedy to be applied when one's boo-shet "falls". Three cloves of garlic must be tied carefully in a knot of hair at the top of your head. This will restore the boo-shet to its proper place in quick time, guaranteed.

In Grenada the word **brag-gat** is often used instead of the word "fly" for the flap at the front of a man's trousers. It is derived from the French *braguette* which also means the flap at the front of a man's trousers and it has an amusing connection with Martinique.

In that island, as a part of the Government's social service, a grant of money (*l'argent* in French) is given to a woman for each child she bears. Accurately reflecting the realities of the situation, the Martiniquan slang expression for that grant is *l'argent braguette*.

The Spaniards never occupied Grenada but, operating from the Spanish Main (Venezuela) they had strong trading links with the island especially after it was made a "free port" in the eighteenth century.

Evidence of the influence on the Grenadian language of these trade contacts can be seen in words which have been borrowed from Spanish and are still in use today.

For instance, a person who pretends to be very important, who goes to great lengths to try to impress everybody but who, nevertheless, is recognised as a fraud, is referred to, derisively, as a **hay-fay**.

Undoubtedly, this is a word the Spaniards gave Grenada.. Why it should be used in a derogatory sense is not clear but hay-fay comes directly from the Spanish *jefe*, meaning "a chief".

The Spanish input is obvious also in the term used when two

politicians are evenly matched in their chances to win an election. Then, you will hear Grenadians say, "They're running **mano mano**". Clearly, the Spanish expression signifying equality, *mano a mano* is the origin of this expression.

Grenada shares with the southern United States the word **crocus-bag** which is a large bag of coarse, brown hemp used to bag agricultural produce. The word crocus-bag probably comes from the fact that this hemp was used originally to make bags to contain saffron, the product of the crocus plant.

A North American word which has enriched the Grenadian vocabulary is associated with the Reverend Ira David Sankey, the nineteenth century American evangelist singer and composer. In 1873, he published a collection of sacred songs which were so popular that, both in the United States and Grenada, a sacred song became known as a **sankey**.

And the United States is responsible for yet another Grenadian word. Black residents of Harlem have a slang vocabulary of their own and, early in this century, Grenadians migrating to the United States picked up many of these words. For instance, the Harlem slang to describe excellence is "kopasetee" and, with a slight change to **ko-pa-set-ic** it has become a Grenadian word with the same meaning.

What may be most puzzling to a visitor are the standard English words which, in Grenada, have been given a special non-standard meaning.

Such a word is the noun **set** which, in its standard meaning, your dictionary will tell you, refers to a group of things having something in common. For example, in the standard English meaning, one can have a "set of carpenter's tools" or a "set of books" by a particular author.

In Grenada set has a quite different meaning. Especially when used with the word **whole**, it denotes a large number of people or things which don't necessarily have anything in common. So, in Grenadian English, referring to the island's growing tourist trade, it would be perfectly in order to say that, every year, "a whole set of people" visit Grenada.

Another standard English word with a special Grenadian meaning is **again** which, in the standard dictionary, has a meaning of, "another time, once more".

Imagine circumstances in which you invite a Grenadian friend to accompany you on a trip to the moon. They accept your invitation but then change their mind. They are then quite likely to call you up and say, "Thanks very much but I am not going **again**".

In the standard meaning this is quite incomprehensible. Your friend has never before gone to the moon, so how can they now say that they are not going again? But, in Grenada, what they have said is quite in order because, in this country again does not mean only "another time, once more". It also means, "after all".

Another puzzling statement you may hear in Grenada, as well as in other Caribbean countries, would run something like this. "When you're taking a long automobile trip, you should always **walk with** a spare tyre." Automobile trip? Walk with? If one is driving a car, how does one walk with a spare tyre? But, not to worry, everything is in order because to walk with means to carry along.

A common Grenadian word and, indeed, one used throughout most of the English-speaking Caribbean, is **lime**. The origin is obscure, but this word first became current in the 1940s when it had a very restricted meaning.

In those days, lime was a verb only, and was used solely in connection with uninvited people standing in the road outside somebody's party. That was "liming the fete". Soon, however, people who limed a fete became limers and then, in a derogatory sense, limers became idle people who stood at street corners.

Today, the word is still very much in use but it has evolved. In addition to its original meaning, it now means to enjoy leisure time. One limes when one visits a friend or spends idle hours in relaxation. Indeed, thousands of people come to Grenada every year just to lime on the island's beautiful beaches!

Your stay on the island will be enriched if you listen carefully for the non-standard English words which Grenadians use. These words exist **by the grap**. You're certain to be fascinated by what you hear and unless you're quite **too-tool-bay** you're going to recognise and enjoy them.

Illustrations courtesy: 'Grenada Sketches in Black and White' by W. Dieterle, 1986.

Other non-standard words

Acid   Alcohol
Alpagat   Slipper with leather sole and coarse woven top
                 (Spanish - *Alpagata*, sandal made of hemp)
Ashum   Pounded parched corn with sugar
                 (African Twi - *O-siam*, pounded parched
                 corn mixed with sugar)
Bargee   Edible shrub similar to spinach
                 (Hindi - *Bhaji*, name for spinach)
Bub-bul   Dishonesty
Cog   To cheat at school by copying from another's work
Dan-Dan   Clothes (childish)
Day Clean   Dawn
Doctor Shop Pharmacy
Dougla   Person of Indian and African descent.
Drevay   To move from place to place aimlessly
                 (French - *Derive*, to drift [of a ship])
Fire One   Have a strong drink
Frupse   To drink noisily (especially of soup)
Ma-Boo-Ya   A small lizard with large bulging eyes
                 (Amerindian - *Mabuya*, evil spirit)
Peg   Segment of a citrus fruit
Soul Case   The human body
Tayche   Large metal container for boiling sugar
                 (Spanish - *Tacho*, sugar-boiler)
Travo   Road worker, especially one breaking stones
                 manually (French - *Travaux*, work)
Wall House   Concrete house
Zut   Cigarette butt

CULTURE
Carnival

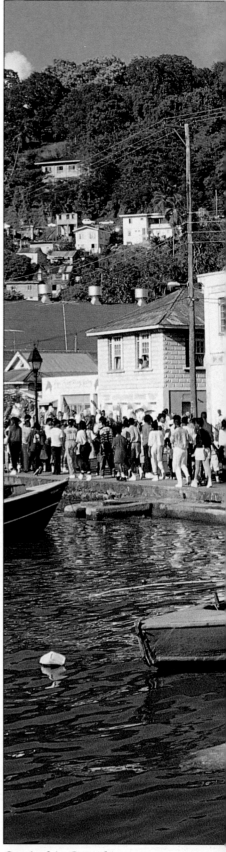

Carnival in Grenada
Courtesy: Jim Rudin

Carnival seasons vary with both local and national traditions. Originally, in some countries it began on January 6 (Epiphany) and continued through to Ash Wednesday. In other countries it was limited to midnight on Shrove Tuesday.

Carnival played a significant role in the development of popular theatre, vernacular songs and folk dances. Any treatment of the subject of Carnival and its origin must be regarded as somewhat arbitrary, since the evolution and survival of the festival with its ideas and rituals from the Egyptian cult of Isis, and the Greek, Roman, and Germanic periods, are far from clear; and the evidence may be differently evaluated.

The derivation of the word is uncertain but it can possibly be traced to the Medieval Latin *Carnem Lavare* or *Carnelaverium* which means, "to take away or remove meat". The early Christians abstained from eating meat during the Lenten period and Carnival was a festival which preceded the austere forty days of Lent. The Carnival processions prior to Lent in many Catholic countries derived from the heathen feasts of Saturnalia, Lupercalia, and Bacchanalia in Italy.

Carnival procession is one of the most basic demonstrations of communal unity. A more sophisticated variant includes imitations of individuals such as rulers, priests, witch doctors, or warriors, who in their person represent the interests of the community at large or their own particular status or function. It is characteristic of pageantry to represent in symbolic form the various classes and castes of the society. The common people developed forms of pageantry that proclaim their own interests. The word pageant derived from the Latin *pagina* - 'page' which means 'kind of illustration'.

This festival is today celebrated in societies that were at one time influenced by both French colonists and African slaves. The cordial relations that existed amongst the French plantocracy were expressed in concerts, balls, dinners, hunting parties, and 'fete champetres' and these were especially concentrated in Carnival season which lasted from Christmas to Ash Wednesday. This was the driest and coolest period of the year and the frantic rush to cut the cane crop would not be experienced until after the Festival. The gatherings of the Carnival season were characterised by 'a contagious gaiety', brilliant verbal sallies, and comic buffoonery which was the subject of conversations for many days after.

The French sought and found recognition among their ranks by excelling in elegance, sophistication, and their ability in the fine arts, conversation, dress, music, and hospitality according to their provincial standards. These French, unlike the English planters and absentee owners,

did not look at their Westindian colonies merely as places to be tolerated for the sake of a quick fortune, the fruits of which might be enjoyed in the metropolitan country, but as a new way of life.

Grenada's Carnival development underwent several serious periods of neglect because of the frequent changing of colonial ruler; from French to British (1650-1762) to French (1762-1779) to British (1779-1783). Under the Treaty of Versailles, 1783, the island was ceded to the British and Carnival took on a different appearance. Most of the French aristocracy and freed slaves migrated to Trinidad after 1783 because of victimisation by the British. For the few French who remained, conditions forced them to keep a low profile and the standard of costume Mas dropped to estate festival levels.

Although the standard had dropped, Carnival between 1784 and 1833 remained an important institution for the upper class whites, particularly in the towns. Christmas and New Year were seasons of rowdy celebrations.

Even on islands not controlled by France but with a French community, the habits and customs of the people resembled those of France and naturally this included Carnival.

Those of French and African descent, referred to as "free persons of colour", were subjected to stringent regulations and, although not forbidden to wear masks, were compelled to keep to themselves and not join the amusements of the privileged classes. The slaves, except as onlookers, or by special favour when required to participate, had no share in the Carnival, which was confined exclusively to the European upper classes.

It would be unwise to say that Carnival came to the region in 1783 since, at that time, it was a festival of the exploiters and not the oppressed people's Carnival which developed from 1834. There was a fundamental struggle on the cultural front which took place from the earliest days - the struggle of the people's culture against the oppressive culture. This has been, and continues to be, part of the struggle for freedom, which was extremely violent at times, and was waged from the earliest days of slavery, through indentureship and the whole period of colonisation.

Prior to Emancipation, slave revolts often took place during the period from Christmas to Ash Wednesday. It became a practice in the British colonies to proclaim martial law from Christmas through to the New Year holidays. On December 24, each year, guns were fired from the forts on the island, red flags were hoisted, civil tribunals were suspended and martial law was enforced. The entire militia was placed on duty, and business literally came to a halt. There were also troop parades and mock engagements.

Junior Carnival participant
Courtesy: The Informer

Carnival in Grenada
Courtesy: Jim Rudin

OPPOSITE
Carnival celebrations in Carriacou
Courtesy: Julia Emerson

Cannes Brulee (Canboulay)

In the eighteenth century, the early Canboulays were part of the slaves
end of harvest celebrations. After Emancipation, the people began to
represent this scene as a kind of commemoration of the change in their
condition, and the procession of Canne Brulee (Burnt Cane) used to take
place on the night of August 1 (Emancipation Day).

During slavery, when fires broke out on estates, slaves from the
surrounding properties were immediately mustered and marched to the
fire accompanied by the tooting of horns and blowing of shells. Upon
collection, they were harassed by slave drivers cracking whips and striking
blows, urging them on in the dangerous work of trying to quell the fire.

For a time slaves were permitted to carry sticks to use as a tool to
assist in cutting cane. Of course, these sticks were used for other purposes
and could be dangerous weapons. Eventually, in 1810, sticks were
prohibited. The severe whipping that slaves received while being force-
marched to cane fires were remembered with intense hate. The inhumane
circumstances surrounding work on the estates led them to regard the
plantation owners as devils and during Canboulay the idea of slavery
was generally symbolised by the Jab Molassi (Molasses Devil). Canboulay
and stick-fighting dominated Carnival until late in the nineteenth century.

From the time the character of Carnival changed, from the frivolous
gaiety of the upper classes to a Festival of Protest of the oppressed people,
the colonial masters tried to stop the festival.

The festival changed its social form three times. After Emancipation,
those who had predominated formerly withdrew, whilst those who were
hitherto debarred from participation joined in tentatively and
experimentally.

About thirty years later, Canboulay became established as the midnight
overture to Carnival. From the end of the nineteenth to the beginning of the
twentieth century the festival began to move back towards the upper classes,
however, by playing on carriages and subsequently on trucks.

The Canboulay festivities have now merged with Carnival celebrations.

*'Jab-Jab' Mas in Carriacou, a sight that is becoming increasingly rare, has its
roots in the 'Jab Molassi' (Molasses Devil) during slavery, where the plantation
owners, because of their vicious treatment of the slaves, were symbolised as devils*
Courtesy: Julia Emerson

Traditional Mas

A look at the origins and evolution of the festival, as a key strand of local history, throws up many setbacks in the course of its long development. From 1783-1983, two hundred years of struggle changed the face of Carnival. Here is a selection of some Traditional Mas.

Pissenlit or **Pizali** or **Pizane** (meaning "Stinker!") - This Mas was usually played by masked men and dressed women. The women wore long night gowns (transparent), decorated with ribbon and lace. Others wore very small undergarments liberally stained with 'blood'. One member collected money. The dancing was coupled with sexual horseplay, including use of a poui stick protruding between the legs, or a shirt gathered together in front in the manner of the Chiffone dance of Carriacou.

Jamet Band - The women wore beautiful dresses with many starched petticoats over which their skirts were draped and caught up into their belts. Large hats, decorated with lots of flowers and feathers, were also worn. They danced in the streets, throwing open their bodices and exposing their breasts. This was particularly a feature of the Trinidad Carnival.

The man was referred to as the sweet-man. He wore trousers of serge or flannel low over the hips, and held up by two belts, rope or leather, from which hung multicoloured silk shirts unbuttoned to display chains and other jewellery around the neck. They completed their costumes with Panama hats decorated with feathers.

Moko Jumby (The Stilt Dancer!) - This was played nearly always by men. They positioned themselves on stilts as high as 10 - 15 feet. They were brightly painted in stripes and the masker wore a full length skirt and a jacket of brightly coloured satin or velvet. His hat was made of tosho, the fried pulp of the wild cucumber. Moko Jumby was sometimes accompanied by a dwarf in similar costume but without stilts to accentuate the Moko's height. His dance was similar to a jig and was usually accompanied by a drum, a triangle and a flute. Moko has virtually become extinct.

Grenada Carnival
Courtesy: Jim Rudin

Calypso

Calypso is a very popular form of song that originated in the French Westindies, and which has been developed to an art form in Trinidad. Calypso is also widely known throughout the region. The roots of Calypso came from the peasant and tribal culture. In Venezuela the 'cariso' and in West African topical songs called 'wuso' have had an influence on Calypso. The most acceptable derivation of Calypso is the West African word *Kaiso* which means well done. The lyrics are usually topical and satirical and are performed by calypsonians with fanciful names.

'The Mighty Sparrow'

Grenadian-born Slinger Francisco, known as 'The Mighty Sparrow', is considered by many as the father of modern Calypso and has maintained his reputation as a worldwide entertainer. His arrival in 1956, when he won his first Calypso crown with 'Jean and Dinah', marked a new era in which presentation and stage performance became a crucial part of Calypso. Sparrow combines powerful lyrics, often highlighting social and political issues, with sweet melodies which suit his powerful and sensuous voice. Sparrow captured 'Road March' honours six times between 1958 and 1984 and was crowned 'Calypso Monarch' eight times, most recently when he made a comeback in 1992.

LEFT & OPPOSITE
Carnival in Grenada
Photos courtesy: Jim Rudin

The 'Olde' Carnival:

Jab-Jab, History Mas, Wild Indians, Shortknee and Pierrot

By John Benjamin
Courtesy of *Rainbow City Magazine*

'Jab-Jab' (Devil Mas)

An encounter never to be forgotten was the 'Devil Mas' or 'Jab-Jab'. Blackened to the hilt with stale molasses, tar, grease, creosote or mud and scandalously attired, they were as grotesque in appearance as they were repulsive in their dance.

They paraded serpents and frogs in order to terrify onlookers and so obtain payment for their quick departure. It was not uncommon to see living serpents serving as their belts or necklaces. 'Jab-Jab' dressed with everything wrong: rusty chamberpots, cattle horns, cow chains, frightful moustaches, owlish goggles, burnt tin pots, phantom hats and old basins to name but a few. From the back of their trousers hung an extended wire tail, often with a hemp brush. Some carried big dirty books, on the pretext of teaching their 'little sons' to read and spell, though such reading and spelling were nothing more than worthless garbage. This was much to the amusement of some in the crowd, who responded to the 'Jab-Jab' performances with uncontrollable, raucous laughter. But there were 'good' Jabs, too, who were witty and tolerable entertainers.

A man plays the 'Jab-Jab' Mas in Grenada's Carnival
Courtesy: The Informer

'History Mas'

'History Mas' masqueraded in pairs, each player vying with the other in an engaging narration of English history. Their accurate recall of chronological events was impressive.

As one player narrated the facts (swinging with appropriate movements), he was regularly complimented by his companion with the words 'Bold Speaker!'

'History Mas' were men, but grandly dressed in ladies' outfits. Crocheted white petticoats gleaming from their brilliant skirts, rich crowns dazzling in the sun. Entire costumes were bedecked with glittering mirrors and jingle-bell trinkets termed 'glows'. In those days people listened with admiration and rapt attention. And many a penny or half-penny was joyfully surrendered to the impressive historians. (A penny at that time could purchase what five dollars will today!)

OPPOSITE
An encounter never to be forgotten -
'Jab-Jab' Mas as played in Carriacou
Courtesy: Julia Emerson

'Wild Indians'

Another celebrated group of past male revellers were the sword-bearing 'Wild Indians '. And wild they were, but for entertainment value they were superb! Their showmanship was compelling and dramatic. Their costumes were gorgeous - scant bodice, short skirt, magnificent colours, long trailing ropey hair. They wore strings of wild Indian beads, bracelets and armlets; brilliant earrings, tinkling 'glow' balls and the best of crocheted petticoats! Such was the 'Wild Indians' grooming. In short, they were captivatingly apparelled! Moreover, a bull-ring suspended from their nostrils increased the impression of power and wildness.

'Wild Indians' dyed their skin purple with the seed of the ochre plant. This provided them with a tan of special and irresistible appeal. Their crowns were tall and shaped like two or three-masted schooners trimmed in all the colours of the rainbow, with flying red and gold streamers.

Behind the line of 'Wild Indians' came their 'Eloina' or queen. The leader formed the head of the line and led his followers in sensational acts of pelvic gyrations, wild gestures and intense ceremonial dancing. At the sight of an approaching vehicle, they all would flee into the bushes! Howls and shrieks of nervousness ensued. They only resumed play after the vehicle had completely disappeared.

One didn't hand money to them. For payment, a coin or coins were tossed at any member of the band during performances. On contact with the coin, a 'Wild Indian' fell to the ground. The 'Wild Indians' gathered over their fallen comrade as though he were dead and an intense ceremony began straight away accompanied with gladdened chants and frenzied motions. Expressions of thanks and gratitude followed as the coins were picked up and the ceremonial dancing resumed with a show full of gratification.

'Shortknee'

Like the Jab-Jab, the 'Shortknee' is the only other Carnival character that dates back to around the end of the sixteenth or beginning of the seventeenth century. It derives from the 'Pierrots', a once popular Carnival Mas, occasionally found in areas of Carriacou. Few can deny they were a class by themselves. And fewer still will deny that they had proven to be a source of concern on Carnival Day. They always appeared restless and threatening. They banded together in numbers, everyone dressing

The masked dancers of the 'Shortknee' Mas, the powder once used to whiten their faces is now thrown at onlookers
Courtesy: The Informer

identically. Worst of all, they were tightly masked, so that individual identity was hard to discover.

With Arab-like head coverings, jumbo collars, batwing sleeves and three-quarter baggy trousers tied above the knee, they pranced the roads aggressively, passionately chanting and boxing the air. They were not such a colourful group, but what they lacked in colour they easily made-up for in action.

St Patrick in particular had many of them. Every generation related to the Carnival feuds that plagued the 'Shortknees' on opposite sides. At the centre of these feuds were the villages of Chantimelle and Mount Rueil, although they were miles apart.

The town of Sauteurs was chosen as the meeting point for the commencement of the battle. Often there would be chase and counter-chase across their respective borders. Each side boasted a fearless captain who directed the course of combat. Needless to say, these were serious disturbances. Many performers were hurt over the years, some badly. This was certainly not a game. However, after a prolonged conflict, the two rival villages did finally reconcile their differences and bury the hatchet for good.

Shortknee is a more subdued character at Carnival today, though many remember the past with trepidation. The trousers which are worn today are of their own creation. All the revellers agreed that each leg of the trousers should be as baggy as ever, but there was not a consensus about the length. Some understand the name of the Mas to come from a reveller's suggestion that the length of the trousers should reach just below each reveller's knee, hence 'Shortknee'. Revellers of the 'Shortknee' throw powder at onlookers - a remnant of the powder used to whiten the faces in the 'Pierrot' Mas of old.

'Pierrot'

What is known today in Grenada's Carnival as 'Shortknee' is the remnant of the 'Pierrot', a once familiar sight in Grenada's Carnival.

At the time in Grenada's history when Carnival belonged exclusively to the plantation owners and their families, particularly the French, one of the most familiar sights in the celebrations was the 'Pierrot', an entertainer with whitened face and loose white fancy dress. The characters did not confine their performances to Carnival celebrations only, but were very much sought after for performances at lavish plantations which were then

Great House

The name used in the English-speaking Westindies to refer to a large spacious house built on a sugar plantation in the seven-teenth and eighteenth centuries for the use of the estate owner. Some of these 'Great Houses' had up to forty rooms

ABOVE, OPPOSITE & OVERLEAF
The 'Pierrot' Mas, once popular throughout Grenada, is now played in parts of Carriacou
Photos courtesy: Julia Emerson

the most common of the Great House revelries.

By the time Emancipation came, the former slaves, especially those of the Great Houses, were very good performers. They used to mimic their former "owners" mannerisms and cruelties, and had accumulated a huge literary repertoire.

The rejoicing at Emancipation contained skilful displays of European dances, reciting of literature and a drastic change in the 'Pierrot' costumes. Their faces were painted white with powder to disguise themselves in the manner of French pantomime characters. This was later to become a full head-mask, but the container which carried the powder remained, as a weapon with razor-sharp edges.

Now that they were free to participate in the Carnival celebrations, the revellers used their costumes to hide weapons with which to harm their enemies from opposing camps.

The revellers chose to wear bright colours and their designs inspired awe among both maskers and spectators alike. They retained the head-piece, the shirt sleeves were long and wide enough to conceal weapons with which to hurt their opponents whenever clashes between bands occurred.

Such behaviour could not be condoned by the authorities and laws were passed regulating their manner of dress at post-Emancipation Carnival celebrations. During the 1920s and 30s the law decreed that further trimming of the costumes was necessary, with the hope of minimising the violence which had become so much a part of the Carnival celebrations.

The confrontations took the form of face-to-face literary recitals, usually Shakespeare. This literature was learnt and passed down through the generations as it was all that was available to the slaves, becoming re-interpreted and distorted, taking on its own form. If one made a mistake, the other would strike him on the head with a stick called a "bull".

Today the stick strikes an elaborate head-dress, heavily padded, which makes more noise than it causes pain. The revellers move from village to village challenging any others who dare to compete.

Disappearing Carnival

Extracts from 'Rules made by the Governor-General under the Authority of Section 5 of the Carnival Regulation Act, Cap. 41 of 1990', as published in *Grenada Today*, July 29, 1994:

"During the Carnival no person shall:

Throw any substance, matter or thing likely to cause damage, injury or discomfort to anyone;

No male person shall in public place appear dressed or disguised as a female person;

During the four weeks preceding the Carnival and during the Carnival no person shall make, sell, distribute, wear, carry, have in his possession or in any manner deal with masks, dominoes, sticks, whips, spiked footwear, or other offensive weapons;

During the Carnival no person shall play the masque known as 'jab-jab' or 'vie cour'."

Dance

Folk and Dance Groups

Grenada's National Folk Group was formed for the specific purpose of harnessing the potential talents in Grenada in respect to the performing arts.

The group consists of members from four of the island's most outstanding cultural groups, namely Cariawa Folk Group, Spice Island Youthquake, Veni-Vwai La Grenade Dance Company and Impulse Dance Company.

Despite its recent formation this multi-talented group comprises artists who have made international appearances in the UK, Ireland, Canada, the United States and Guadeloupe.

An outstanding feature of the group is the blending of youthful talents with experienced senior artists. Members of the National Folk Group are all amateurs with a desire to learn and to improve their skills in creative arts.

The group hopes to inspire in Grenadians living abroad a feeling of nostalgia so they will have an ardent desire to return home. The group also aims to give Europeans and people of other nationalities, a vivid insight into certain aspects of Grenadian folk-life, through song, dance and drama.

The Cariawa Folk Group are from the parish of St Patrick. This group specialises in the singing and choreographing of folk song, especially those in Grenadian patois. Cariawa won the folk singing and creative dance sections of the National Festival of Arts in 1982 and they were also winners in the folk song category for adults at the 1985 Grenada Festival of Arts. Cariawa enjoyed a highly successful tour of the UK where they produced and presented a folk opera. They were also selected to perform at a number of prestigious functions - such as the visits of Queen Elizabeth (1985) and of President Reagan (1986).

Veni-Vwai La Grenade Dance Company are from the parish of St George and were formed in 1974. They started a new repertoire of dances, presenting traditional folk dances in a creative and exciting form. Veni-Vwai have performed in the United States, Cuba and Canada. The group achieved first place at the International Year of the Youth Cultural Competition staged in Grenada in 1985. The company also performs on visiting cruise liners.

Spice Island Youthquake, from the parish of St John, concentrate mainly on religious and folk songs. They have made several successful tours abroad including the UK, the United States and Canada.

Impulse Dance Company, from the parish of St George, specialise in modern dance, performing folk and classical ballet. Impulse were formed in 1986 and have thrilled many audiences throughout Grenada.

OPPOSITE
The National Folk Group, harnessing the talent of Grenada's performing arts
Courtesy: Grenada National Folk Group

Traditional Dances

Bongo

There are many versions of the Bongo, yet, each version tells the same story. It is usually performed at 'Wake Houses' with the express purpose of affording the soul of the dead the safest transportation to the heavenly kingdom. It is performed by both sexes, but there are times when some versions use men only. It is rather pleasing to watch the dancers whose gesticulations leave not a spectator in doubt as to what the dance is meant to convey.

Bongo, which is of African origin, has been greatly 'Westindianised', more so in Trinidad where movements have been modified to give it a better look on the Westindian stage, and at the same time, to show the intricate and graceful movements of the dancers. At Grenadian national dances, it is not uncommon to see ten, twelve or even more people dancing the Bongo at the same time. But on stage a cast of two, four, six and even eight may perform.

Stick Fight or Kalinda

The Kalinda or Stick Fight was formerly danced at "Wake Houses" to ensure the passage of the dead person through purgatory to heaven.

After a time, however, it became the dance used by liquor dealers on the occasion of the formal opening of their shops. The idea was to attract customers since many people, chiefly men, turned out to witness the dance and share in the entertainment provided by the stick fighters. The dance reached its climax when either of the stick fighters sheds the blood of his opponent.

Belle Air or Bele

This dance, the origin of which is uncertain, seems to have come from the Westindian slaves. It strikingly resembles the Lancers and Quadrille dances except that the movements of the feet are different. There is the popular belief that Westindian slaves, seeing the masters and mistresses perform the Lancers and Quadrille with such grace and skill, created this dance which they performed at national celebrations, making sure to retain most of the African footwork.

It is performed with four couples whose costumes should reflect the bright colours usually worn at any Westindian festival or celebration. Two versions of the Belle Air are usually performed - the Bele (plain) and the Grand Bele. Brightly coloured headscarves are worn by the women together

Wake Houses

The burial gathering or wake takes place at the Wake House where the deceased body remains for the night. People gather from all over the island and the men and boys build a coffin while the women and girls prepare clothes for the corpse and headties, ribbons and clothes for the mourners.

Hymns are sung and Anansi stories are told. Tea, coffee and bread or biscuits are served. Jack Iron rum is also served. Neighbours and friends share the domestic chores of sewing and preparing food for the mourners.

with long-sleeved dresses and long white-laced petticoats that complete the costumes, while the men wear gaudy shirts, a red head-band, white trousers or dungarees and a single or pair of bracelets. The dance is performed barefooted.

The Lancers

The Lancers originated in France. It was danced in England where it underwent certain changes to suit the national taste. It made its appearance in the Westindies through the English, and the slaves were quick to adopt it. They made a few changes to 'Africanise' it and performed it with music.

It is performed by four couples who comprise a set, and as many sets as possible can perform, according to the size of the hall. Five figures are danced, after which there is the 'heel and toe' which is danced by Lancers and spectators alike.

Costumes for the Lancers are usually made in the fashion of ballroom costumes of the Victorian era. The ladies are in long flowing gowns and flat-heeled shoes, with rosettes worn on the right-hand side of their hair. The men are usually in tail-coats, low-heeled shoes and a frilled neck-piece worn in the fashion of a Spanish aristocrat.

The Bele Dance, as danced by the National Folk Group
Courtesy: Grenada National Folk Group

Folk tales

By Christine David

Ever since the beginning of time, the creation of the human race and the development of languages, storytelling has been closely related to the African people. The stories usually contain folklore, folk traditions, rituals, sayings and beliefs. Usually the story is told by that notorious individual who possesses that ability to depict the essence of the narration with warmth and volubility.

Forbidden to play the African drums, the Caribbean black slave population engaged, depending on the level of restrictions, in telling stories in the guise of amusing and entertaining the *Masa* and his offspring. *Masa* saw the activity as childlike and insignificant.

However, they contained concealed messages of escape plans and philosophies on survival in a foreign land under unbearable circumstances. Most of the stories told, even today, at wake nights and prayer meetings, are told with accuracy and judgement.

In the process of suppression, the African slaves were forced to adopt a new religion, a new set of beliefs, in short, a whole new personality. Yet despite this suppression they managed to incorporate some of their past rites into their new and developing culture.

The stories began to reflect this environment with its different experiences. The ancient myths, explanatory tales, *Masa* tales, dilemma tales, animal tales, warrior legends and moral tales of African folklore merged into slave Anansi stories.

The folk tales of the people are guides to the understanding of their past. Many present a point of view and emphasise a moral. Taken as a whole folklore shows the wit and philosophy of a people.

Zyeh and the water-hole
A Grenadian Anansi story

Supplied by Shirley Robinson, *Chief Cultural Officer,*
Grenada & Carriacou National Folk Group

Zyeh was a very disagreeable little character who used to do a lot of wrong things. In those days there were no pipes to convey water and people used to get water from ponds, springs and water-holes.

Once upon a time a man had a water-hole on his land and all the neighbours and villagers used to go there to get water to cook, wash,

Anansi legend

There are many legends of Anansi; the most relevant and convincing is that Anansi Kojo (Cudjoe) was an Ashanti leader of the Kromantin tribe. These people were thought to assemble frequently on social occasions to sing and to dance each others dances. Kojo is venerated by Carriacouans in the Big Drum rites.

Today, Anansi is the name for the chief character in Westindian folk tales, a simple yet intelligent being, reduced to playing the role of a cunning trickster. He is able to overcome all difficulties and dangers by using his wits. The stories symbolize the triumph of the artful and quick-witted over brute strength and ponderous might.

bathe and do everything they needed water to do.

One day when the people went to collect water, they found that the water was dirty and they could not use it. The next day they went to the hole, again the water was dirty. This went on for a few days. 'Who could be playing this trick on us?, they wondered, angrily.

The owner of the water-hole made up his mind to catch the culprit at all costs. He made a plan. He made a beautiful woman out of tar and stuck her up on the land not too far from the water-hole: close by her side he put a waiter (tray) with some bakes and fish-cakes and a cup of cocoa-tea.

Zyeh came to the water hole as usual, when he saw the bakes and fish-cakes he looked at the tar-baby and said "Good morning mam." The woman did not answer. "Good morning mam", he repeated, but the lady still did not answer.

"Ah nice, nice lady like you ah telling you a nice howdy do an you doh sayin nuttan; ah bet you ah box you." Saying so, he slapped the tar-baby and his hand stuck.

"Leggo me han nuh, leh me go: ah likkle joke ah make wid you, you holin me han." He said again, "Leggo me han; if you doh leggo me ah go give you a harder box dis time you know."

But the tar-baby wouldn't let go. Getting angry, Zyeh slapped the tar-baby with the other hand and it stuck fast too.

"Leh me go. Man leh me go. Leh me go ah tell you" shouted Zyeh more angrily: "If you doh leh me go ah go butt you". So saying he gave the tar-baby a head butt and his head stuck fast. Eventually his whole body got stuck on the tar-baby.

The land-owner passed by the water-hole to see if his plan had worked. There was Zyeh well caught in the trap.

"Eh heh! ah hole you. Zyeh you mean all de time is you dat doin dat wickedness in de water hole? Well, now is me turn, wait for me, ah coming bac wid you present", said the landowner, and he went away.

While Zyeh was waiting Compere Tig came for water and saw him there. "Wat you doin dey?" asked Tig.

"Ah waintin to marrid de landowner daughter." said Zyeh. "Compere, ah doh want to marrid, because, as you know, ah marrid aready: but he say ah mus marrid, udderwise..."

"Zyeh," said Tig. "Ooh behave so; de got is a prutty likkle gal, any man woulda glad to marrid wid her."

"Den why you doh marrid her?" asked Zyeh.

"Is not me dey ask." said Tig. "If you gi me de opportunity see if ah do marriding wid her."

"Wid all pleasure. Compere," said Zyeh. "Just put me down an leh me stick you up in me place, an de prutty likkle gal is all yours."

Tig was glad to hear that. He fought with all his might to loosen Zyeh from the tar-baby, then took Zyeh's place.

Zyeh was so happy he didn't wait to see Tig's present. He ran off as fast as he could and as far away from the water-hole as possible. When he had reached a good distance away, he climbed up a tree to rest. As he sat on the tree he laughed "Ha! Ha! ah wonder if Tig get he present aready? Ah wonder wat de present is?"

Meanwhile Tig was patiently waiting to get marrid to the beautiful young lady.

"How dey takin so long to come? he said to himself.

Just then, he heard, "Zyeh! you dey?" It was the landowner's voice.

"Yes" replied Tig.

"OK ah comin wid de present, but you mus close you eyes an doh open it until ah tell you," said the landowner.

"Alright," said Compere Tig.

"Ready?" said the owner. "Close you eyes tight, tighter, tighter still."

"Woye! Bonjai!" screamed Tig as he felt the hot iron on his bottom. He broke loose from the tar-baby and ran away as fast as he could, saying as he went, "If ah ketch Zyeh today, ee dead!"

Did Tig catch Zyeh? Ah doh know. Ah de so fraid far meself dat ah run like hell. De story en and de wire ben, and ah want ah pen to write me nennen.

Ring games

Once a popular pastime, 'Ring games' were a part of the after supper recreational activities of families. The games were played mainly by the children on 'moonlit nights' in the early evenings while the elders looked on or enjoyed a friendly gossip.

Although these games were recreational, bringing fun and laughter both to the players and onlookers alike, they were also quite competitive and involved a good deal of concentration.

One of the most popular games was 'Pound stone'.

Pound stone

This game was played with stones, one stone to each player. Each player of 'Pound stone' carefully selected their stone and sat, stooped or knelt in a circle holding that stone. The players, and sometimes the onlookers also, sang the 'game' songs while the rhythm was kept by tapping the stones on the floor. At a certain point in the song, towards the end of the verses, the stones had to be passed around the circle, beginning with the immediate right.

The object of the games was, while singing and passing the stones, to keep the timing and avoid being struck on the hand.

The person or persons who failed in this were eliminated. The game was restarted and the same procedure continued until a victor emerged.

The Grenada National Folk Group keeping the traditions alive. (Top) a clapping 'Ring game' played usually by children and (Bottom) a re-enactment of 'Pound stone'

Carriacou Dance

By Christine David
Courtesy *Folklore of Carriacou*

Dance on Carriacou is the nucleus of communal activities. It is an integral part of the Saraca, Maroon and Tombstone feasts. It is also part of the Boat Launching ceremony.

A legacy of European cultures have to a greater extent been superimposed on the traditional art forms in the Caribbean. The fusion of Caribbean folklore evident in the Caribbean Festival of Arts has broadened the scope of traditional art forms.

The culture of ancestor worship was widespread among the Kromantins, the Ibos, the Chamba, the Banda, the Moko, the Temne, the Arradah and the Hausa-speaking peoples who were prevalent on Carriacou during the slave era. Dances relating to these nations or tribes are still considered as ritual and the Carriacouan can, up to this present time, identify with his nation of origin.

Whenever a Carriacouan holds a dance ceremony, the Nation Dance (or Big Drum Dance) takes priority, second only to the Kromantin or the Chief Beg Pardon Dance.

Other dances, secular or old Creole are the Bele Dances (Gwa bele, Bele Kane, Bele Tuba) also the Hallechurde, Bongo and Kalinder.

There are also dances that are neither ritual or old Creole, referred to as frivolous dances - the Chiffone, the Checcup, the Pike which may have been copied during the post Emancipation period.

It is correct to say that the Kromantin Dance is the most significant. The Kromantins, who came from Ghana, were the foremost nation to come to Carriacou. It is believed that the spirits of the Kromantins are strong, since they were usually leaders of rebellion.

This dance is performed primarily for the purpose of begging the ancestors to partake of the sacrificial plate and to witness and participate in the ceremony. It is the chief of the Beg Pardon Dances and at any Big Drum rite the opening and closing of the ritual is done with Kromantin Dances. Anansi Kojo, honoured ancestor of the Kromantin tribe, is venerated. The ringing of an old hoe accompanying mainly the cot drum, the total drumbeat, the shac-shac and the songs are to beckon the spirits of the ancestors into the dancing ring with the Kromantins in the lead. A popular African saying is that "the dead are never gone, they are in the thickening shadows". Other Beg Pardon Dances are the Ibo, Hausa and Mandingo.

The Ibos of Nigeria danced when they thought they had offended their God and therefore had to make restitution.

The Mandingo Dance, also originating from Nigeria, is performed for healing. The Mandingos are believed to be earth worshippers, so the

An 'Ibo' drummer on Carriacou
Courtesy: Winston Fleary

Shac-shac

The shac-shac tree, which has many names, grows to a height of 30 feet, produces a long flat seed-pod of about twelve inches. In the dry season the seed-pod dries and the seeds rattle in the wind. These shac-shac pods are used by musicians who cleverly use a variety of techniques to produce spectacular sound effects - much the same as the South American maraca player

OPPOSITE
The costume of the Big Drum Dance
Courtesy: *Folklore of Carriacou*

dance is known as the Thunder and Rain Dance for fertility of the soil.

The Arada Dance is for healing the sick and casting out evil spells. It is known as a serpent dance as the body movement depicts. The people of Benin worshipped the serpent Dangbe, or Dam-bala as it is called in other parts of the Caribbean.

As for the old Creole dances, they are mainly for entertainment although some of them depict warfare. Of these secular dances, the most popular is the Bele Kawe. It contains European extracts but it may have originated as an African court dance, as has been suggested - a mock fight between two women. The women in the dance represent either two hens or a Queen and second wife of the King. It is called the Queen Dance or the Hen Dance of ancient Benin. The male dancer who takes the ladies in and out of the dancing ring represents either the famous cock or a King over whom the women fight in more or less the form of a challenge. This beautiful dance demonstrates dignity, spirit and gracefulness.

The Quadrille Dance

The Quadrille originated in France but became popular in England. The eighteenth century English influence is revealed in the Quadrille Dance which is now prevalent in Carriacou, especially in the village of L'Esterre.

There are three kinds of dance - English Quadrille, Albert Quadrille and Lancers Quadrille. Up to 1930 the Lancers Quadrille was very popular and was danced in homes. The throwing of a bouquet at the end of a dance session showed that the next sponsor was the person who caught the bouquet.

The Quadrille is second in popularity to the Big Drum Dance. It lacks the variety and significance of the Big Drum, but surpasses it in the quality of its rhythm.

The dance is performed by four men and four women. The head couple stand close to the musicians and the tail couple opposite. There are six pieces of dance to every set. The first four pieces are special, the last two could be different, usually the fifth is a fast rhythm and the sixth either a Polka or Cacian.

A tambourine, a bass drum, a violin and a triangle are played.

OPPOSITE
Quadrille Dance musicians -
bass drum, violin, tambourine
and triangle
Courtesy: *Folklore of Carriacou*

The Big Drum Dance

A significant feature of the Carriacouan folk culture is the extent to which the African connection has been preserved, as is evident in the African Nation Dance - popularly known as the Big Drum Dance. The drums are called Big Drums because when that tide of humanity moved across the Atlantic in the seventeenth century, when the Caribbean became home to a transplanted race, the Africans were found to have the biggest drums in existence at that time.

In Carriacou, cultural practices have emerged from the melting pot of African and European ancestral cultures, but the African influence is predominant. Colonialism tried to eradicate the indigenous cultures and created a plantation economy based on exploitation of the African forefathers, who gave their lives but not their dreams, and who faced the inhuman slave regime. But the African people have a controlled, yet rebellious, assertive nature that guarantees their survival and propels their struggle for self-determination.

Drummers and singers of the the Big Drum Dance
Courtesy: Maria Hamlet

The fact that the Nation Dance survived as a common dynamic practice among Carriacouans is not merely due to absentee European land-owners but because of the determination of the African people to preserve their identity.

The slave, though taciturn and sad all day, found escape in joyful and meaningful recreation in the drumbeat, the songs and the dances. The dance, the drumbeat and the songs ring out a tradition of resistance to oppression as is evident in the secular dances of the Bongo, the Hallechurde and the Kalinda.

Today, when there is an endless search for new forms of dance based on cultural roots, the African National Dances continues to regenerate the cultural heritage in schools, in homes and at social functions. A tangible feeling of togetherness emanates among young and old - a symbol of roots, identity and liberation. This tradition is an integral part of communal activities.

In Carriacou, life is centred around the drums particularly in the southern and eastern sections of the island. It cannot be over emphasised that it was the drums that the missionaries and authorities tried to eradicate by persuasion on one hand and legislation on the other. It is fortunate and significant that the drum continues to make its noisy entrance into our lives, our culture; and what is more significant is the recognition given to the authenticity of the exercise. A visiting doctor from Sierra Leone identified the drumming in Carriacou as Mandingo drumming. Other

From across the Atlantic I come,
With my drum, my story and my
  song,
And though I lost my tongue,
I couldn't even frown,
I so wanted to drown'
But the drum was my tongue and
  my crown.
So let the drums beat!
(*Verse from 'Me and My Drum' by Christine David*)

visitors have referred to the forward-leaning movement in some of the dances as a distinctly African posture.

The drums are used primarily for rhythm - the basis of all African music. It is believed that music has its own magic to bind all members of a community together.

The origins of wooden drums
Wooden drums originated in Guinea and Liberia and other parts of Africa, where they were used for initiation dances. The wooden drums were the principal instrument of communication. They symbolised above all else the secret rites that were practised there

The drums

Drums of varying shapes and sizes were, at the inception of slavery, carved from wood from the forest as was customary in Africa. Later estate casks or rum kegs were used.

The drums are called "Lapeau cabrit" (goat skin) drums. The goat skin when stretched and dried is further prepared and lashed over the mouth of the small rum barrel. According to the famous veteran Ferguson Adams, popularly known as Sugar Adams - drum maker, drummer, "chantrell", dancer - to produce a drum from the large rum casks now available, the staves made from oak or pine wood are thinned so as to produce the right sound. They are fitted together in a hole dug in the ground, the circumference representing the open end of the finished product. These fourteen, fifteen or sixteen staves are held tightly together with iron rings and glue or paste made of flour and water. Holes are put in the sides of the drum for sound effects.

The goat skin, stretched out to dry with nails or pegs, is soaked, cleaned on either side and lashed over the mouth of the keg. The bottom is left open, unlike the Quadrille Dance bass drum which has goat skin on one end and sheep skin on the other end to produce alternate sounds. Famous drummers of the 1960s, like Sugar Adams, tuned their drums by pounding around the edge of the top with a wooden peg, stone or hammer.

Big Drums can be seen in the Carriacou Museum

Among other renowned drummers were the Lambert brothers, Haynes, Williamson, Corneal and Titus. According to Adams, he learnt the art of drumming from his relative, Elisha John, becoming so skilled that he received visitors from the sciences of musicology, anthropology and ethnography. He made two trips to the United States in 1975 and in 1980 visited England. Adams, partially crippled with rheumatism, died in 1983.

The centre drum is called the Cot (cutter) drum. Because of the complexity of the rhythm it takes a very qualified middle drummer to ring out the intricate beat. The two side drums are called Bula drums. They are also called Babble or Fule drums. These side drums are held tilted between the knees of the side drummers. The Cot drum rests fully

on the ground. In the construction of the Bula drums, the skins of ram goats are used, but for the Cot drum the skin of a young ewe goat is used to produce a higher note. Over the top of the Cot drum is attached a piece of cotton thread with three or four straight pins. The vibrations of the pins as the drummer plays add a sort of raspy note to the drumbeat.

The songs

Like the stories, the songs reflect parables of troubles or repressions, warfare and gossip. The African is not only a person with a drum but a person with a song. The songs are sung in Creole French or Patois as well as in English, with African phrases incorporated.

They are usually sung in a statement and response pattern, the subjects being both serious and moral. The lead singer is called the chantrell. Some songs reflect a longing to go back to West Africa, but the Atlantic waters are seen as an obstacle. Some songs lament the singers tragic life, while others ridicule the oppressor. Songs are also based on gossip and challenge. To every dance there is a set of songs and a distinctive drumbeat. The old hoe and shac-shac evoke and beckon the spirits of the ancestors into the dancing ring and emphasise rhythm.

The Big Drum Dance
Courtesy: Maria Hamlet

The Feasts of Carriacou

By Christine David
Courtesy *Folklore of Carriacou*

According to the beliefs of most Carriacouans, the dead and the living are inextricably linked. Dream mythology and the concept of life after death dominate the culture of the island and dreams are believed to be the interaction with the living by the dead. Most dreams are thought to be requests for sacrifices. If the requests are not carried out, punishment will follow the dreamer. The culture has developed to respond accordingly and different feasts are held depending on the dream, which act as sacrifice or celebration to the spirits of the dead.

'Plate' and 'Saraca'

It is believed that if one dreams of a dead person requesting food, the dreamer, if a poor person, has to make a meal, usually consisting of a few pounds of rice, and sacrifice one or two chickens. The food and a quarter gallon of rum are placed on a table with a lighted candle. The dead person is then believed to visit the house and partake of the food. This custom is called a 'Plate'.

If the dreamer is prosperous, then a much larger sacrifice is made. Friends and relatives are usually invited and the large quantity of food they all bring, including goats, chickens and pigs to sacrifice is collectively called a 'Saraca'.

The people of Carriacou seem to dream most in the dry season, and on most days at this time there is a 'Saraca' or 'Plate' being sacrificed for the dead. Most sacrifices are accompanied by the Big Drum celebrations.

'Maroon' feast

A 'Maroon' feast is held by people on Carriacou either in response to an interpretation of a different type of dream to that which promotes the 'Saraca' or 'Plate' feasts, or as an annual custom.

It is believed that if someone dreams of a big gathering where food is being served - that dream is interpreted to mean a 'Maroon', and therefore a feast is held. These feasts are very large and will involve the supplying of food, the 'Saraca'. Like the dreams that require the 'Plate' or 'Saraca' sacrifices, it is during the dry season that most 'Maroon' feasts are held.

'Maroon' are also held in response to a grand annual event, such as a harvest celebration. The whole population will become involved as those responsible for the celebration issue public invitations. The food is taken and presented to the Big Drum dancers and drummers, who always perform at the 'Maroon'.

170

Tombstone feast

A Tombstone feast is the ceremony accompanying the laying of a tombstone (or headstone) on a grave and requires months of preparation. A mason is given the job of making and inscribing the tombstone. This will be done at least a month before the feast is held and the tombstone erected.

It is believed that after burial, a ritual cycle begins which only closes when the headstone is placed, or tombed. The tombing can take place months after or twenty years later, no specific time is observed. Whenever it occurs, the tombing is celebrated by a Tombstone feast for the setting of the tombstone.

Relatives overseas are informed well in advance so that they may make their contribution in cash. Materials for the setting of the stone - water, stone and sand - are stored at the cemetery a few days before the feast.

On the day of the feast, relatives and friends and other invitees donate, as is the custom, food to the person in charge, and they assist in the preparation of a 'Saraca'. Others remain in the cemetery to assist with the making of the 'body' of the tombstone, into which will sit the 'head' or tombstone itself.

The entire occasion, involving much work by many people is done without pay. Only the work of the mason is paid for. When the 'Saraca' is prepared, it is shared. After sending some to the cemetery, those who donated food get their bowls and dishes filled and partake of the food themselves. More food is taken by the owners to nearby homes to be shared around. The rest of the 'Saraca' is left for the drum beaters and dancers. On the following day, some extra food is cooked along with a pig's head. The person responsible for the feast then prepares a sacrificial plate for the dead called the 'Parents Plate.'

The sacrificial plate or plates are filled with a variety of the food and are taken inside the house and placed on a table prepared with tablecloths and candles. Then, the remains of the cooked food can be eaten. Sometimes the sacrificial plate is rested at a particular spot outdoors according to the request made by the spirits to the 'dreamers'.

The tombstone is then carried to the house where the death occurred. It is placed on a bed and covered with a white bedsheet. The relatives of the dead speak to the stone (or 'head of the tomb') believing the dead person is present and sprinkle rum and water around it. A few hymns are sung and eventually the 'head' is taken to the cemetery to be fitted to the 'body' of the tomb.

On the following day finishing touches like smoothing and polishing are done. A tombstone feast is usually accompanied by Big Drum or Quadrille since it is a time for rejoicing and often occurs long after the mourning has been done.

At the government cemeteries interesting inscriptions can be read. At Brunswick Cemetery, it is said that a Duncan Blair, who was a doctor, surgeon and probably a mason erected many tombs. He could have been the uncle to Hector Blair of Harvey Vale, whose father, a Scotsman, was an overseer on the slave estate. At Tibeau Cemetery it is also said the name Tom Carriacou is inscribed on a tomb. Such a name could have belonged to a Carib. He died in 1844. Eighteenth century tombs can be seen at Lanse La Roche.

At the Harvey Vale cemetery the largest tombstone carries the following inscription:

Sacred to the memory of John
   Dallas Esq.
Who departed this life 3rd. Dec.
   1831.
Age 48 years.
His latter end was peace.
And he died firmly trusting for
   pardon.
And acceptance.
To the merits of his saviour.
In testimony of affection and
   respect
For the best of men.
And the kindest of husbands.
This memorial is erected by his
Disconsolate widow Eliza Baillie
   Dallas. LUX VENIT

OVERLEAF
Tombstones in a small cemetery at Cassada Bay, Carriacou

171

CULTURE

Local Artists

Winston Thomas Fleary

Born in the 1940s, Winston Thomas Fleary, an anthropologist by profession, began his association with the Big Drum culture in 1962. He started as a trainee with Sugar Adams, a Big Drum specialist, who inherited the tradition from his grandfather.

Fleary became determined to carry on the traditions of his homeland, both locally and abroad. After working with community and church groups in Carriacou he migrated to the United States in 1965. While there, he organised the Big Drum Nation Dancers before returning home.

In 1975, he went to the US again, this time with a group of Carriacouan artists to participate in a programme at the American Museum of National History with Pete Seeger - the international folk singer.

In 1977 and 1981, Fleary, on invitations from the Grenada High Commission and under the patronage of the Governor General, Sir Paul Scoon, led a group to England to participate in the Commonwealth Foundation Programme.

In Britain, Fleary produced the first black programme ever staged at the Dominion Theatre, London, a venue where the Royal family sometimes attends cultural events. He also produced programmes at the Birmingham Odeon.

In 1979, Fleary's work was recognised by the Washington based Smithsonian Institution and he was funded for three years by the National Endowment for the Arts (USA) to promote and produce programmes for the Caribbean and African-American communities. Fleary's Big Drum and cultural production expanded to the Avery Fisher Hall, Lincoln Centre, where he and his group performed at the Caribbean Artist's Award Night; at the Kennedy Centre for the Performing Arts - Washington DC and at the National Folk Life Programme.

Again, in 1986, he led another group of Carriacouans to the Commonwealth Institute's nationwide Caribbean Focus festival in London, England.

Fleary's involvement with the Big Drum gained international media exposure for Carriacou, with features in *National Geographic* magazine and on the British Broadcasting Corporation's (BBC) "Black Londoners" radio programme. He also presented cultural folklore on "Voice of America" radio and programmes on WLIB Radio, New York. The national press in the United States featured his activities, with articles in the *Washington Post*, *Daily News* and *New York Times*. In the British press he was featured in *The Times* and the *Caribbean Times*, as well as in leading entertainment journals. Fleary also worked relentlessly with the local tourism authority in their promotional ventures.

Fleary continues his work with schools, colleges and community groups, endeavouring to keep the Big Drum culture alive in Carriacou.

Jackie Miller

In the late 1960s, self-taught Grenadian-born artist Jackie Miller painted pictures of cowboys and Indians. Not an auspicious start but visiting tourists and locals were impressed and purchased his efforts which boosted the young artist's confidence.

Miller then turned his attention to subjects closer to home and had his pictures exhibited at the Yellow Poui Art Gallery, in St George's.

Hollywood actor Lloyd Bridges became one of his patrons, but he still had to overcome his lack of formal training and the annual drop in sales at the close of the tourist season.

However, he survived it all and is an inspiration to the students who admire him. He is truly versatile and able to paint and draw with a variety of materials from charcoal to acrylic. Even though he is an accomplished artist, Miller feels that education is an ongoing process and that he is still mastering his craft.

Joseph Rome

At the age of ten, Joseph Alexander Alexis Rome began sculpting as a result of circumstances rather than design. He was shy, and found teachers at school threatening, and decided to teach himself.

Rome learnt his craft by utilising available material such as brown and white clay which he dug out of the ground and hog plum tree bark. Later he used red cedar, mahogany, breadfruit and white cedar from the local woods. The encouragement shown by visitors to Grenada towards his work was instrumental in boosting his confidence.

In the early 1990s, Rome won a Canadian scholarship to study with fellow sculptor Vincent Udivick, and another scholarship that took him to Taiwan, both of which broadened his artistic horizons.

Rome's early work can be considered raw, but over the years his style has evolved as his skills at handling the material improved. However, his art still shows his trademark, a sense of humour.

Joseph Rome and his work
Courtesy: Jim Rudin

Canute Calliste

Canute Calliste better known as C.C., was born in the village of L'Esterre, Carriacou on July 16 1916. He was educated at the Harvey Vale Government School and started painting at the age of nine.

In 1986, Calliste won the first prize at an art exhibition held at Marryshow's House for best native painting. He was show-cased at Barbados National Museum in 1988. One hundred of his paintings were placed on exhibition and for sale. He considers this the high point of his career.

In 1992 he was awarded the British Empire Medal for service to the community. In that year, he was also recognised by the Grenada Board of Tourism for his contribution to the development of tourism in the field of art and culture. In 1993 he received an award from the L'Esterre Youth in Action Organisation Inc. for his contribution towards the growth and upkeep of culture.

Calliste is also a well known musician, shipwright and carpenter. He has travelled to London and the United States, accompanying a group in which he specialised as the violinist.

Calliste, 78, is still painting at his art gallery in L'Esterre. He sees his painting ability as a gift from God and intends to utilise it as long as he has life.

Michael Paryag

Grenadian artist Michael Paryag, despite limited formal training, has had many accolades bestowed on him and is a recipient of the Most Promising Young Painter Award.

His paintings are legendary in his native land, and are proving popular in Europe as well. "Carenage in St George's", a 'work in progress', was seen by a German tourist passing Paryag's home. So overwhelmed was the art lover that he insisted on purchasing the picture in its unfinished form.

Born in 1969 in Sauteurs, Paryag was initially inspired by the watercolour paintings of his mother who encouraged him to paint. Later, he befriended two of Sauteurs' finest artists, Elinus Cato and David Paterson, and the trio would frequently debate the merits of art.

Another influence has been Jamaica School of Art graduate Gordon Hamilton, who regularly monitors Paryag's progress.

Canute Calliste in his studio
Courtesy: Julia Emerson

Trish Bethany

In the late 1960s, Trish Bethany, then a travel agency manager, visited Grenada and has remained on the island ever since. The images of the Carenage, St George's, that she captured on her simple camera proved to be a catalyst; awakening her dormant artistic flair while intensifying her interest in social concerns.

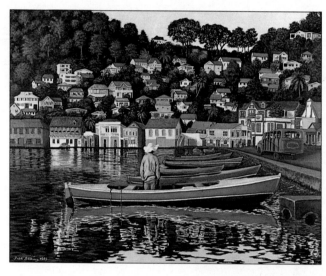

Painting by Trish Bethany
Courtesy: Jim Rudin

To subsidise her change of direction she became a school teacher, later specialising in art and literature. The designing of sets for musical productions satisfied her artistic cravings.

From reproducing her photographs of Grenada into paintings, which won acclaim in the community, she gravitated to 'self generating images.' Ed Povey, a British artist in residence on the island, was instrumental in tutoring her in this new venture.

Bethany has recently given up teaching and now devotes her time to painting. She is evolving as an artist and her new style is just as popular.

Frankie Francis

Frankie Francis, born in L'Esterre, Carriacou, has successfully channelled his spare time into creating works of art. Francis started drawing whilst a primary school pupil at the L'Esterre Catholic School. His interest continued during his Junior Secondary days where art became part of the curriculum.

Francis used to sketch in his spare time while at work for a telephone company, and that was where Frances Brinkley and Lee Katzenbach spotted his efforts, recognised his potential and encouraged him to paint. Katzenbach also provided him with his first set of paints and brushes.

Francis' paintings capture the beauty around him and this often inspires his public to do likewise. In his paintings he attempts to represent most aspects of cultural life in Carriacou, including Big Drum Dances, Quadrille Dances, regattas and Boat Launching.

His pictures are on view at the Museum in Hillsborough and at the Yellow Poui Art Gallery in St George's. His latest work is a mural at Tanki's Place in L'Esterre Beach.

When asked of his plans for the future, he says he would like to go to

Art collectors

Serious art collectors and dealers will find the canvases of local artistes and those from Jamaica, Guyana and Trinidad & Tobago on display and for sale in the art galleries in St George's an art college to improve on his skills and learn new techniques. To young people he says, "drawing or painting keeps you from being bored, but to succeed you must be patient, and never give up."

Elinus Cato

Elinus Cato was born in 1933 in St Patrick, Grenada. A now successful painter his works are among the most popular in Grenada. Over the past decade he has won many prizes and in 1985 his painting 'People at Work' was presented to Queen Elizabeth II in honour of her visit to Grenada. However, art is not his only pursuit, farming, spear-fishing, street cleaning and helping his neighbours in 'maroons' occupy a greater part of his time. Living in relative seclusion, his work now shows considerable maturity, with landscapes of the Grenadian countryside often featured.

Artist, Elinus Cato and (below) one of his paintings 'The Carenage'
Courtesy: Jim Rudin

'Maroon' on Grenada

A 'Maroon' on Grenada, as compared to Carriacou with its attachment to dream mythology, is a community occasion when people get together and offer assistance for specific tasks such as harvesting their crops, clearing some land, digging a pond or extending or moving a house. The person who is receiving the assistance provides a 'Saraca', an amount of food.

Carriacou's seafaring culture

By Christine David

For as long as men have been building roads, farming or writing symbols, men have been going to sea. There is the urgent call back to nature, back to the kick of the wheel and the song of the wind, back to a life in which the main thoughts are not of other people or on trivial matters but rather on what type of weather is foreseen or forecast; and where and how to find shelter. It is a life of unknown chemistries and whirling planetary laws whose origins seem to lie with creation.

Carriacouans, a virile and hard-working people with a strong attachment to the sea, (dating back to the Scottish shipbuilders who came to the island during the nineteenth century) and faced with a limited landmass, took to the sea in ships built by men with no formal shipbuilding experience, with no power tools (only a bit, axe and adze) and no lengthy mathematical planning. These shipbuilders, with enviable, incredible talent, have produced, and continue to produce, sloops (a single masted vessel) that are both seaworthy and durable.

The Carriacouan mariner realises, like all other seamen, that sailing is no mere sport. Despite years of sailing experience, a sailor is never blessed with the gift of knowing the true relationship between sails, seas, wind, sun and moon. When the weather is in full fury, the mariner, no matter how skilled, will experience some gruelling moments.

The merchant marine is manned by men of the soil who have braved the angry seas and raging winds, men who have the zeal for challenge, who face danger head-on, men who especially during the hurricane season have escaped disaster by the skin of their teeth and braved the elements in truly devastating weather. Such men always have thrilling stories to tell, of broken booms, broken gaffs, of men getting down on their knees to try a prayer. Many of these men have steered themselves into the halls of regional fame.

Boat Launching

It is Boat Launching Day, and the little crowd that gathers at dawn go through their religious observances with seriousness and precision. There is the customary libation (the pouring of wine or spirits), the sprinkling of rice grains around the vessel to be launched, and the preparation of fire stones for cooking. This is to beckon the ancestral spirits for their support, and to cast away evil spirits. Usually a "saraca" and Big Drum Dance precede the launching exercise. Following the

ABOVE & OVERLEAF
Boat building in Carriacou

libation, a traditional rite of West African society, animals are slaughtered in ritual fashion as part of the food that is needed to feed the crowds that gather at a Boat Launching ceremony.

Chickens are killed in the galley while a ram goat is killed on the stern so the ship may be butted along by fair winds. A sheep is slaughtered over the bow to make steering easy. This is accompanied by the pouring of spirits, a second libation, from stem to stern. Several large pots are used for cooking the wide variety of foodstuffs; and considerable effort is required to remove the pots from the fire. Launching is one of the activities that attract island-wide participation and by 9.30am there is a growing crowd to witness the Blessing of the Boat - the first of three main Boat Launching activities.

A priest officiates at the blessing. As he ascends to the deck he is followed by specially dressed individuals who represent the godparents of the sloop. The priest makes a petition for God's benediction with prayers and the sprinkling of the holy water. Following this the flag attached to the bow is unfurled, revealing, for the first time, the name by which the boat will be identified. The beating of the drums opens the way for the boat's virgin entrance to the sea. The crowd swells as everyone is anxious to witness the next exciting stage, the 'Cutting Down' of the boat.

For this, men line themselves alongside the sloop with axes to cut down the upright posts on which the boat rests. This calls for co-ordinated movements, for expert and tactful handling of the axes, and a strong nerve to remain underneath the vessel.

The chopping begins amid loud cheers, and chants echo the movements, a fascinating piece of coordination. Gradually the vessel is lowered and rests on its side awaiting the grand finale, the most difficult part, the Floating of the Boat.

By now, the crowd has reached the peak of excitement and there is real pandemonium, the tooting of horns, shouts from old boatmen, the laughter and clamour of the spectators, the appetising smell of the food, the constant flow of liquor; all intermingle making Boat Launching Day what it is.

Prior to Launching Day an anchor will be buried in the sea. The builders put special rollers in the path of the moving vessel. A block and tackle is attached to a boat offshore and the end of the rope brought ashore. The men now place themselves at vantage points around the sloop and give instructions for the operation of the tractor at the back, and the pulling

Hillsborough jetty, Carriacou

and rearranging of the ropes. Amidst the heat and excitement, the crowd gives vent to well-known sea shanties, which accompany the operations to move the sloop.

> "Captain Shanty Doe
> Way ye store the liquor?
> You give the sailors water
> But you drinking wine."

This is a very trying period for the owners and boatmen. Even with the use of a tractor, ropes may burst or rollers may shift out of line. With every move the spectators shout out their approval. And as the stern reaches the edge of the water, bottles of champagne are smashed on the side of the sloop with jubilation. When finally afloat and anchored, small boys climb the deck and dive into the sea until they are too exhausted to continue.

The rest of the day is spent consuming the food and drink prepared. On the vacant spot where the boat rested, another will be built. The assistance in cash or other donations, which relatives and friends contribute, bear testimony to the communal assistance with which Carriacouans are identified.

ABOVE & LEFT
The sloops on Carriacou are made from timber that is skilfully fashioned without the use of power tools

RIGHT
Sunset over Hillsborough Bay, Carriacou

NATURE
Geological history

Grenada is the last remaining portion of the Grenada Bank - a volcanic entity, with sheer submarine cliffs stretching from the island of Bequia in the north to Reindeer Shoal in the south. Deep water separates Grenada from all other major islands, which indicates that it is a purely volcanic island which rose from the sea never having had a land bridge between any other land mass other than the Grenadines.

The geology of Grenada is complex. Reconstructing Grenada's geological history is a formidable task for the geologist as most of the island is covered by soil and dense vegetation, many rock types have been juxtaposed with others through volcanic shifting and rock exposures are often severely weathered.

Grenada's geological history began 38 million years ago in the Upper Eocene Period. At that time, there was only a shallow sea where Grenada now exists. The sediments deposited were composed of sand, silt, mud and calcareous mud; the rock formed from this deposition is now known as the Tufton Hall Formation. Volcanic activity became more frequent in the Oligocene Period (37 to 26 million years ago). The volcanic activity during and following the deposition of the Tufton Hall Formation deformed and uplifted the rock, resulting in the folding and faulting which can be seen just north of Levera Beach.

The oldest of the volcanic rock series are the andesite domes of northern Grenada which formed in the Miocene Period (26 to five million years ago). These andesite domes (Mount Alexander, Mount Rodney and Mount William) have been estimated to be 21 million years old. The andesite domes of Levera Hill and Levera (Sugar Loaf) Island represent volcanic activity near the end of the Miocene Period. During this time, the first eruptions to the south occurred at the centres of South East Mountain and Mount Lebanon.

The Pliocene Period (five to two million years ago) witnessed the advent of Grenada's most intense volcanic activity. In the south west of the island, basaltic lava flows estimated at 3.5 million years old are interlayered with reworked volcanic sediments. The source of the basaltic lava was probably the Mount Sinai Centre. Most of the deposits in southern Grenada are thought to be 'lahar' deposits of various ages (a lahar is a massive mud slide from the sides of volcanoes). The massive in-filling character of lahar deposits is thought to be responsible for the relatively subdued topography of southern Grenada.

In the northern central parts of the island, major eruptions recurred in the Pliocene Period and continued into the Pleistocene Period (two million to

Large areas of central Grenada consist of steep hills covered in thick vegetation

Local guide, Shaba, at the Levera National Park Centre at Bathway

OPPOSITE
Levera National Park viewed from the Welcome Stone with Levera Pond below and the three islands; Levera (Sugar Loaf) Island, Green Island and Sandy Island; in the distance

10,000 years ago). The island's interior was the scene of intense activity as a series of eruptive centres shifted southward from Mount Granby towards Mount Qua Qua, emitting pyroclastic products and a series of basaltic and andesitic lavas. The final stages of this activity formed the andesitic dome summits of Fedon's Camp and Mount Qua Qua, and probably ended with the extrusion of basaltic lava on the western ridges of Mount Qua Qua.

The Mount St Catherine massif represents the youngest major volcanic structure on the island. Activity at this centre probably began in the Pliocene Period and continued throughout the Pleistocene Period. Initially, a vent near the Plaisance/Malagon area extruded basaltic lavas, which were overlain by a series of andesitic and diacidic lava flows. As the vent migrated southward, andesitic and diacidic lavas were deposited to the northwest of the present summit. The pyroclastic flows to the west of the present summit are the most voluminous deposits of their type on Grenada. The one and a half kilometre diameter crater to the southeast of Mount St Catherine (2,756ft) was partially filled in by an andesitic dome which probably concluded the eruptions in the area.

The final stage of volcanic activity involved the formation of explosion craters throughout the island, most notably at what is now Lake Antoine, the Carenage in St George's and Grand Etang Lake. Lake Antoine is a well-preserved crater and has been described as the best example of a true "tufaceous ring" on the island. The Carenage in St George's and the Queen's Park are both believed to be explosion craters, giving the island its best harbour and best source of scoria gravel. The three closely spaced explosion craters at Grand Etang are generally thought to be the youngest volcanic structures on the island, having formed approximately 12,000 years ago.

In recent times, volcanic activity on the island of Grenada has been virtually non-existent, with the minor exception of some hot springs which occur in the Mount St Catherine area and emit sulphurous water and vapour. Other springs such as the River Salee and Peggy's Whim Springs are not sulphurous to any extent.

About seven miles to the north of Grenada, however, is one of the most active volcanoes in the Lesser Antilles. It is Diamond Island, a submarine volcano, 160 metres below sea level, known locally as "Kick 'em Jenny". This is derived from the French expression *cay qu'on gene*, referring to the rough seas which normally surround it. It has erupted at least eight times this century, with the last eruption occurring in 1978. It is possible that the volcano may emerge during its next eruption. Scientists

"Kick 'em Jenny"

Diamond Island, or "Kick 'em Jenny", is a submarine volcano. The summit is 160 metres below sea level and is located about seven miles north of David Point, Grenada. This volcano is one of the most active in the Lesser Antilles, having erupted at least eight times this century, and some scientists believe it may emerge above sea level during its next eruption. The last eruption occurred in 1978.

Evidence of lava flows at Prickly Point

OPPOSITE
Lake Antoine occupies about sixteen acres within a near perfect crater. It represents an excellent example of a crater lake. The water level is normally not more than twenty feet above sea level

in Trinidad & Tobago are currently monitoring this area for seismic disturbances, which might indicate renewed activity.

Carriacou and Petit Martinique, like other islands in the Grenadines, are the exposed summits of volcanic peaks on a single narrow bank of submerged volcanic mountains. Carriacou lies 23 miles northeast of Grenada, separated by a channel 600 feet deep and Petit Martinique lies two and-a-half miles northeast of Carriacou. The geology of Carriacou is two-thirds volcanic in origin and one third fossiliferous limestone (from the Eocene and Pleistocene Periods). Erosion, uplift and faulting have all contributed to Carriacou's varied topography. It is thought that the original volcanic activity formed Carriacou, Petit Martinique and the other Grenadine islands in the late Oligocene Period (38 to 26 million years ago) and sank or were eroded away during the Pliocene Period, becoming completely submerged during the Pleistocene Period. Since that time, the regional uplifting of the sea floor has raised the islands above sea level.

Carriacou's fascinating natural landscape
Along the southern coast, Saline Island and White Island present examples of fascinating geology. Columnar jointing of the rock formations indicate major volcanic activity. Saline Island has a brackish lagoon salt pond surrounded by a mangrove ecosystem.

View of Petit Martinique from Carriacou. The island, like others in the Grenadines, is an exposed summit of a submerged extinct volcano

Natural vegetation

The existing vegetation in Grenada has largely been influenced by land-use history and differences in soil types and rainfall regimes. The principal peak, Mount St Catherine (2,756 feet), rises in the northern half of the island as the centre of a massif surrounded by lesser peaks and ridges. From these central mountains the land descends fairly regularly to the sea. There is not strictly a coastal plain, though there are lowlands in the northeast at Levera and in the southwest where a long low peninsula runs out to Point Salines.

Except in the higher parts of the mountains, the slopes are not excessively steep. As a result, with the small size of the island's land mass, large areas have been cleared for agriculture including fruit, cocoa and nutmeg.

In the interior practically all the land was originally sold to estates and cultivation was pushed to the highest practicable limit in most cases, though some owners reserved belts of forest on ridges for protective purposes. The Government began the consolidation of a forest reserve in 1897 and today the Grand Etang Reserve contains over 3,800 acres. Most of this area has been protected from cutting since then, the only major damage was caused by hurricane "Janet" on September 22, 1955. These areas were subsequently planted with blue mahoe (*Hibiscus elatus*), a tree noted for its value in watershed protection.

The slopes of Mount St Catherine are extremely steep and the central massif is clad only with palm brake. At the summits of the mountains elfin woodland is found, a repressed growth ten-feet in height, gnarled, mossy and containing species typical to this environment. The palms are stunted and the tips of the leaves appear scorched. Owing to the steep slopes and young shallow soil, landslides are frequent.

South of Mount Qua Qua the forest growth is more diverse and includes the last remnant of the lower montane rainforests in Grenada. In the sheltered lower elevations the forest is mature and comparable to the type of rainforest to be found in other islands of the Caribbean. Some trees in this area reach 110 feet in height and form a closed canopy. Ascending towards the main ridge forest, their size is progressively reduced and along the crest, montane thicket predominates. Nearly all the big trees in the montane thicket area are bois (*Micropholis chrysophylloides*) and some of them are up to six feet in girth. There is virtually no shrub layer at all in the montane thicket. There are small orchids and ferns, and while there are few climbers, the forest is extremely mossy. Ground vegetation is knee-high and thick beneath seedlings, ferns, and razor grass (*Scleria*).

Rainfall

Annual rainfall in Grenada varies from approximately 50 inches in dry coastal locations to 160 inches in the wet central mountains. The length of the dry and wet seasons varies greatly depending on location, but there tends to be a dry season from January to May and a wet season from June to December. About 75 per cent of annual average rainfall occurs during the wet season. In Carriacou and Petit Martinique annual rainfall is variously estimated at between 40 and 60 inches. These drier conditions predominate because of the inability of the mountains to cause condensation. The scarcity of water is overcome with an elaborate system of cisterns and water catchment schemes.

Volcanic landscape

The islands are of volcanic origin and extinct explosion craters can still be seen in many parts of the island of Grenada. This accounts for it's numerous hills and valleys and lush tropical vegetation. Elfin woodland and tree-ferns adorn the peaks, the highest of which, Mount St Catherine, rises to a height of 2,756 feet above sea level.

OPPOSITE
Grenada's high rainfall feeds its many rivers

OVERLEAF
Grand Etang Nature Reserve is very important because it is the major catchment area for domestic water for southern Grenada, including St George's

The flora was profoundly modified by felling of the valuable timber species during the nineteenth century. Most of the original species are now extinct and have been replaced by second-growth rainforests which have grown into a mature structure since the establishment of the forest reserve. This secondary growth mainly occurs along the Mount Sinai ridge and in the Mount Sinai water catchment.

Crowning Morne Delice, an isolated, conical hill, 900 feet in height, two miles inland from the south coast, is the only example of intact dry scrub woodland. Tree growth has evidently been allowed to remain due to unsuitability of the terrain for cultivation, but has been subject to frequent felling. At the bottom of the hill there are young secondary thickets of mahogany *(Swietenia mahagoni)* and white cedar *(Tabebuia pallida)*. Nearer to the coast, in the dry belt, only very impoverished growth remains. At best there are woodlands 30-40 feet high on rocky hilltops.

Very little remains of littoral woodland in Grenada. At Levera in the northeast the littoral hedge is formed of, among others, white cedar *(Tabebuia pallida)*. The woodland behind has specimens of sea grape *(Coccoloba uvifera)*, mapou *(Pisonia fragrans)* and manchineel *(Hippomane mancinella)*.

There are some small mangrove swamps, chiefly at Levera Pond in the northeast and at the head of the various deep inlets of the south coast. These contain the usual red mangrove *(Rhizophora)*, black mangrove *(Avincennia)*, white mangrove *(Laguncularia)* and button mangrove *(Conocarpus)*. In all cases they are recommended for National Park protection.

The vegetation on Carriacou and Petit Martinique, as with all the smaller islands of the Grenadines chain, is hugely influenced by seasonal variations due to the scarcity of water. If periods of drought are short, then the vegetation will hardly be affected, but longer droughts - as are characteristic of the dry season between December and June - adversely affect the flora. Typical flora during this season are dry thorn scrub, cactus and legume.

Areas of deforestation, particularly on the leeward side of Carriacou, have come back in pure stands and vegetation tufts such as croton *(Cordia)*. On the windward side sea grape, manchineel and coconut *(Cocos nucifera)* are found on the beaches on the moist lowlands which descend to the sea. The most dominant tree in the open woodland is the gumbo limbo *(Bursera simaruba)* and also present are two species of the pineapple family *(Tillandsia utriculata* and *Tillandsia flexuosa)*.

Carriacou's agriculture

When Carriacou was colonised, a deep fertile soil was found. This resulted in the use of the island for sugar cane production and, thereafter, cotton. Later, limes were also grown on Carriacou until the mid-1970s. During this period of intense cultivation, soil erosion caused a loss of fertility and water retention ability. Today livestock, corn and pigeon peas are the primary agricultural crops.

Mangrove swamps

The mangrove ecosystems at Carriacou's Petit Carenage Bay are among the most developed in the country. Both the mangrove swamp formation and the littoral sand beach vegetation are found. Few signs of cropping for charcoal are visible. As a result, this is one of the finest mangrove and mud flat ecosystems found in the whole of the nation. Here numerous migratory and shorebirds can be found. The area is one of the best bird watching spots in the country.

Giant cactus on the cliff edge at Prickly Point, Grenada's most southerly point

High North Peak

High North Peak, at 955 feet above sea level, is the highest point in Carriacou. Containing important watersheds for the northern part of the island, this National Park encompasses the complete spectrum of ecological systems in Carriacou. It includes L'Anse La Roche, the most scenic and private beach in Carriacou, where coral reefs and outstanding volcanic and uplifted sedimentary formations are clearly visible. The littoral vegetation of sea grape, manchineel and coconut is well developed. The park is the most undisturbed area of Carriacou.

Species of interest found in Carriacou

There are two trees in Carriacou unknown, in Grenada, the dogwood and the white immortelle. The dogwoods may be seen along the road from Beausejour to Craigston, and the white immortelles at Top Hill. Tamarinds grow here, a fruit much in demand in Trinidad. Bougainvillea and flamboyant flourish. There are many varieties of cacti. Coconuts and almonds line the beaches. Sugar apples are common, as are papayas. Limes, which used to be a paying crop, are still abundant.

RIGHT
The gumbo limbo, the most dominant tree in the open woodland of Carriacou. As with all small islands, the vegetation on Carriacou is hugely influenced by seasonal variations due to the scarcity of water
Courtesy: Julia Emerson

Wildlife

Because Grenada and the Grenadine Islands may have been an 'oceanic island' since the Pleistocene Period (two million to 10,000 years ago) when the sea level is estimated to have been between 300 and 900 feet lower, plants and animals may have been able to spread throughout the Grenada Bank.

The oceanic islands such as Grenada (volcanic) or Barbados (uplifted coral) have a simpler biological diversity than that of Trinidad and Tobago, which were at one time connected to the biologically rich South American continent. In Grenada, animal and plant migration would have only occurred by flight, winds or as part of a large vegetation mat which would form in the Orinoco River and float to Grenada and other islands. Interestingly, the majority of winged insects and birds are of North American origin, indicating the island is on the Northern Antillean migratory route.

Invertebrates *(Without a backbone)*
No endemic invertebrates have been discovered in Grenada with the possible exception of the weevil *(Diaprepes)*. The centipede whose bite causes a swelling, is the only dangerous animal in Grenada.

Amphibians *(Living both on land and in water)*
Present on Grenada are the giant toad *(Bufo marinus)*, the piping frog *(Eleutherodactylus)* and the highland piping frog *(Eleutherodactylus johnstonei)* which is confined to the remnant forests of the Grand Etang as is the Garman's woodland frog *(Leptodactylus wagneri)*.

Reptiles *(Cold blooded and scaly)*
There is one reptile endemic to Grenada, a species of lizard *(Typhlops tasymicris)*, which is known only from the parish of St David. Other reptiles include: the house gecko *(Thecadactylus rapicauda)*, an object of superstition; the spinous gecko *(Hemidactylus mabouya)*, introduced from Africa; the common anole or wall lizard *(Anolis aeneus)*, found from Trinidad to St Vincent; the crested or tree lizard *(Anolis richardi)*, found only from Tobago to Grenada and in some of the Grenadines; iguana (of the family *Iguanidae)*, are becoming increasingly rare due to hunting and its reputation as a culinary delicacy; Garman's ground lizard *(Ameiva ameiva)* or zaggada, now found only in Grenada and the Grenadines, the male of which is a handsome blue colour, is sun loving and was almost brought to extinction by the mongoose; Allen's ground lizard *(Bachia heteropus alleni)*, is found throughout the Grenadines; the Antillean

Orinoco River
A river in the north of South America, 1,280 miles long, flowing from the Guayana Highlands through Venezuela to the Atlantic Ocean

The endemicism of Grenada
Grenada is such a geologically recent volcanic island, that it is remarkable it should have some five species peculiar to itself: the Grenada Dove - regularly recorded, but rare; a sub species of snake; a weevil; the mountain cabbage palm and one of the Grand Etang ferns

OPPOSITE
There are no wild parrots in Grenada. This macaw, from Guyana, is in captivity at the Grand Etang Nature Reserve

slippery back lizard *(Mabuya mabouya)*, was thought to have been extinct, but its numbers are increasing.

Snakes *(Limbless reptiles)*

None of the snakes found on Grenada are venomous. They include; the white headed worm snake *(Leptotyphlops margaritae)*; the tree boa *(Corallus enydris cookii)*; Boddaerts's tree snake *(Mastigodryas bruesi)*; the cribo *(Clelia clelia)*, a powerful constrictor feared locally for its strength, is also an excellent rodent exterminator.

Birds

150 species of birds have been identified in Grenada and the Grenadines. The avifauna is primarily tropical North American. Compared to Trinidad, bird life is remarkably different considering the islands are less than 100 miles apart.

The absence of a parrot *(Amazonas)* in Grenada is interesting, especially as islands to the north such as St Vincent, St Lucia and Dominica all have their own endemic species. Parrots were recorded in the 1600s, and may have been driven to extinction by the introduction of the aggressive African mona monkey *(Cercophithecus mona)*, perhaps through predation of the eggs in their nests.

Ornithologists attribute the peculiar distribution of birds to the hurricane frequency as some species are noted for the first time after a hurricane and others may never be seen again.

All wild birds and their eggs are given absolute protection throughout the year, with the exception of 19 species for which there is an open season from September to February. Ducks, waders, waterfowls, pigeon and doves may be hunted. The broadwing hawk, malfini or chicken hawk *(Buteo platypterus)*, the most common hawk in the region and the peregrine falcon *(Falco peregrinus)* may be legally shot in defence of domestic chickens.

Three species of birds are listed as endangered species. These are: the Grenada hookbilled kite or snail hawk *(Chondrohierax uncinatus murus)*; Euler's flycatcher *(Lathrotriccus euleri)*, and the Grenada Dove *(Leptotila wellsi)*, very rare and limited only to scrubland in the southwestern coast of Grenada. There are no estimates available of population size for the Grenada Dove, the country's national bird. The reasons for the rarity of this species are unclear, although it is possible that the population has been low throughout this century, or that it has been reduced by competition with one or more of the other species of dove that occur in

The rarity of Grenada's national bird

The possible impact of predation by monkeys and mongooses on the Grenada Dove has not been investigated quantitatively. However, the mongoose is known to be destructive to poultry, lizards, turtle eggs and hatchlings and ground nesting birds and may be a contributing factor to the rarity of Grenada's national bird.

Petit Carenage Bay

The mangrove eco-systems at Petit Carenage Bay, on Carriacou's north coast, are highly developed. Numerous migratory and shorebirds can be found here and this bay is one of the best bird watching spots in the country

Carriacou's fossil beds

The fossil beds at Grand Bay (near Grand Bay village on Carriacou's windward side) are the only known beds in the country which are plainly visible. They provide excellent opportunities for information exposing millions of years of archeology in the rock layers including prehistoric shellfish, some of which are long since extinct.

Shorebirds can be seen searching for crustaceans in the mud flats of the lagoon. The adjacent coral reefs are unquestionably this nation's finest. Panoramic views of the reefs may be seen from various lookout points from both Saline and White Island.

the same habitat. The Grenada Dove and the nine banded armadillo are part of Grenada's National Coat of Arms.

Endemic to the Lesser Antilles are: the rusty-tailed flycatcher *(Myiarchus tyrannulus)*, found in Grenada, the Grenadines and St Vincent; the scaly-breasted thrasher, black-billed thrush or spotted grive *(Margarops fuscus)*, found in the Grenadines; the Lesser Antillean bullfinch or redbreast *(Loxigilla noctis)*, and the Lesser Antillean tanager, hooded tanager or dos-bleu *(Tangara cucullata)*, found only in St Vincent and Grenada.

Information on seabirds is incomplete, with only three species recorded as possible breeders: Audubon's shearwater *(Puffinus lherminieri)*; the laughing gull *(Larus atricilla)* and the roseate tern *(Sterna dougallii)*.

Migratory birds breeding and feeding

Forests, wetlands and coastal habitats in the Lesser Antilles provide critical feeding and nesting habitat for many species of birds migrating along the Westindian flyway between North and South America. The loss of these habitats, especially coastal systems such as mangroves, salt ponds and other wetlands, could threaten the long-term survival of a number of migratory shorebird and songbird species. Over 100 migrant species are regularly recorded in the Lesser Antilles; most of these species nest in North America and over-winter in the Caribbean or South America.

Levera Pond is the northernmost range extension of the scarlet ibis *(Eudocimus ruber)*, an occasional visitor to Grenada. This pond is also an important breeding and feeding area for waterfowl and other migrant birds.

La Sagesse and many of the mangrove-lined bays on the southern coast of Grenada, as well as Point Saline ponds, are important for migratory shorebirds. Calivigny mangrove swamp supports a seabird colony, and numerous seabirds are reported to nest on Glover Island.

The Carriacou mangroves and Petit Carenage mangroves have many resident waterbirds and rare migrants and London Bridge Island has seabird colonies. These areas are legally protected in the National Park system.

Mammals and Marsupials

Four native species of terrestrial mammals occur in Grenada. The armadillo, the agouti, the lesser Chapman's murine opossum and the greater Chapman's murine opossum. The greater Chapman's murine opossum, mouse opossum or manicou *(Marmosa robinsoni)* is strictly a nocturnal animal which uses its prehensile tail for climbing and transporting bedding material. The lesser Chapman's murine opossum or large opossum (*Didelphis marsupialis insularis*) is a common omnivorous animal which may prey upon poultry and is hunted for its meat. This species is thought to have been introduced by Amerindians while making journeys in their pirogues.

Armadillos
The nine banded armadillo or tatou (*Dasypus novemcinctus hoplites*) is confined to forested areas, and is under heavy pressure from hunting. The armadillo is part of the National Coat of Arms.

Bats
There are eleven different species of bats, with feeding habits ranging from insects and fish to nectar and fruits.

Carnivora
The Burmese mongoose (*Herpestes auropunctatus*) was introduced from Jamaica in about 1870 to control rats in the cane belt. Now it is primarily destructive to poultry, wild ground-nesting birds and lizards.

Rodents
The agouti (*Dasyprocta albida or Dasyprocta liporina*) is extinct on the island due to over-hunting and the aggressive mongoose. Hurricane "Janet" in 1955 may have given the final push to extinction. Naturalists of Grenada would like to see it reintroduced

Primates
The African mona monkey (*Cercophithecus mona*) was introduced from west Africa during the slave trade period. It can easily be seen in Grand Etang and St Catherine Upper Montane forests. They have proven to be destructive to the local fauna. The hurricane of 1955 reduced their numbers, but their population has once again reached new proportions, due to the limitations placed on the use of firearms for hunting, during recent years.

Sea turtles
The extensive shallow waters and reefs around the Grenadines are excellent foraging habitat for many species of sea turtle. They nest on the beaches on the Windward side of Grenada and Carriacou. The females crawl up the beaches and lay their eggs in the dry sand of the spray zone. Species include: the green turtle (*Chelonia mydas*) which come to the beaches to

Grenada's extinct species
Several species have become extinct in Grenada since the arrival of the Europeans, including the manatee (*Trichecus manatus*), the Grenada parrot (*Amazona sp.*), the · agouti (*Dasyprocta albida*), Neuweid's moon snake (*Pseudoboa neuweidi*), Shaw's racer (*Liophis melanotus*) and the morocoy tortoise (*Geochelone carbonaria*).

It has been suggested that the introduction of the mona monkey led to the extinction of the Grenada parrot. The manatee and the morocoy tortoise were hunted to extinction for food; the later has since been re-introduced through escapes from captive populations.

Over-hunting by humans and predation by the mongoose led to the extinction of the agouti in the wilds. Hurricane "Janet" may have played a large part in the disappearance of Shaw's racer and the moon snake

OPPOSITE
The west African mona monkey was introduced to Grenada during slavery. It can easily be seen in the Grand Etang and St Catherine Upper Montane forests
Courtesy: Heather Bruce

lay up to 600 eggs in a season; the loggerhead turtle *(Caretta caretta)*; the hawksbill turtle *(Eretmochelys imbircata)* is carnivorous, and like the loggerhead feeds on shellfish and rock encrusting marine animals; the olive ridley turtle *(Lepidochelys olivacea)*; the leatherback turtle *(Dermochelys coriacea)* is the largest of the sea turtles, weighing up to 500 kilograms; and the morocoy or red legged tortoise *(Geochelone carbonaria)* is thought to have been indigenous to Grenada and the Grenadines but was hunted to extinction. It has since been reintroduced.

All marine turtles are listed as endangered, with the hawksbill being the most critically endangered species. Natural factors, such as storm damage to nesting beaches, disease and natural predators have always taken their toll, but the actions of man have had the greatest impact on sea turtle populations. Harvesting of sea turtles, lobsters and oysters have been subject to closed seasons since 1987. This is from May 1 to September 30.

Coral reefs

Coral reefs occur mainly on the north, east and south coasts of Grenada. Levera Bay and the adjacent islands also have large areas of coral reefs.

Large bank-barrier reefs occur on the east coast of Carriacou and Petit Martinique and around some of the smaller islets in the Grenadines. Many of these reefs are strongly dominated by elkhorn coral in the shallow areas, with well-developed boulder coral zones on the deeper forereefs.

Two small algal ridges occur on the south side of Carriacou. Saline and White Islands are said to have "the best reefs in the country". Mabouya Island and Sandy Island also have excellent reefs.

Coral reefs play an important role in Grenada's fishing industry, tourism and storm protection. Much of the seafood eaten, especially snapper, grouper, parrot fish and lobster, live and feed in the sheltered surroundings of the coral reef. Tourists come to Grenada to snorkel and scuba dive in the beautiful coral reef environment. Tourists and Grenadians alike enjoy the white sand beaches which are actually the skeletons and shells of corals which have been broken down naturally by waves and other animals. The reefs also protect the coastlines and coastal communities of Grenada from powerful waves and currents.

Underwater study
The introduction of the 'Carriacou Islander', a 35 foot motor-powered catamaran has opened exciting new sightseeing and study possibilities for both Carriacou and Petit Martinique. This vessel has a ramp which allows safe and easy access direct from any beach and it enables disabled and wheelchair passengers to experience a new world. The 16 x 4 feet underwater observation window, which can be raised and lowered as required has the double advantage of allowing very close views of the tropical reefs and fishes while avoiding possible damage to this fragile eco-system. There is a library and running commentary which provides study opportunities for school children, and those with a special interest in marine life.

Coral reefs off Grenada
Courtesy: Dive Grenada

The protection provided by the coral reef at Bathway Beach allows bathers safe swimming

OVERLEAF
Corals on the reefs off Sandy Island, Carriacou
Courtesy: Niki Weidinger

Whales and other cetaceans

The manatee *(Trichecus manatus)* was extirpated soon after the arrival of Europeans in Grenada.

There is a stock of humpback whales *(Megaptera novaeangliae)* which migrates between Greenland and the Eastern Caribbean. A small group of humpbacks still winters in the waters between St Vincent and Grenada. Their calving grounds are located in the Grenadines and also between Anguilla and Antigua. Humpback whales had been hunted from a station on Glover Island off Grenada from 1857, but were virtually exterminated in this area by American whalers by 1927. Other species of cetaceans formerly taken by whalers operating out of Glover Island and Barrouallie Village in St Vincent included the pilot whale or blackfish *(Globicephala macrohynchus)*, the killer whale *(Orcinus orca)*, the beaked whale *(Zizyphus sp.)*, the bottlenose dolphin *(Tursiops truncatus)*, and two species of ocean dolphin *(Stenella sp.)*.

SPICES
Grenada's spices

By Norma Sinclair

(with the assistance of Cecil Winsborrow of Grenada's Department of Agriculture)

The spice trade between Asia and Europe was flourishing long before the New World was discovered. Indeed, that was the reason that Columbus sailed west - trying to find a new route to the Orient. What he found instead were new lands, new foods and new spices. Gradually, eastern spices were introduced to tropical America and the Westindies. It was found that Grenada's soil and climate was particularly well-suited to these new plants and a thriving spice industry developed. Eventually, the island became known as the "Isle of Spice".

Spices are useful in a variety of ways. In the kitchen, some are used for flavouring meats and vegetables. For example, allspice, cloves, cinnamon, vanilla, ginger, sapote, nutmegs and mace are all put into various cakes, cookies and confectionery. Peppers and allspice help in the curing and preservation of meats, and oils extracted from cinnamon, allspice, clove, vanilla and nutmeg are widely used in the perfume and pharmaceutical industries.

The **nutmeg** is by far the most important spice grown in Grenada. With its twin spice, the mace (which grows around the nutmeg shell), it has become one of Grenada's three major export crops.

This versatile nut is a necessary ingredient in the kitchen for flavouring meat and vegetable dishes as well as cakes and cookies, and in the making of jams, jellies and syrups. In the Victorian era, ladies of the aristocracy continually wore a nutmeg around their necks, enclosed in a specially designed pendant. Gentlemen kept a nutmeg in a special case in their pockets. This was believed to ward off illness. It is still used locally as a cure for colds. The nutmeg is grated on to a 'hot toddy' - a mixture of rum, lime and honey. This is drunk as quickly as possible, preferably at bedtime, and is 'guaranteed' to sweat out all impurities in the blood. The grated nutmeg is also mixed with vaseline and rubbed on the chest.

At the nutmeg processing stations in Gouyave and Grenville nutmegs and mace can be seen in different stages of processing as they are prepared for shipment.

The **bay** tree is native to the Windward Islands of which Grenada is a part. This is an evergreen tree of the laurel family. It grows to a height of about 10 metres and has obovate, leathery aromatic leaves. Bay oil, distilled from the leaves, is used in the perfume industry. Bay rum is also prepared from the oil. This has soothing and antiseptic properties. It is used in some foods, in toilet preparations, as a hair tonic and also as a necessary addition to the sick room to cool fevers, its astringent properties refreshing the body generally.

Three layers surround the nutmeg proper. The outer layer, called the 'pericarp', is used to make nutmeg jelly. The red membrane is dried and ground into the spice mace. The darker shell, when cracked open, reveals the nutmeg. The shell is used for flower bed mulch

A gift of spice

A novel souvenir solution is the local 'spice basket' filled with nutmeg, cinnamon, mace, bay leaf and cloves. They are on sale at most shops, hotels and from the many vendors trading all over the island. Another Grenada special is nutmeg oil, available in various sized bottles and recommended for numerous applications from insect bite to providing protection from the sun.

OPPOSITE
Bedie Jerimiah, selling spices on the Carenage to cruise ship passengers

In Grenada the bay leaves are sold green or dried, and are added to soups, meat and vegetable dishes and pickles. They particularly enhance all tomato dishes. It is essential that the leaves are removed before any dish is served as the spine of the leaf can be dangerous if swallowed by accident.

Some peppers are also indigenous to the Westindies and Central America like the **pimento (allspice)**, which is grown extensively in Jamaica and was later introduced into other Westindian islands, including Grenada. Allspice is the dried berry of the pimento tree, and is believed to combine the flavours of cinnamon, clove and nutmeg, hence its name. The green fruit, about the size of a small pea, changes to dark brown when picked and dried in the sun. It can be used as a pickling spice, in ketchup and sausages, whole or ground, for curing meats or for flavouring wines and meat dishes. It is also added to several other foods, cakes and beverages. Sometimes it is even used to hide the taste of particularly unpleasant medicine. Ground allspice is added to many spicy mixtures, including curry powder. An oil can be extracted from the berry and the leaf. This is used in perfumes and pharmaceuticals.

Capsicum encompasses cayenne, chilli, red, green and sweet peppers, all native to tropical America. They are not actually considered spices, but as peppers they are used extensively in the kitchen for flavouring foods. The chilli or bird pepper is by far the tiniest and the hottest of these. Birds seem to enjoy the pretty red fruit, eating it whole. Human beings unaccustomed to fiery foods should approach this "red devil" with caution.

Pepper *(Piper nigrum)* is one of the oldest and most important of all spices. The fruit begins life as red berries about the size of peas, growing on a vine. They are wrinkled and black when dried and are familiarly known as "peppercorns". They are used either whole, or ground in various meat and vegetable dishes or for pickling. White pepper is obtained from the same fruit which has been soaked in water and the mesocarp removed. This pepper is widely used as a condiment, the flavour and pungency blending well with most savoury dishes. Pepper mills grace many tables where people enjoy the taste of freshly ground pepper in their food. Its stimulating action on the digestive organs produces an increased flow of saliva and gastric juices.

Piper nigrum is a native of the mountains in the Western Ghats, India and has been in use since about 300 BC. From there it spread to other eastern countries eventually arriving in Europe. By the Middle Ages, pepper had assumed great importance. It was used to season insipid food and as a preservative in curing meats. Together with other spices it helped

Special dishes of the Spice Island
Crab and callaloo soup
Oil down (a complete casserole)
Spicy chicken
Grenadian caviar (roe of white sea urchin)
Stuffed jacks (fish)
Rice and peas
Mango mousse
Nutmeg or guava ice-cream
Breadnut souffle
Ginger beer (locally made)
Sorrel liqueur

to overcome the odours of bad food and unwashed humanity. At that time it was also used in medicine as a carminative (drug curing flatulence) and febrifuge (medicine to reduce fever), but it hardly finds a place among our vast array of modern medicines.

Peppercorns were extremely expensive in the Middle Ages. Tribute and rents were often paid with them. This practice still survives in the expression "peppercorn rent", but unlike medieval times, this now means little or no rent.

Pepper oil is distilled from the fruits. It has a mild taste and is used in perfumery.

Cinnamon is an evergreen tree and like the bay tree, is related to the laurel family. The bark is carefully peeled off and often rolled into "sticks" or "quills" before being dried. Whole or ground, the dried bark has a sweet, delicate aroma and is used as a spice or condiment, and for flavouring cakes and all sweet dishes. It can also be found in curry powder, incense, toothpastes and perfumes. It gives a delicious flavour to broiled grapefruit, sauteed or baked bananas or any apple or pineapple dishes. Cinnamon bark oil is distilled from the chips and bark of a lesser quality. This flavours confectionery and liqueurs and is used in pharmaceutical and dental preparations and soaps. Cinnamon leaf oil is distilled from dried green leaves and can be found in perfumes and flavourings, and also in the synthesis of vanillin. Cinnamon occurs wild in Sri Lanka and southwestern India and appears to have reached Egypt and Europe by the fifth century BC. It maintains its popularity to this day.

Another import from tropical Asia is **turmeric**, known in Grenada as saffron. The true saffron comes from the dried stigmas of the crocus, whereas this is an aromatic root, resembling the ginger root, except that it has a rich, orange-yellow colour. It is an ingredient of curry powder and also gives the yellow colour to prepared mustard. Turmeric is also used as a dye, and to flavour and colour breads, meats, rice and some medicines. It is interesting to note that white paper soaked in turmeric is used by chemists to detect the presence of alkalis which turn it brown, and for boric acid which turns it reddish brown. It is called curcuma or turmeric paper.

Clove trees are indigenous to the Molucca Islands in the Malay archipelago, and can grow to a height of about 12 metres. The dried, unopened flower buds of the tree are known to have been used as a spice since the third century BC. The buds are first a pale green, growing darker and eventually changing to a deep red. These are picked and dried to a dark brown colour. Cloves have a pungent aroma and are said to relieve toothache and nausea.

A spice vendor in Market Square, St George's

They can be purchased whole or ground and are used whole for decorating legs of ham and pork. Cloves also flavour meat dishes, cakes and sweet dishes and are an ingredient in some pickles and preserves. The oil of cloves, distilled from the buds, is added to some liqueurs and perfumes.

The **vanilla** plant is a tropical climbing orchid having spikes of large fragrant greenish-yellow flowers. The long fleshy pods contain the beans which, after being distilled, are used in flavouring all sorts of sweet dishes and cakes. It is also employed in the perfume industry.

The **tonka bean** is indigenous to tropical America. The tree grows quite tall and the fibrous pods have a very dark brown almond-shaped seed with a strong fragrance. Soaked in alcohol, it sometimes takes the place of vanilla in certain recipes. It is the source of coumarin which is used in perfumes and flavourings, and as an anticoagulant.

The **ginger** from South East Asia is a plant with a leafy, reed-like stem. Its spicy, hot-tasting root is dried and ground to flavour cakes, breads and drinks. Ginger is popular in many Chinese dishes. Gingerbread and ginger beer are well-known in most households. Oil of ginger is said to allay pain.

The **sapote** is the brown, rough-surfaced fruit of a large tree. The flesh is orange-red and edible, with a rich, cloying taste. It is used for making preserves and beverages. The large seed has three sides. Two of them look like old, polished mahogany, while the third is a lighter brown, and rough. The kernel is creamy white and has an almond flavour. It is grated into cakes and pies.

The Minor Spices Cooperative Society in Grenada handles all spices apart from the nutmeg. They purchase the spices from farmers around the island and arrange for processing and packaging. A small quantity of these spices are also exported.

Spice vendors in Market Square, St George's

214

The Nutmeg Story

By Alister Hughes

When Christopher Columbus sailed past Grenada on the morning of August 15, 1498, he did not see the lush nutmeg plantations which now cover the island's picturesque mountains. The great navigator didn't get near enough to identify the vegetation, but, in any case, there were no nutmeg trees in Grenada at that time.

This plant is not indigenous to Grenada. Its origin lies thousands of miles away on the other side of the world. Many centuries after Columbus were to pass before the nutmeg was planted here and the circumstances of its introduction are curious.

By the end of the twelfth century, Europeans had become familiar with nutmegs. It was a prized commodity of great cost. It was used on special occasions and, once, in 1195, the streets of Rome were sweetened with the aroma of burning nutmegs to welcome the Holy Roman Emperor, Henry VI.

However, the western world did not know where nutmegs came from. To protect the exorbitant prices at which they sold the spice, merchants kept its origin a deep secret. All that people knew generally was that the nutmeg had its source in the "Far East" and was brought to Europe by overland caravan.

It was not until 1512 that Portuguese explorers found the trees growing on the Banda group of islands, part of the Moluccan chain in what is now the Indonesian archipelago. This led to development of a monopoly and a profitable trade in nutmegs for the Portuguese. But that advantage was lost about a century later when Holland annexed the Banda Islands.

The Dutch did everything to maintain the valuable monopoly they had acquired. First, to ensure security, they evacuated the native population. From then on, the plantations were worked with convict labour and, until Emancipation in 1860, any shortage of manpower from this source was made up with slaves brought in from Turkey.

The greatest danger to the monopoly was that, when seeds were exported, they could be planted in other parts of the world. This would have created unwanted competition and the Dutch found a remedy for this problem. They discovered that seeds soaked in lime would not germinate and all nutmegs for export were given this treatment.

But other nations did not give up without a fight. Nutmegs were valuable. They fetched handsome prices and every effort was made to break the monopoly.

One such effort was made by the French when Peter Poivre, the eminent French naturalist and traveller, was commissioned by his Government to organise a clandestine raid on the Dutch nutmeg plantations.

Nutmeg shells are used as flower bed mulch and for covering garden paths

OPPOSITE
Nutmeg trees grow to between 15 and 30 feet in height

In 1770, Poivre mounted a successful expedition to the least frequented parts of the islands and, undiscovered by the Dutch, made off with 400 young nutmeg trees. He also stole 10,000 nutmeg seeds either already growing or ready to grow.

This agricultural loot was taken to the then French island of Mauritius in the Indian Ocean, but, unfortunately for the French, Poivre's efforts came to nothing.

The stolen nutmegs were planted out in several different kinds of soil in Mauritius and in the French South American colony of French Guiana. Careful attention was given to the trial plots. Every effort was made to tend them, but most of the plants died and those which survived did not do well.

Some 25 years later, the British had more success. Following the French Revolution of 1789 and the rise of Napoleon Bonaparte, Britain was drawn into hostilities with France and her ally Holland.

In the war which resulted, Britain ousted the Dutch from the Moluccas in 1796 and, until 1802, when the islands were given back to the Dutch under the Treaty of Amiens, had full control of all the nutmeg plantations.

Seizing this golden opportunity, the British East India Company collected large quantities of nutmeg plants, some of which were set out in the British colony of Penang off the Malay peninsula. These cultivations did very well and, by 1812, nutmeg was a major crop of Penang.

Other plantings were attempted with varying success in Calcutta, Madras, Brazil and several Westindian islands. This experiment did not extend to Grenada and, at this time, the nutmeg did not achieve any economic importance in the Caribbean.

Grenada's connection with the nutmeg was created by a curious link between sugar producers of the British Westindies and their counterparts in British colonies in the Far East.

The sugar industry was then much more important to the Westindies than it is today and, in these islands, the system of sugar extraction had been developed to a fine art. The method used in the Far East was not as efficient and, to upgrade that system, arrangements were made for a transfer of Westindian technology.

Competent sugar plantation overseers, including some from Grenada, were identified for secondment to British Far East sugar plantations and, in 1840, they were sent out to Penang to do a stint as managers, introducing their system of sugar extraction.

These agriculturists, returning home, brought nutmeg seeds with

The Nutmeg

The nutmeg tree (*myristica fragrans*), grows to a height of 15 - 30 feet. The nutmeg when mature and while still attached to the branch, splits open to expose a scarlet netlike membrane known as mace which enwraps the shiny dark internal shell. Inside this shell is a tiny oily seed - the nutmeg. The mace is soft to touch and even while drying it retain its powerful fragrance.

Plants spring up from fallen seeds of the parent tree and are transplanted to an area of rich, well-drained soil with an annual rainfall of between 40 - 70 inches.

Nutmeg plants normally take five to six years to flower and it is only then that the 'sex' of the tree can be determined. This is because the male flower grows on one tree and the female grows on another. Male trees are usually planted on the windward side of the plantation for efficient pollination and planters usually have about one male tree to every 12-14 female trees.

After the disastrous impact of hurricane "Janet" on the nutmeg, a new, faster method of producing females trees was introduced and this quickly restored the nutmeg estates. The new tree starts bearing in two-three years and does not grow as tall, therefore making harvesting more efficient.

The nutmeg fruit ripens about five months after flowering and in the mountain areas harvesting takes place throughout the year. Nutmegs are harvested after they fall to the ground and by picking with a long rod or cocoa knife (a curved knife attached to a bamboo rod).

The collected nutmegs are taken to a processing station

where workers remove the mace using their fingers or a knife. The mace is flattened and put to dry in the sun for a few days. The nuts are left in their shells to air for two weeks, after which they are cracked open and the shell removed, ready for use locally or for shipment.

The soft yellow pods, called the nutmeg pericarp, are used by the De La Grenade Industries to make nutmeg syrup.

The world produces about 7,000 tons of nutmeg and 1,000 tons of mace per year. Indonesia supplies about 70 per cent with most of the remainder supplied by Grenada.

Nutmeg drying in the sun at the Dougaldston Estate, Gouyave. The racks are designed to be pushed under cover if it rains

them as a curiosity, and it is believed the first nutmeg tree in Grenada grew from seed that was brought from the Banda Islands by one Frank Gurney and planted, in 1843, at Belvidere Estate on Grenada's west coast.

There is also the story of Captain John Bell of the Royal Navy who, it is said, brought nutmegs from the Far East "because he liked his punch". Captain Bell put out his seedlings on his estate which, significantly, he called Penang, a name it still carries today.

However, although the future of cane sugar was already being threatened by European beet-sugar and alternative crops were being sought, there is no evidence that, at this time, Grenadian farmers were planting nutmegs as an economic crop.

In fact, the tree was probably still just a curiosity. Nutmeg adds great taste and the trees were, no doubt, planted conveniently close to the estate Great House to provide flavouring for the Sunday morning rum-punch.

But fate was to change all that when, in 1851, disaster struck the nutmeg plantations of the Far East. A nocturnal worm attacked the trees and, by next morning, the top branches withered and all the leaves fell off. The trunk then disintegrated in a remarkably short time and the tree fell.

This was catastrophic for the plantations of Singapore which were reduced suddenly from 56,000 trees to a few hundred. Other areas like Penang were not so badly affected at first, but, over the next 90 years, their plantations diminished from an estimated 14,500 acres to a few small garden plots.

The news of these Far East disasters reached Grenadian farmers and they saw in them an opportunity to diversify the agricultural base of the island's economy. A great deal of soil and climate experimentation was done and, sometime after 1860, the nutmeg began to be planted in Grenada as an economic crop.

This spice is used in the pharmaceutical industry and in the meat and food processing industries, and, generally, is a lucrative crop, but initial development was slow. The first exports were not made until 1881 and there was no significant increase in production until after World War I (1914-18).

Nor were there any important developments until 1942 when there was a move to change radically the method by which the nutmeg crop was marketed internationally.

Until that time, cut-throat competition between independent local exporters kept market prices low and deprived nutmeg farmers of a fair share of the profits.

To remedy this situation, the Grenada government decided to become involved and, after much planning and debate, passed an ordinance creating the Grenada Co-Operative Nutmeg Association (GCNA).

GCNA came into being on March 27, 1947 and was an association of nutmeg farmers. It was given the monopoly for the export of all nutmegs and was designed to bring maximum benefits to the farmer.

But there was no peaceful transition from the traditional marketing method to the new system. The middle-man profits of the independent local exporters had evaporated with the creation of GCNA, and they did not give up easily. These exporters had powerful support in the Legislative Council and carried on the fight for several years.

For a while, the outcome was in the balance but the issue was settled finally in 1951. In that year, a Commission of Inquiry, appointed by the Legislative Council, recommended continuance of the export monopoly of the association and the independent exporters had to admit defeat.

The Nutmeg Processing Station, Gouyave

Four years later, Grenada's nutmeg industry faced another gigantic hurdle when, on September 22, 1955, hurricane "Janet" struck the island. The nutmeg tree, with its heavy head and shallow root system, is ill-adapted to withstand 150 mile-per-hour winds, and "Janet" demolished an estimated 75 per cent of the plantations.

The industry slowly recovered from this disaster but international market fluctuations, over which Grenada had no control, made the future unpredictable. The obvious solution was a marketing co-operation agreement with Indonesia, the only other supplier of nutmegs in commercial quantities.

The international market is shared by Indonesia and Grenada in the ratio of about 70 per cent to 30 per cent in favour of Indonesia, and a marketing co-operation agreement would have provided absolute control over prices

For years, GCNA tried unsuccessfully to come to an arrangement with Indonesia's nutmeg exporters. Indonesia had no association similar to GCNA which could control the exports of nutmegs, and it was not until 1987 that an agreement was finally achieved.

The beneficial results were dramatic. Competition having been removed between the two countries, prices soared. Earnings rose by over 50 per cent as compared with pre-agreement figures and the industry seemed poised for an attractive future. Within three years, however, the agreement came to an end.

At that time, Indonesia was negotiating an IMF loan and that organisation is opposed to cartels. It is alleged that one condition for the granting of the loan was abandonment of the marketing co-operation agreement with Grenada, and Indonesia had no choice.

Whatever the facts, the failure of the agreement had devastating effects on the industry and GCNA was bought to near-complete economic collapse. Fortunately, however, that hurdle has been overcome. Financially assisted by the government, the GCNA made a slow recovery and, among other measures, the association continues to penetrate markets which have not yet been exploited.

Cost saving measures have been put into effect, belts have been tightened and there are new horizons which promise attractive avenues for success. One such avenue is the proposed distillation plant which will produce nutmeg oil. This operation will add value to the raw material and put more money into the pockets of the nutmeg farmers.

Another avenue is the successful utilisation of the fruit (pericarp) of the nutmeg which largely went to waste. A local manufacturing plant, De La Grenade Industries Ltd, now converts this raw material into jams, jellies, liqueur and syrup which enjoy a growing world-wide reputation and a consequent export boom.

And there has been an even more radical departure from the traditional practice of selling only the raw material produced by the nutmeg tree. Research is being conducted on extracting two valuable industrial chemical compounds from the nutmeg.

One is *trimyristicin,* which is low in volume but high in value, and the other is *oleo-resin,* a substance used extensively in the cosmetic trade.

Just over a century and a half has gone by since Frank Gurney planted the first nutmeg tree in Grenada and, since then, in spite of many adversities, the nutmeg industry has contributed a great deal to the economy of the island. That contribution is acknowledged by incorporation of the nutmeg into the design of the national flag and is the basis on which Grenada can claim to be the "Spice Island of the Caribbean".

Mace, the membrane around the nutmeg shell, drying in Market Square, St George's

There's a secret in the Nutmeg

By Alister Hughes

Grenadians have always known that there's more to the nutmeg than the export of a fragrant spice. They know lots can be done with the pericarp, the yellow, fleshy, outer covering of the nutmeg. They know it can be candied. They know, too, that it makes delicious jam, jelly and syrup.

For many years, however, no attempt was made to produce these exotic delicacies on a commercial scale. Each housewife made nutmeg jam and jelly for just her family or friends. But this made use of only small amounts of the pericarp while most of this resource rotted where it fell to the ground under the trees.

Sometime around 1970, however, a pioneer Grenadian entrepreneur, Sybil La Grenade, decided to do something about this waste. Surprisingly, her initial aim was not to produce nutmeg jam and jelly. She looked in another direction. She had a priceless advantage which no one shared, and she set out to exploit it.

The fact is that the La Grenade family has a secret formula for production of a top-class liqueur from the nutmeg pericarp. That secret has been in the family for many years and there's a fascinating story behind this.

According to family legend, one of the La Grenade ancestors once did a favour for a Dutch missionary who had worked in the Banda Islands - present day Indonesia - where the nutmeg originated. It seems that, while in the Far East, this missionary, by some means, had acquired this closely guarded formula and, in gratitude, he disclosed the secret to the La Grenade ancestor.

Since then, the formula has been developed, improved and handed down from generation to generation. The rule is that, in each generation, only one member of the family is allowed to know the formula and, in her generation, Sybil was the person entrusted with the secret.

Until recently, the secret formula had never been exploited for commercial purposes, production having always been limited to just a few bottles for family use. But, Sybil saw a golden opportunity in this situation. The time had come, she felt, to share the exquisite taste of this product with others, and she launched a cottage industry with production of La Grenade Liqueur geared to supply the local market.

It was an instant success. Demand grew and, soon, nutmeg jam, jelly and syrup were being produced under the brand name of "Morne Délice", the "Mountain of Delight", the verdant peak which stands near the La Grenade factory.

Success followed success, production expanded to include exports

Jams, jellies and syrup can be made from the nutmeg's yellow outer covering, the pericarp

throughout the Caribbean, to Europe and the United States, and, in 1990 came international recognition.

In that year, Morne Délice Nutmeg Syrup was honoured by "Monde Selection, International Institute for Quality Selections", the official institution established in 1961 by the Belgian government for universally maintaining high standards of beverages and food produced for human consumption.

Each year, applying quality criteria laid down by the European Union, and after exhaustive laboratory tests and analyses by experts, Monde Selection awards three categories of medals, Gold, Silver and Bronze. Above these, products of absolutely superior quality receive the Grand Gold Medal.

In 1990, Morne Délice Nutmeg Syrup became the first Caribbean food product to receive the Grand Gold Medal. In that year also, another La Grenade product was recognised by these quality experts. Monde Selection presented La Grenade Liqueur with its Gold Medal.

In 1992, the La Grenade and Morne Délice products passed out of the "cottage industry" category when a modern food processing plant was commissioned. And that plant has been very carefully laid out. One section is devoted to the Morne Délice products and is open to all the workers. Visitors are also welcome, but the other section of the factory lies behind closed doors.

That's where La Grenade Liqueur is produced. Now under the management of Cécile La Grenade, Sybil's daughter and the present custodian of the secret, this section of the factory is carefully guarded from intruders. Stainless steel pipes convey the finished liqueur from this sanctuary to the bottling division on the main floor, but only Cécile knows what happens behind those locked doors.

The range of products made by De La Grenade, including syrups, liqueur, jams and jellies

"Many attempts have been made to get the secret from us", she says, "but we have always managed to preserve it."

Cécile disclosed that the production process involves careful selection of ingredients to complement the nutmeg component, but declined to give any details of the distillation process or say whether there is any ageing of the product.

The domestic use of nutmeg to create exotic products was given a boost when, in the latter part of 1993, the Grenada Board of Tourism launched a contest in the United States for the best cake recipe using nutmeg as a major ingredient.

This contest marked the 150th anniversary of the planting of the first nutmeg tree in Grenada, and the winning entry was appropriately named "Numero Uno Nutmeg Cake".

Recipes using Nutmeg

Numero Uno Nutmeg Cake

> 1 cup cake flour
> 1 teaspoon nutmeg
> Quarter cup cornstarch
> 2 teaspoons baking powder
> 1 cup almonds, toasted and ground
> 1 knob butter
> 1 cup sugar
> Half cup milk
> 5 egg whites
> *also required* 3 firm ripe bananas

Preheat oven to 350º F (180ºC). Grease and flour a nine inch spring form pan. Sift flour, nutmeg, corn starch and baking powder together. Mix in ground almonds. Cream butter with sugar in mixing bowl. Beat in milk alternatively with dry mixture. Add egg whites and beat until batter is fluffy. Pour into prepared pan. Bake for 50-60 minutes until cake tests done. Cool on rack.

To serve. Remove sides of cake pan. Cut cake into eight slices. Top individual servings with nutmeg-rum cream and top with banana slices. Serves 8.

And here are some suggestions guaranteed to tickle your palate with a genuine Grenadian flavour:

To make nutmeg syrup

2 tablespoons sugar
2 tablespoons water
1 tablespoon dark rum
1 teaspoon nutmeg
Bring sugar and water to boil in small saucepan. Cook and stir until sugar dissolves. Stir in rum and nutmeg. Use when cool.

To make nutmeg-rum cream

2 cups whipping cream
Third cup powdered sugar
1 tablespoon dark rum
Quarter teaspoon nutmeg syrup
Beat whipping cream with powdered sugar until stiff. Beat in rum and nutmeg syrup.

Nutmeg Brigadier

2 ozs (60g) Morne Délice Nutmeg Syrup
4 ozs (100g) La Grenade Liqueur
8 ozs (220g) Club soda
Stir, add cracked ice and serve with a twist of lemon or lime

Nutmeg Delight

2 ozs (60g) Morne Délice Nutmeg Syrup
6 ozs (170g) Club soda
1 slice of lemon
Grated nutmeg
Mix Nutmeg Syrup with club soda and add cracked ice. Top with grated nutmeg and serve with twist of lemon or lime

Spicy Nutmeg Chicken

8 chicken legs (or wings)
Half teaspoon pepper sauce
Quarter cup soy sauce
Quarter cup grated onions
2 cloves garlic (crushed)
Half teaspoon salt
Half cup Morne Délice Nutmeg Syrup
Quarter teaspoon ground ginger
Season chicken with salt, pepper, crushed garlic and onions. Bake for 15 minutes at 400º F (200ºC). Remove chicken from oven and baste with mixture of nutmeg syrup, soy sauce, and ground ginger. Lower oven to 300º F (150ºC), and continue baking for one hour, basting frequently. Serve hot.

To achieve that unique nutmeg flavour with its soft finish and clean taste, top your ice cream, pancakes and fruit salad with nutmeg syrup. Nutmeg syrup also adds a special touch to your sweet and sour pork and barbecue chicken.

INDUSTRY AND COMMERCE
An OECS first

Local Talent

Local architects, Tomlin Voss Associates (TVA) were appointed by Marketing & Reservations International (MRI) operators of Rex Resorts Properties, as architects and prime consultants for the 212-room **Rex Grenadian Hotel**. The design was carried out by TVA's Managing Director and Senior Architect, Grenadian Nigel Renwick in close collaboration with MRI's Managing Director.

Other major projects carried out by this local firm of architects include **The Calabash Hotel**, the **Grentel** building on the Carenage, the **Learning Research Centre** and the **Grenada Trade Centre**. TVA is also responsible for the restoration of the **Financial Complex** on the Carenage. This historic Georgian building was partly destroyed by fire in 1990.

Caribbean Agro Industries is now registered to the International Quality Management System, ISO 9002, that ensures that all services regularly and consistently meet the complete requirements of the customer. Accreditation to the standard is a pre-requisite to any company pursuing the goal of Total Quality Management or TQM as it is colloquially referred to.

Caribbean Agro Industries is the first company in the OECS and CARICOM to successfully meet the requirements of the standard and as such, leads the way in total quality management in the region.

In conjunction with a quality consultant, a new company has been formed to meet the needs of other companies in the region who are also trying to gain registration to the standard. Based in the region the new company can offer a Caribbean resource for quality minded companies.

Jonathan Bradshaw, regional manager for the company recently commented on the success of Caribbean Agro Industries saying "Quality cannot just be left to testing the finished goods, it must be built into the company and its employees to make sure the raw materials are supplied correctly, the work processes are carried out correctly and efficiently and to ensure the customers needs are always satisfied. It must become a part of everyday life that all those concerned with the manufacture of a product believe in, and strive continuously to improve quality in all aspects. Operating a company to the requirement of ISO 9002 means exactly that. We make sure that we get it right, first time and every time. Without this ethic the customer has no guarantee of quality."

OECS Expo

The OECS Expo '94 was hosted by Grenada, Carriacou and Petit Martinique at the new Trade Centre in Grand Anse, St George's. A wide variety of companies were represented, promoting their services to other OECS businesses.

Vanel's Enterprises   *Sissons Paints*   *Grenada Sugar Factory*   *LIAT*   *Geest Industries*

General information

W hen it comes to providing investors with an attractive and viable environment for business development, the facts in Grenada's favour speak for themselves.

Population - Total population 95,000; Average rate of growth 0.25%; Reproduction rate 3.5%; Population density 263 per square kilometre; Adult literacy 90% (English speaking); Ethnic divisions: 82% African descent; 13% mixed; 1% white; 4% others.

Currency - Eastern Caribbean Dollar EC$2.70 = US$1.00. Grenada is a member of the Eastern Caribbean Central Bank which consists of eight countries. Since no member can make any decision affecting the currency without the express approval of all countries, the EC dollar is among the most stable currencies in the Caribbean.

National Commercial Bank of Grenada

Banks - There are several banks around the island and in the capital, St George's which offer a wide range of banking and financial services:
Barclays Bank Plc Tel: 440 3232
Bank of Nova Scotia Tel: 440 3274
National Commercial Bank (NCB) of Grenada Ltd Tel: 440 3566
Grenada Bank of Commerce Tel: 440 3521
Grenada Development Bank Ltd Tel: 440 2382
Business hours are generally 8.00am to 4.00pm, Mondays to Friday.

Territorial waters - There is a claimed limit of 12 nautical miles (22 km). The economic zone includes fishing of 200 nautical miles (370 km).

Telecommunications - Grenada's modern telecommunications system is a leader in the Caribbean. Grenada Telecommunications Limited (Grentel), a joint venture company, operates both domestic and international services. There are approximately 20,000 telephone connections throughout the country. The telephone system is fully digital, with worldwide dialing available to all residential and business customers, and from public pay phones and card phones. An 800 Toll Free service for international outgoing and incoming calls is available. Also provided are international telegraph, telex, and facsimile services, leased voice and data lines, and a mobile cellular phone service (USA Amps) for land and marine use, payable by major credit card. USADirect service is obtainable from pay phones and hotels by dialling USA (872).

Electricity
Power on Grenada is supplied by Grenada Electricity Services Ltd. (GRENLEC), from diesels. Upgrading of the system is continuous. The non-industrial current is 220 volts, single phase, 50 cycles. For industrial use, 40 volts, three phase, 50 cycle power is available.

Water
The country's water is supplied by the National Water and Sewerage Authority from a series of catchments, rivers and deep wells. The water is clean and safe to drink. Residential and industrial consumers are metered, plus a tariff based on 17.5% of the annual imputed value of the property.

Driving

Non-Grenadian citizens must present a valid international or national driving licence to the traffic department to obtain a local licence which costs EC$60 (approximately US$22). Cars drive on the left side of the road. There are several car rental agencies in St George's. Local licences can be obtained through these agencies.

Access

Grenada, Carriacou and Petit Martinique are easily accessible by sea and air. Point Salines International Airport (below) is one of the largest airports in the Caribbean.

Airlines of Carriacou at Lauriston, Carriacou

OVERLEAF
Point Salines International Airport today, and (inset) early on during construction

The media - Radio Grenada is owned by the Government of Grenada and operated by Grenada Broadcasting Corporation (GBC) with 20,000 watts transmitting to the Caribbean on the medium wave band. Spice Capital Radio is a privately owned and run 5,000 watt FM station, also on the medium wave band. There is also Young Soul FM.

Grenada Television, also owned by the Government and operated by GBC, was formed in 1980 and transmits on chánnels 7 and 11. Lighthouse TV is a privately-owned, non-profit making station which broadcasts religious and light-entertainment family programmes. Channel 6 - Cable TV is a non-commercial community facility with the emphasis on culture.

There are six newspapers published in Grenada which appear either weekly, monthly or bi-monthly.

An on-going investment in the local infrastructure is a major feature of Grenada. From roads to communications, power to airports, these resources reflect the country's progressive policies and long-term commitment to development.

Roads - Grenada has approximately 750 miles of roads, many of which have been newly resurfaced or rebuilt.

Seaport - The country's major port is St George's, the capital, where the sheltered natural harbour features an 800 feet pier with berth space for two to three vessels at a minimum depth of 30 feet. A general ports development provides a 250 feet schooner berth with 18 feet depth, a container park and other operational improvements. The port has 27,500 square feet of transit shed space and supporting warehouse and bond storage facilities.

Ocean freight service is provided by shipping lines such as Anglican Shipping, Geest, Nedlloyd, Wisco, Mitusi-Osk Lines, TEC Marine Lines, NYK (Nippon, Yusen, Kisha), K-Line, Bernuth Agencies, Star Caribbean, RMC Lines, and TMT (Trailer Marine Transport). Shipping agents include Geest Industries (W.I.) Ltd, Geo. F. Huggins, Jonas Browne & Hubbard, Star Agency, and St John's Agencies.

Airports - Grenada has two airports, a 2,700 feet airstrip in Carriacou, and the 9,000 feet International Airport at Point Salines capable of servicing the largest aircraft in the world. Regular passenger and air cargo services to regional and international destinations are provided by several companies. There is potential for further air transportation by reopening Grenada's former airfield at Pearls.

227

Commercial outline

Like most other small island states, the Grenadian economy is open and dependent. The principal sectors which fuel economic activities in the tri-island state are: Government services, transport and communications, agriculture, wholesale and retail, tourism and manufacturing. Tourism is measured by the contribution of hotels and restaurants.

Total Real Gross Domestic Product (GDP), which has been growing constantly over the last few years, increased from an estimated value of EC$282 million in 1986 to EC$457.4 million in 1992.

All of the major components of aggregate demand, with the exception of government expenditure, have been registering significant increases. In an attempt to contain the deficit situation, government expenditure has therefore been squeezed, especially since 1994.

Grenada is an extremely attractive location for new investments in agro-processing, electronic data processing (already the country can boast one of the most successful offshore data entry [high speed scanning] operations in the region), electronic assembly, apparel and sewn goods, wooden furniture and toys, health care products, costume jewelry, light manufacturing and financial services.

Agriculture. The agricultural sector is the backbone of the Grenadian economy in terms of its contributions to GDP, employment and export earnings.

The principal products which generate foreign exchange earnings are the traditional export crops - bananas, cocoa, nutmegs and mace. Fresh fruit and vegetables and fresh cut flowers' performance over the last few years also account for some measure of these earnings. Production of the traditional export crops, except cocoa, has been increasing over the years.

The prospects for the Grenadian banana industry, like those of many other Caribbean banana producing islands, are fraught and heavily dependent on the type of arrangements which can be made with the European Union.

The strengthening of inter-sectorial linkages, particularly between the agricultural and tourism sectors, greater emphasis on agricultural diversification and land utilisation, superior farming techniques, better marketing and distribution arrangements and improved storage facilities, are the main planks of government strategy aimed at servicing a significant advance in this sector.

Tourism, which accounts for roughly 8.25% of GDP, is a major sector in the Grenadian economy, especially in terms of its foreign exchange earning capacity. In recent years large dollar investments have been made

The natural foodbasket
Grenada grows everything from cabbages, tomatoes, bananas, mangoes, papayas (pawpaw), plantain, melons, callaloo (spinach family), okras, yams, breadfruit, oranges, tangerines, limes, christophenes, avocados and many others.

In addition, fresh seafood of all kinds, including lobster, oyster, prawns and shrimps are plentiful. Conch, locally known as 'lambi' is extremely popular and appears on most menus.

Horticultural Society
Over the past few years the Horticultural Society of Grenada has taken part in the renowned horticultural show in Chelsea, London. In 1992 and 1993, flowers and foliage from Grenada were stunningly arranged by a member of the society, based in the UK. On both occasions, a silver medal was awarded the display.

The Grenada National Museum in St George's was once an old French prison and administration building

Horse Shoe Beach Hotel, Lance Aux Epines, Grenada

Grenada Breweries factory, bottling the famous Carib Beer

in this sector. The bulk of these investments have made a significant contribution by increasing the number of hotel and guest house rooms available on the islands.

Having displayed uneven growth during the last ten years, occupancy levels have started to climb to more acceptable levels. The number of stay-over visitors and cruise ship passengers have been registering reasonable increases. The ultra-modern Point Salines International Airport, infrastructural development and increased airline service, have all helped to improve the performance of this sector.

Over the next few years the government intends to focus its attention on increasing the number of rooms on the island, embark on strong marketing and promotional campaigns, improve the number and quality of tourist attractions, and engage in further infrastructural developments. These objectives, when implemented, will certainly benefit the tourism sector and the nation in general.

The area of hotel development has been greatly enhanced with the opening of two large luxury hotels during the last quarter of 1993 - the Rex Grenadian (212 rooms) and La Source (100 rooms), thus increasing the hotel room capacity in the state to 1,400. The target is 2,500 rooms by the year 2000.

Manufacturing. Grenada's manufacturing sector, which is still in the early stages of development, currently accounts for roughly 5-6% of GDP. Garment manufacturing, which has accounted for a great deal of economic activity in this sector, still remains at the forefront. Recently, however, greater industrial diversification has been taking place and new industries to Grenada, such as industrial gases, paints and varnishes, flour and animal feeds, food processing and assembly type activities of garments, handicrafts, furniture, appliances and mufflers have begun to make an impact.

In addition to the wave of new industrial activities, older industries in Grenada like beer, rum and cigarette production continue to make their contributions. The beer industry, in particular, has seen a huge investment in plant and equipment in an effort to increase production levels, improve product quality and upgrade the level of efficiency.

The strategy for upgrading the performance of this sector, which has the potential to ease the pressures of unemployment, is inextricably linked to the government continuing to provide generous concessionary incentive packages to entrepreneurs, improvements of infrastructural and financial facilities, technology transfer, taking advantage of skill level improvement and other assistance programmes, as well as continuing to work on winning consumer confidence for locally manufactured products.

Business, investment and industrial organisations

Grenada Industrial Development Corporation (IDC)

The Industrial Development Corporation, IDC, established by an Act of Parliament in February 1985, is a statutory body with direct responsibility to the Minister of Finance, Trade, Industrial Development and Planning, whose primary objective is to "stimulate, facilitate and undertake" the establishment and development of industry in Grenada.

A significant proportion of the corporation's work is associated with the promotion and development of the tourist industry, particularly hotel development, and other support services in that sector.

The activities of the corporation are directed by a nine-member board of directors with representation from the private and public sectors, and a small core of professional and support staff.

Some specific activities of the Industrial Development Corporation include:

Large investments have been made in increasing the performance of manufacturing industry

- Local and overseas investment promotion.
- Evaluation of investment proposals and recommendation for the granting of concessions.
- Identification of investment opportunities.
- Assistance to businesses in areas such as factory space provision, technical assistance, arranging joint venture partnerships and the identification of export marketing possibilities.

Each year the IDC interviews several hundred prospective investors and businesses and receives project applications, most of which are reviewed and sent to Cabinet for approval. Local project sponsors account for nearly 80% of all project approvals.

Secret Harbour Hotel

Grenada Chamber of Industry and Commerce (GCIC)

The GCIC was formed in 1921 to provide a unified voice for the business and industrial community in its effort to promote economic growth and development in Grenada.

With its office and Multi-Media Training Centre located in the DECO Building, Mount Gay, about a mile from downtown St George's, the GCIC continues to play a stimulating role in upgrading and maintaining services to the community.

The fourteen-member board of directors meet regularly to formulate

Shell Oil Refinery

Grenada Chamber of Industry & Commerce
Standing (l-r): Earl Carter, C K Sylvester, Joseph Charter, Geoffrey Commissiong, Colin Little, Omar Al Shariff
Seated (l-r): Deodatt Singh, Allan Bierzynski (1st Vice-President), Aaron Moses (President), Edwin De Caul (2nd Vice-President), Cheryl Kirtin (Executive Director)

the policy of the organisation as well as to provide direction for the chamber.

The GCIC is able to join in regional efforts through its membership in the Caribbean Association of Industry and Commerce (CAIC), which assists the continued growth and development of Grenada.

The business community also benefits from technical assistance and training with funding from the Small Enterprise Assistance Project (SEAP), a USAID-funded programme for small and medium-scale Eastern Caribbean productive businesses. SEAP is managed in the region by CAIC and by GCIC in Grenada.

Grenada Bureau of Standards

This body was established by the Standards Act Number 6, in 1989. Its main purpose is to promote higher standards in goods, services, practices and processes.

The bureau encourages producers to make good quality products without limiting the consumer's choice, or restricting freedom in design or manufacture. Consumers can help to improve quality by buying goods made to declared standards, whenever these are available. This will encourage manufacturers to produce better products to meet consumer demands at home and in foreign markets.

Grenada's Non-Governmental Organisations (NGOs)

Grenada's development has been boosted by the role of NGOs who have been fostering the nations's growth.

The National Development Foundation (NDF) has given small entrepreneurs the financial kickstart and technical assistance needed to get a variety of businesses off the ground. NDF's main criteria for loan assistance stipulate that funded organisations be of productive value to the community, stimulate exports and generate employment.

Other NGOs contributing to Grenada's prosperity are the Agency for Rural Transformation (ART) and the Grenada Save the Children Development Agency (Grensave). ART promotes and assists in the development of women, youth, farmers, fisherfolk, craft producers and agricultural workers, and supports programmes that will promote the development of a sustainable society.

Grenada's NGOs support the development of many local craft industries

235

The GCIC Junior Achievement (JA) Programme

Junior Achievement, JA, is an economic education programme sponsored by the Grenada Chamber of Industry and Commerce which gives secondary and senior primary school students hands-on experience of the free enterprise system. By running their own small company one afternoon each week for 25 weeks at the Junior Achievement Centre, the young people gain practical knowledge of the operations of a business.

All previous Junior Achievement Companies have been manufacturing companies. Their product list includes: tye dye T-shirts, picture frames, greeting cards, hair accessories, delicacies, scatter cushions, stationery holders, paper-weights, place mats, belts, key rings and memo pads.

These products are sold to friends, relatives and school friends, with the bulk being sold door-to-door and at Open House. There are plans to include a trade fair.

By helping them understand the free enterprise system, Junior Achievement enables young people to see a future for themselves in the economic life of the country. In their JA companies the young executives discover what they enjoy most in business - developing and marketing products, keeping books, making decisions as part of a team, putting leadership qualities to work - and their experience helps them in their choice of a career. Those who don't go on to a career in business will become better educated citizens and consumers.

Small Business Incubator

The Industrial Development Corporation, IDC, in its continuing efforts to stimulate local entrepreneurship and facilitate economic development in the country, has embarked upon a novel concept called a Small Business Incubator (SBI), the first of its kind in the countries of the Organisation of Eastern Caribbean States (OECS).

The IDC, in conjunction with the Small Enterprises Development Unit (SEDU) of the Grenada Development Bank, have put together a comprehensive package to help and guide small scale entrepreneurs from the concept of projects to the point of their implementation. The concept of the SBI is one which provides a conducive environment under controlled conditions to assist in the cultivation and successful development of small businesses.

The provision of these controlled conditions will enable the SBI to

J A Companies give young people practical business knowledge

Young achievers, not in the field of business, but in athletics, receive their awards at the Intercol Sports Day

Sunsation Tours specialists in island-wide guided tours

promote under one roof an effective linkage of entrepreneurial talent, technology know-how, capital and infrastructure support.

The IDC has sub-divided a twelve thousand square feet factory building at the Seamoon Industrial Park into eight units exclusively for small business, with factory space ranging from four to eight hundred square feet. Preference will be given to manufacturing operations in the areas of agro-processing, handicraft and other light industries.

The Nutmeg Restaurant on the Carenage

The Grenada Hotel Association

The Grenada Hotel Association, a non-profit, limited liability private sector organisation was established in 1961. Regionally, the association is a member of the Caribbean Hotel Association, and locally, it is a member of the Grenada Chamber of Industry and Commerce and the Grenada Board of Tourism.

The affairs of the association are conducted by a board of directors which includes a president, first and second vice-presidents and six other directors. Meetings are held on a monthly basis, or are convened when necessary.

Ade's Dream Guest House, Hillsborough, Carriacou

The association employs a manager and secretary who manage the day-to-day affairs of the association, carry out public relations functions, handle all secretarial duties and operate a facsimile and telex reservation system, which is linked into a Grenada reservation clearing house in the United States. The principal aims, objectives and functions of the association are as follows:

- The regulation of the tourism industry, both internal and external.
- Public relations and promotions on an industry basis in existing markets, in addition to introducing the product into new markets.
- Lobbying government with regard to advancement of industry interests.
- Operation of a membership telex reservation system.
- Educational training programmes for hotel management and staff.
- The improvement of labour relations and the bargaining strength of the industry.

The Siesta Hotel, Grand Anse

- Fostering the support of, and interaction with, other private sector enterprises, with the purpose of joint benefits.
- Public education on the benefits that accrue from the tourism industry.

Grenada Employers' Federation

The Grenada Employers' Federation, GEF, was registered on September 24, 1962, under the Trade Union and Trade Disputes Act No 20 of 1951. The initial membership was ten. Now there are about sixty members in three categories, ordinary, associate and affiliate. These include commercial business places, hotels, airlines, electricity and telecommunications, industry and agricultural concerns. The rules of GEF are patterned along the lines of similar bodies in the Eastern Caribbean.

The principal services include advice and information on local and regional trends in unions' demands, progress of negotiations, wage rates, fringe benefits, labour legislation and future industrial development likely to affect employment levels or redundancy. Under the rules of the GEF, provision is made for negotiating together with members.

The affairs of the GEF are handled by a committee representing member organisations. A president and vice-president are elected by the committee, from among its members and an executive director is employed who, along with the committee, handles the affairs of the organisation.

National Development Foundation of Grenada

The National Development Foundation of Grenada (NDFG) is a local, private, non-profit making, dynamic, community-oriented organisation, dedicated to providing opportunities for the establishment and expansion of micro-enterprises in Grenada. The NDFG is registered as a company limited by guarantee under the Companies Ordinance of Grenada for the following principal purposes:

- Serve the micro business sector through technical assistance, funding, business consultancy and training.
- Assist enterprising men and women who are business oriented, imaginative, ambitious, trustworthy and interested in building a new Grenada.

Towards positive industrial relations

In 1979, Grenada became a member of the International Labour Organisation (ILO), a body with its headquarters in Geneva, that aims to bring together government, employer and employee representatives, in a tripartite forum to exchange views and hold discussions with a view to making recommendations for labour legislation, and all matters relating to smooth and equitable industrial relations. The federation is a member of the regional body, the Caribbean Employer's Confederation, which meet once a year, rotating from country to country.

Help is available for small businesses striving to build a new Grenada

Caledonian Airways improve Grenada's worldwide connections

On Thursday, 16 December 1993, Caledonian Airways became the first European charter airline to operate flights to Grenada via Tobago.

Using a wide-body, 353-seat DC10-30 aircraft, the weekly service operates between Gatwick, Tobago and Grenada on Thursdays.

A number of the UK's major tour operators as well as leading specialists including Hayes & Jarvis, Kuoni, Thomson, Caribbean Gold, Caribbean Connection, Tropical Places and Cosmos, utilise the flights to offer an extensive range of new tourist packages.

Pictured below at the inaugural flight reception, Hon Tillman Thomas, Minister of Tourism; Paul Slinger, Chairman of the Grenada Board of Tourism; and Clare Hollingsworth, Marketing Director Caledonian Airways

If you have a viable project or business idea or wish to expand an existing business, but do not have access to credit, collateral, or business assets over EC$25,000, then you may qualify.

Grenada Development Bank

The Grenada Development Bank, formerly the Grenada Agricultural and Industrial Development Corporation was established in February 1985. The Development Bank is a statutory body working in close co-operation with the private sector and government of Grenada for the mutual benefit of all, and more specifically for the country's economic development.

In keeping with its objective of facilitating and stimulating economic development, the bank has among its responsibilities the following:

- Assisting borrowers in establishing or expanding development enterprises by granting loans and other forms of financial assistance to eligible persons or enterprises.
- Assisting persons in pursuing courses of higher education by making loans and other forms of financial assistance available to such persons.
- Mobilising and co-ordinating available resources to be utilised in financing agricultural, industrial and tourism projects in Grenada.

Any citizen of Grenada, company registered in Grenada, co-operative, partnership, or credit society is eligible to apply for assistance in any of the areas listed below:

- Agricultural development, fishing and livestock.
- Industrial development.
- Tourism development.
- Higher education.
- Housing.
- Consultancy service, including project preparation and business plans, training for new and existing entrepreneurs through the Small Enterprise Development Unit.
- Other approved development projects.

The interest rate chargeable on GDB loans is determined by the degree of risk involved in the project being financed, the form of financing applicable, the size of loan, and current interest rates. A grace period appropriate to the loan project is normally given. The repayment period is usually based on the earning potential of the project, its viability and expected lifespan. The type and amount of security required will depend, in the final analysis, on the nature of the project and other pertinent factors.

The Grenada Co-operative Bank, St George's

Water projects

The National Water and Sewerage Authority (NAWASA), formerly the Central Water Commission, was established in 1990 to take responsibility for wastewater in Grenada. The Grand Anse Sewer System was funded by a grant from the United States Agency for International Development (USAID) and turned over to NAWASA upon completion. NAWASA own, operate and maintain the system.

The main purpose of the Grand Anse Sewer System is to reduce the wastewater being discharged into the Grand Anse Bay and in addition, to collect wastewater from the primary industrial area in south St George's. The objective being to improve conditions in the Grand Anse area of Grenada for the benefit of residents, businesses and tourists.

The system consists of some 15 miles of force main and gravity collection lines, four pump stations and a marine outfall 1,145 feet long. The collection, which includes all grey water (baths and sinks), begins just above DeFreitas Cottages and collects all the sewage from residential, commercial and industrial establishments in the Falege, North Grand Anse, Camerhogne and Frequente areas. It has been designed to handle all future expansion in the entire south St George's area.

Before the project started, USAID commissioned an environmental assessment which was completed by Bellairs Research Institute, Barbados. They concluded that due to several characteristics, Point Salines was considered the best location for an outfall.

The characteristics included: fast and consistently offshore currents, even bottom with relatively deep water access close to shore, and no large-scale productive marine communities in the immediate vicinity. Bellairs further concluded that treatment of sewage beyond the preliminary stage was not necessary at present but a monitoring programme should be established to detect environmental changes that may occur following implementation of the system. NAWASA continuously monitors the water quality of many sites along the south and west coasts, including Point Salines.

Water supply improvements benefit all of Grenada's industries

Due to the costs associated with the operation and maintenance of the system, a monthly sewage rate is charged to consumers. There is also a fee for hooking-up to the system. The costs include electricity for the pump stations, labour and transportation to visit each pump station daily to perform routine maintenance and clean the screens, spare parts inventory, system management, environmental monitoring and emergency repairs.

Grand Etang Water Supply Project

The Grand Etang Water Supply Project was developed to improve the water supply shortfall in the capital and south St George's area.

A dam constructed on the outlet stream has raised the existing lake level by five feet. This increased water capacity will be used to supplement the supply to the Annandale Treatment Plant by pumping approximately 500,000 gallons during the four critical months of the dry season.

A pump house constructed 200 metres downstream from the dam houses three electric centrifugal pumps. These pumps carry the water uphill to a point adjacent to the forestry house, from where it flows by gravity into a tributary of the Beausejour River, source of the Annandale Treatment Plant.

The project was funded by the French Development Agency, Caisse Francaise de Development (CFD), at an approximate cost of EC $1 million.

Seven Sisters Falls, an hour's drive from St George's

Most hotels, like the Coyaba Beach Resort, Grand Anse, require a constant supply of fresh water and will benefit from further development in Grenada's water utilities

The damming of the outlet stream from the Grand Etang Lake will supplement Grenada's water needs during the dry season

Fishery resources

Courtesy of *Mahon Study*, 1988

G renada has the second largest oceanic shelf area in the OECS countries as well as substantial fishery resources in comparison to many other Caribbean islands. The major fishing centres on the island of Grenada are at St George's, Grand Mal, Gouyave, Victoria, Duquesne Bay, Sauteurs and Grenville. With the exception of Grenville, all are on the west coast. Fishing is also an important activity in Carriacou and Petit Martinique. Fishing is mainly conducted as a means of earning a living and about 2,000 full and part-time fishermen operate almost 600 boats. There are two fishing seasons during the year, the 'low season' from July to December and a 'high season' from November to June, when offshore pelagic [upper ocean layer dwellers] species become more abundant.

The major types of 'traditional' fishing gear and other methods used in Grenada and other countries of the Eastern Caribbean include:

- bottom hand lines (in depths from 20 - 200 metres, with monofilament lines and several baited hooks)
- trolling lines (with artificial feather lures or baited hooks, deployed at 100 metres or more while the boat is drifting or at the surface with outriggers when underway)
- fish traps or 'pots' (usually Z-shaped with one or two funnels, made from chicken wire or sometimes wicker reinforced with wooden stakes and weighted with stones)
- beach seines (set from a rowing boat to enclose schooling fish and then hauled to shore)
- gill nets (primarily used for catching pelagic flying fish and occasionally used for both demersal [ocean bottom dwellers] and other pelagic species)
- trammel nets (consisting of three panels of netting - an inner panel hanging between two larger-meshed outer panels attached to common float and lead lines; typically set in shallow reef areas where lobster, conch, and a wide variety of fish may be captured)
- diving (often with scuba equipment; live lobsters are caught by fishermen using snares, conch are taken by hand.

Wooden-hulled boats with outboard motors are the main vessel for professional fisherman

Four categories of fishing are recognised. The major category concentrates on the oceanic pelagics such as tuna, billfish, flying fish and dorado during the traditional 'ocean season' from November/December to June/July.

This fishery accounts for approximately 50% of national landings and is carried out principally by fishermen from the area around Gouyave,

Nearshore beach fishing on Hillsborough Bay, Carriacou

using 18-28 foot wooden-hulled canoes and pirogues powered by gasoline outboard motors. These professional fishermen use long lines of some 1.5 to 3.5 miles long to exploit this resource.

The second type is fishing for bottom-dwelling (demersal) species on the deeper shelf and ocean drop-off, where groupers, snappers and other tropical rockfish are caught from June to November. The same vessels which target the oceanic pelagics during the 'ocean' season are used in this fishing method. Additionally, off Carriacou and Petit Martinique, 25-40 foot sailing sloops are used to catch demersal fish. This demersal fishing accounts for approximately 15% of total landings.

The third type is the nearshore beach seine fishing which uses encircling nets to harvest small schools of fish such as scad or sardines. Nets vary in length from 500 to 750 feet, with the deepest section being 30-36 feet, and this fishing accounts for approximately 30% of national landings.

The fourth type comprises the shell fish, game-fish, and dive fisheries for species such as white sea urchin (or Westindian sea egg), turtles, lobsters and conch, together with some fin fish. This fishing accounts for approximately 5% of national landings, of which less than 1% at present is landed by sports-fishing tourists.

There are six established public fish markets in Grenada, but the majority of the catch has not traditionally been sold through these outlets. In the past, most of the fish catch was marketed directly at the landing site without processing or was transported without refrigeration to individual buyers. This situation is changing. There has been an increase in the availability of ice and cold storage facilities, and a greater proportion of the catch is now sold to buyers for export.

In Carriacou and Petit Martinique, most of the catch (about 90%) is sold to fish buyers who export it to Martinique, and the local retail market has become negligible. Because the exporters offer a higher price than local buyers will pay, only a few fishermen sell locally.

About 12-15 locally made sailing sloops from Carriacou and Petit Martinique go out daily to fish for shellfish and demersal species such as snappers, parrot fish, groupers, grunts and other reef fish; but they only fish whenever there are boats with ice available to buy their catch. There are about thirteen of these buyer boats, powered by both engines and sails. Each has a capacity of 10,000lbs of ice and 6-12,000lbs of fish. There are roughly five boats on stand-by in the Grenadines in any given month. Each buyer from Carriacou and Petit Martinique must have an agent in Martinique who is licenced by the authorities there.

Boatbuilding on Carriacou

Boat building is a skill for which the people of Carriacou are famous. It was introduced by the Scottish shipbuilders who came to the island during the nineteenth century.

In that era, frequent calls were made by merchant ships for a cargo, chiefly sugar. With the decline of the sugar industry, these ships were withdrawn from service and the people were forced to find means by which they could keep in touch with other parts of the world.

There was the need to export their products and there was also a need for basic commodities like food, clothing and implements which the people could not produce themselves. Because of this, necessity became the mother of invention. People began building their own sloops and schooners. They were made from strong timber similar in structure to those withdrawn from service. They were boats which had to be durable and seaworthy from their inception.

OVERLEAF
Nearshore beach fishing at Gouyave, Grenada's main fishing town

Despite the seasonal availability of the same offshore pelagic species that are caught in Grenada, fishermen do not exploit this resource because they have not developed a market for it. During November to July, fishermen in the French-speaking island of Martinique can catch enough pelagic species to supply that island's demand (the importation of pelagics to Martinique is strictly prohibited at this time and the trader boats will buy only demersal fishes).

After July, boats from Carriacou and Petit Martinique are allowed to take both demersal and pelagic species to Martinique, but the availability of the latter is then low. Therefore Grenadian fishermen concentrate on demersal species year-round.

Fisheries development

A Government of Grenada, GOG, ice plant/fish storage facility at Windward in Carriacou provides small volumes of ice at low cost to fishermen, as well as fishing equipment. The plant was built with funds from the International Fund for Agricultural Development (IFAD).

Fishing off the St George coast
Courtesy: Gary-John Norman

The Organisation of American States (OAS) Integrated Development Project for Grenada stationed a consultant in Carriacou to provide assistance with several fisheries development projects, such as the renovation of the fish market in Hillsborough, a seamoss mariculture project, development of the mangrove oyster bed in Tyrrel Bay, improvement of the fish marketing and distribution system, development of pelagic fisheries and marketing for pelagics in Grenada.

The Artisanal Fisheries Development Project operates under the Ministry of Education, Culture, Youth Affairs, Sports, and Social and Security (which includes Fisheries) as a semi-autonomous agency dealing with the commercial aspects of the fisheries sector. With the opening of the new fish processing facility in St George's, funded by the Venezuelan Investment Fund, the emphasis of this project is on buying surplus catch from fishermen at the Government markets, processing it, freezing it and reselling it to retailers and exporters. Grenada is also a participant in the Food and Agriculture Organisation of the United States (FAO) sponsored Caribbean Technical Cooperation Network in Artisanal Fisheries and Aquaculture.

Fishermen with a catch of sea urchins (or Westindian sea eggs). Urchins are important as they eat the algae which can sometimes smoother the coral reefs. The eggs (or roe) of the urchin are eaten raw or roasted

Mariculture

Seamoss (red alga) is harvested and used as an ingredient in a popular drink in many Caribbean countries. It seems to grow best on windward

coasts which are not too exposed, but where agitation of the water by wave action is sufficient to keep the plants free of epiphytes. In volcanic islands, such as Grenada, available nitrates appear to be the main limiting factor for the growth of seamoss.

The Grenada Seamoss Project aims at the establishment of small commercial farms in a five-phase strategy: training of the staff biologist at the Artisanal Fisheries Development Project in seamoss cultivation; site identification; set-up of a pilot project; workshop for potential farmers; and the establishment of commercial farms. In 1987, a survey was carried out of the coastlines of Carriacou and Grenada to locate bays which are best suited to seamoss cultivation. A test raft for growing seamoss was installed in Grenville Bay, Grenada, and species of Gracilaria harvested by the local people was identified. There is also a private seamoss aquaculture venture in Carriacou.

Shrimp farming

The Agricultural Mission from the Republic of China on Taiwan headed by Dr James Tsay established a shrimp farming hatchery (above) at Paradise in St Andrew.

The US $450,000 facility was formally opened in August 1994. Apart from the hatchery, the administration office and shed, the shrimp producing installation has an engine room, fresh water and salt water settling tanks. There are also treatment tanks and ponds, where the juvenile shrimp are transferred for development after they move through the different stages from the eggs in the hatchery.

Although the main focus of the project is on shrimp production, and some samples of Grenada crayfish, the hatchery is capable of working on the fresh water fish 'tilapia'. For the second phase the saltwater white prawn will be introduced into half-acre ponds which will be added to the present infra-structure.

The shrimps which would be harvested at the end of five to six months would require about 15 pieces to the pound, while the tilapia is expected to reach sizes that weigh about half-a-pound each.

At present, the production capacity of the hatchery is one million juveniles per year.

Trade Agreements

A variety of beneficial bilateral trade agreements established between Grenada and the US, the European Union, Canada, Venezuela and other Caribbean Community (CARICOM) member states, serve to open the door for business investors to a world of lucrative markets.

UNITED STATES

Caribbean Basin Initiative (CBI). Under the terms of this initiative, products grown, produced or manufactured in Grenada and exported to the US qualify for preferential treatment. The following criteria apply:

- Products must be imported directly from Grenada.
- At least 35% of the appraised value of the article must be derived in the beneficiary country. (US-made components may account for up to 15% of this amount provided 20% of the final value is CBI-added).
- Products must be substantially transformed into new or different articles of commerce. Products excluded for treatment under CBI are textile and apparel articles, canned tuna, petroleum products, footwear, luggage, handbags and flat goods, certain leather, rubber and plastic gloves.

Tariff Item 807. A provision granted by the US Customs which permits a reduction of duty on imported goods containing components of US origin. The imported items are assigned a dutiable value from which the value of the US components is then deducted. This allows component parts to be sent offshore for assembly with reimportation duty paid only on the value added in the CBI region.

936 Funds. Projects located or contemplating location in Grenada can access 936 Funds providing they meet the necessary stipulations. These funds are profits deposited in Puerto Rican banks by subsidiaries of US corporations operating in Puerto Rico, and which are exempt from US income tax under Section 936 of the Internal Revenue Code and from Puerto Rican income tax. Under the Tax Incentive Act, companies making the deposits accept a lower rate of return on their earnings.

Tax Information Exchange Agreement (TIEA). A mutual and reciprocal obligation between the United States and signatory countries to exchange information relating to the enforcement of tax laws. For companies to gain access to 936 Funds, the countries in which the projects are or will be located must be a party to the TIEA. Grenada is among the first six Caribbean countries to have signed the agreement.

Trade agreements between Grenada and Europe benefit companies who rely on the supply of goods to service their customers

Caribbean Basin Initiative (CBI)

The name given to the trade and tax measures approved by the US Congress in 1983 in an attempt to promote the economic revival of the countries in the Caribbean region.

Grenada's many shipping companies are crucial to the country's import and export trade

CARICOM

The Caribbean Community or CARICOM, is the regional organisation created among the states of the Commonwealth Caribbean to promote economic integration, to coordinate foreign policy, and to provide common services in areas such as shipping, health, education and women's affairs. It was established in 1973 by the Treaty of Chaguaramas. The member countries are: Antigua & Barbuda; Bahamas; Barbados; Belize; Dominica; Grenada; Guyana; Jamaica; Montserrat; St Lucia; St Kitts-Nevis; St Vincent & the Grenadines; Trinidad & Tobago.

A brief history of the Geest Line

The Geest Line was established by John Van Geest, born in Holland in 1906. He went to England in 1930 with a view to develop his family's horticultural interests, by exporting dutch bulbs. After World War II, the company's rapid expansion was marked by the decision to market bananas and in 1954, a ten-year agreement was made to purchase all bananas of exportable quality grown in Grenada, Dominica, St Lucia and St Vincent. The success of this agreement led to the construction of purpose-built ships and the company currently provides a regular freight shipping service (with a limited passenger capacity) between Britain and the Caribbean. John Van Geest was held in the highest esteem throughout the West-indies, he died in July 1994.

EUROPE

Grenada has preferential trade agreements with the member countries of the European Union (EU) under **LOME IV** and with the African, Caribbean and Pacific States (ACP) group. Products meeting certain source and value-added criteria may be exported to the EU duty free under the convention.

CANADA

Grenada has preferential trade agreements with Canada under the terms of **CARIBCAN**.

CARIBBEAN

Grenada-based manufacturers have preferential access to a regional marketplace embracing over five million people throughout the **Caribbean Community** (CARICOM) and the **Organisation of Eastern Caribbean States** (OECS). Locally produced or manufactured goods may be imported duty free into any of the 12 CARICOM member states, subject to certain value added specifications.

INDUSTRY AND COMMERCE

Incentives

Investors find a great deal of incentives to establish their business in Grenada. A competitive package of benefits and concessions for specific enterprises ensures the best possible environment to build on success.

The **Fiscal Incentives Act**, 1974, grants incentives to enterprises involved in a manufacturing or processing industry, including deep-sea fishing and shrimping, which form part of an integrated processing operation. Agricultural and tourism industries are excluded.

An enterprise is defined as "a company incorporated under the laws of Grenada engaged, or about to engage, in an industry."

Incentives available:

- Benefits will be granted to enterprises with a minimum value of 40% except in cases where a lower value added is stipulated in the Rules of Origin (eg, car assembly - 30% value added; computer assembly - 35%). In such cases, benefits to be given will be similar to those granted to a company with a minimum 40% value added.
- Tax Holiday Periods range from 7 to 15 years.
- Enclave Enterprises - 15 years minimum Tax Holiday when the enterprise is producing exclusively for export to countries outside the CARICOM market. The Tax Holiday Period guarantees the waiver of payment of the business levy.
- Relief from import duties and taxes on plant, equipment, machinery spare parts, raw material and building equipment, packaging materials and vehicles will be available to all enterprises granted incentive under the Fiscal Incentives Act, 1974.

The **Hotels Aid Ordinance Cap 139** of 1954 grants relief of custom duties to entrepreneurs investing financially in the construction of hotels in Grenada and equipment for use in hotels, and for other related purposes.

A hotel is defined as a building or group of buildings containing no less than ten rooms to be used for accommodating guests. It includes the land and any structure within it, or any building or group of buildings accepted by Cabinet which fulfil the purpose of a hotel.

Concessions available to approved hotel enterprises:

- Duty free importation of hotel equipment and building

Hotel development
The Grenada government strictly regulates the size, type and design of new hotels and apartments. High rise development is banned and no building can be 'higher than a palm tree'. Pictured is the Secret Harbour Hotel, L'Anse Aux Epines.

Real Estate
There are several real estate offices in St George's specialising in residential and commercial sales. All non-nationals or firms wishing to buy property in Grenada must apply to the Government under the Alien's Land Holding Ordinance for a licence. This is a straightforward procedure requiring little documentation.

250

The Association of Caribbean States

Grenada is a founding member of the Association of Caribbean States (ACS) which was launched with the signing of the treaty in Cartagena, Colombia, on July 24, 1994. The membership of the Association comprises Antigua and Barbuda, The Bahamas, Barbados, Belize, Colombia, Costa Rica, Cuba, Dominica, Dominican Republic, Grenada, Guatemala, Guyana, Haiti, Honduras, Jamaica, Nicaragua, Panama, St Kitts-Nevis, St Lucia, St Vincent and the Grenadines, Suriname, Trinidad and Tobago, Mexico, Venezuela and the French Republic in respect of Guadeloupe, Guyane and Martinique.

El Salvador is eligible to become a member of the grouping. Thirteen small non-independent islands in the Caribbean are eligible to become Associate Members.

The ACS will seek to promote integration and cooperation among the States in the economic, social, cultural, scientific and technological spheres and enhance coordination in external relations. The grouping will have a population of some 200 million and an estimated GNP of about US $500 billion.

The number of airlines using Grenada as a destination has increased rapidly with the development of Point Salines International Airport. Communication between Grenada and Carriacou has also been improved with the extension of the airstrip at Carriacou's Lauriston Airport

materials exclusively for the construction and operation of the hotel.

- Exemption of custom duties on equipment and building materials purchased in Grenada for the hotel enterprise.
- Complete or partial exemption from payment of tax on income derived from the operation of a hotel which has been granted concessions for a specified period not exceeding ten years.

The **Customs Ordinance SRO 35** of 1960 allows approved enterprises to be exempt from duty or charged a lower rate laid down by the custom tariff regulations.

An enterprise not entitled to benefit under the Fiscal Incentive Act 1974, or the Hotels Aid Ordinance 1954, may benefit under the Customs Ordinance SRO within the following categories: Industrial, Educational and Cultural, Agricultural, Governmental, Fishery, Diplomatic Personnel, Shipping, Personal Movement, Airlines and others.

Business contacts

Ask the people who know best about investment opportunities in Grenada. For further information on any aspect of business development, contact the following island-based or overseas organisations:

GRENADA
General Manager
Grenada Industrial Development Corporation
Frequente Industrial Park
St George's, Grenada, WI
Tel: (809) 444 1035/40
Fax: (809) 444 4828

Grenada Chamber of Industry & Commerce
De Gaul Building
Mount Gay, St George's, Grenada, WI
Tel: (809) 440 2937/4485
Fax: (809) 440 4110

Export Development Unit
Ministry of Trade
Lagoon Road, St George's, Grenada, WI
Tel: (809) 440 2101
Fax: (809) 440 4115

USA
Embassy of Grenada
1701 New Hampshire Avenue, NW
Washington, D.C. 20009 USA
Tel: (202) 265 2561
Fax: (202) 265 2468

Grenada Mission to the United Nations
820 Second Avenue, Suite 900D
New York, NY 10017 USA
Tel: (212) 599 0301
Fax: (212) 808 4975

Eastern Caribbean Investment Promotion Service
(ECIPS)
1730 M Street, NW, Suite 901
Washington, DC 20036 USA
Tel: (202) 659 8689
Fax: (202) 659 9127
Telex: 4976444 ECIPS

CANADA
High Commission of the Eastern Caribbean States
112 Kent Street, Suite 1610
Ottawa, Ontario K1P 5P2 Canada
Tel: (613) 236 8952
Fax: (613) 236 3042

Consulate General of Grenada
Phoenix House
University Avenue, Suite 830
Toronto, Ontario M5G 1Y8 Canada
Tel: (416) 595 1343
Fax: (416) 595 8278

UNITED KINGDOM
Grenada High Commission
1 Collingham Gardens
Earls Court
London SW5 0HW England
Tel: 0171 373 7808/00
Fax: 0171 370 7040

REST OF EUROPE
Embassy of Grenada to the European Union
Avenue de Arts 24
Box 2 B 1040
Brussels, Belgium
Tel: (011) 32 2 230-6265
Fax: (011) 32 2 230 3963

VENEZUELA
Embassy of Grenada
Edificio Los Frailes
Piso 3, Oficina #34
Calle La Guariga
Urb. Chuao, Miranda
Caracas, DF
Venezuela, SA
Tel: (011) 582 911237/912359
Fax: (011) 582 918907

For the record

Lord Pitt with his wife Lady (Dorothy) Pitt

Lord Pitt - stalwart, activist and aristocrat

Lord Pitt of Hampstead in Greater London and Hampstead in Grenada - the very name indicates the continuing identification with, and commitment to, Grenada on the part of this most unlikely British aristocrat.

David Thomas Pitt was born in Grenada in 1913 and in 1933 went to Britain to study medicine at Edinburgh University.

A political activist since his student days, he became a stalwart in Trinidad and Tobago's West Indian National Party before returning to Britain and to the British Labour Party, that he first joined in 1936.

Both as a general practitioner and as a political activist, Lord Pitt came to know and make friends with many of the towering figures of Pan-Africanism and the freedom movements of Africa and the Caribbean. He stood unsuccessfully for Parliament on two occasions, but his many positive achievements include serving as the Chair of the former Greater London Council (GLC), the President of the British Medical Association (BMA) and Deputy Lieutenant of Greater London. Leading members of Britain's Caribbean community spearheaded the formation of the charitable Lord Pitt Foundation on the occasion of his 70th birthday.

Photo: Rex Features, London

Miss Grenada to Miss World

In 1970, Grenada had the distinction of producing a world winner. Miss Grenada, Jennifer Hosten became Miss World and was crowned by celebrity host Bob Hope. Jennifer, now Mrs Hosten-Craigg, lives in Canada and works in television.

253

Sport and leisure

Grenada's first Test cricketer

Junior Murray created history when, on January 2, 1993, he became the first player from Grenada to represent the Westindies in Test cricket, replacing David Williams, from Trinidad as wicket-keeper for the Third Test against Australia at the Sydney Cricket Ground.

He made an impressive start, taking 19 catches in the three remaining Tests and when the Westindies were in trouble in the Fourth Test match, which decided the series in Westindies' favour, he played a crucial innings of 49 not out, made in over three hours at the crease to save his side.

Murray played for Westindies Under-19's in the Youth World Cup in 1988, and was soon wicket-keeping regularly for the Windward Islands and he gained selection for the Under-23's against the touring Australians in 1991/2.

He has his own batting style and likes to play his shots, hooking and driving particularly well. He is tall for a wicket-keeper but is athletic and has quickly established himself as Westindies' first choice behind the stumps. In 1993 he toured South Africa, Sharjah and India for one-day competitions, Sri Lanka for the inaugural Test against that country, and played in the home series against Pakistan in 1993 and England in 1994.

Murray, who made his Test debut two weeks before his 25th birthday should have a long international career ahead of him, now that it seems likely that he will be the long-term replacement for Westindies' great wicket-keeper, Jeff Dujon. Strangely, he is the third Murray, none of them related, to have kept-wicket for the Westindies.

The main venue in Grenada is Queen's Park, St George's which is rapidly improving thanks to a number of multinational donations, and it should not be long before Grenada hosts its first international. Both Pakistan and England have already played four day matches at the ground.

Murray's success has spurred great enthusiasm on the island. Already there is talk of Rawle Lewis, a young leg-spinner who took nine wickets in the 1994 match against England, being the next to gain international honours.

The 'Hurricanes' sweep Caribbean football

In Victoria, in the parish of St Mark, a football team by the name Hurricanes (now known as Courts Hurricanes) was formed in 1958 by a British Catholic priest, Father Dowring. He sought to pull the community together after the devastation of hurricane "Janet", which hit the island in 1955, with Victoria

Sponsorship opportunities

In Grenada, there are golden opportunities for companies offering sponsorship of sports competitions and sports coaches, and in providing sports facilities. Because, outside the hotel complexes of Grenada there is a shortage of sporting facilities and this has been reflected in the country's limited sporting achievements in the regional and international arenas.

However, a visitor would hardly believe such a statement, because virtually everywhere one travels around the country - sport is being played enthusiastically. On the beaches, in the water, on the water, in the streets, in the fields and parks. Women are as active as the men and they take netball and cricket, in particular, very seriously.

The limited sporting facilities are constantly being improved and some of the country's politicians are campaigning for a modern national stadium, complete with swimming pools and indoor facilities, to allow training to continue during the rainy seasons.

OPPOSITE
Junior Murray, in his debut playing for Westindies against Australia, January 1993, at the Sydney Cricket Ground
Photo: Joe Mann/ALLSPORT

254

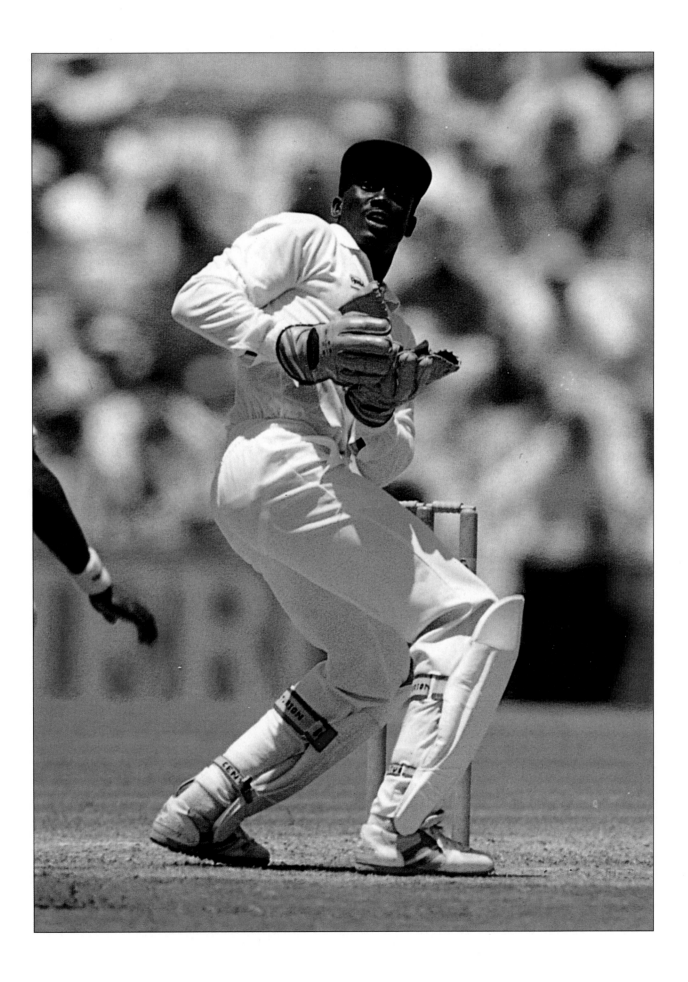

suffering particularly badly. Thus the Hurricane Football Club was formed.

Some of the most historic games were played against neighbouring St John's Sports, who hail from Gouyave, three miles from Victoria. In one match Hurricanes were trailing 2-0 with only two minutes to go in the game, but Hurricanes swiftly hit two goals to draw the match. On another occasion playing against the same team at Gouyave, supporters of St John's Sports left Gouyave at half-time for Victoria, celebrating, blowing their shells, ringing bells, to tell everyone in Victoria of the Hurricanes' imminent defeat, as they were trailing by 4-0. By the time those same supporters returned to Gouyave to continue their celebration, they found that the final scoreline was 5-4 to Hurricanes.

Hurricanes have won the Grenada National Championship more times than any other club. Between 1969 and 1976, Hurricanes won the championship eight times consecutively. Furthermore, they were undefeated for four years and in the 1970 season only one goal was scored against them. In the 1992 season they were again undefeated in the Premier League, whilst back in 1989, during the Shell Caribbean Competition, one player, Steve Mark, stood out from the rest. Mark was then voted Caribbean Footballer of the Year; since then he is still rated as one of the best footballers in the Caribbean, playing professionally for teams in Chile and in Barbados.

The coach of the team is Norris "Bouza" Wilson, one of many ex-players who still encourage today's team. Although the team is now known as Courts Hurricanes, in the past they have had two other sponsors, Arnold John & Sons Ltd., and Colonial Life Insurance Company (CLICO).

Between 1959 and 1993 the following players from Hurricanes made the Grenada national team: (*most of the players in Hurricanes and in Victoria traditionally have nicknames, these are included as many Grenadians would know them better by these names!*) Western John, Gerald 'OJ' Hosten, Raymond 'Little Boss' Arthur, Don 'Eyoye' George, Alston 'Heads' George, Oswald 'Boucus' Clovey, Ashley George, Lincoln 'Mertel' Charles, Pat 'Dukey' Fletcher, John 'Prengey' Patrick, Norris 'Bousa' Wilson, Anthony Paul, Justin Jerome, Don 'Billy' Frederick, Mike 'Skylark' Charles, Steve Mark, Raphael 'Rampa' Forsyth, Andrew 'Brother' Munro, Bernard Morris and John Williams.

Hashing - Grenada style

Visitors to Grenada should not be alarmed if they are approached by a character, resplendent in jogging attire, who proposes a Hash. Your enquirer

OPPOSITE (TOP)
Hurricanes Football team pictured in August 1968, when they won the first Windward Islands Cup Competition, played in St Lucia.

Back row (L-R): T C Crosby (Manager), O Mitchell, L Charles, Als George, O Clovey, T George, E Modeste.

Front row (L-R): L Marshall, P Fletcher, Ash George (Capt), U Romain, D Greasley, F Welsh, V Patrick
Courtesy: D Greasley

OPPOSITE (Bottom)
Courts Hurricanes - present team members.

Back Row: (L-R): Reynold 'Killer' Francis, (Patron), Steve Mark, Hycinth 'Tanner' Fraser, Charlton 'Bookas' Mark, Andrew 'Brother' Munro, Roland John, Norris 'Bouza' Wilson (Coach).

Middle Row: Stron 'Mackas' Barry, McKosker 'Moppa' Charles, Lynden Phillip, Raphael 'Rampa' Forsyth, Asif Fletcher, Reynold Elahie, Andy Augustine.

Front Row: Danley 'Bumble' Fraser, Rohan Joseph, Michael 'Pintay' Julien, Robert 'Chaplay' Bishop, Foster 'Gorgan' Charles, Francis 'Zeg' Munro

is not making an illegal suggestion but inviting you to run in the Hash.

To the uninitiated, Hashing is best described as a hybrid of a fun-filled adventurous cross-country run incorporating an assault course, and a treasure hunt without the treasure. Still, the trail does culminate at a local drinking establishment, usually a rum shop, and seeing as you would have acquired a serious thirst it is a fitting finale. Incidentally, the winner is the first to order a well deserved drink.

The sport originated in Malaysia during the years after World War I. It was conceived as a reprimand for young men who had embraced the party 'spirit' with a little too much enthusiasm at the weekend. That Monday morning cross-country retribution run evolved into a more humorous activity and subsequently became the popular event it is today.

As Hashing has developed it has acquired its own language which can be confusing for the novice. Hares are those individuals who devise the routes for the run, set the trail marks, signposted by shredded paper, often intentionally misleading the front runners from making too much headway. The unwritten law of Hashing is that it is not a competitive run. It is more enjoyable and in keeping with the original concept if the runners stay reasonably close together.

Colourful personalities take part in this ritual every other Saturday afternoon in various parts of Grenada and they are diverse in their age range and background. It is not uncommon for teenagers to find themselves Hashing with more mature persons, or truck drivers and estate agents negotiating a difficult terrain that has been set by a sadistic Hare. Equally, you may even find yourself in the company of some veteran Hashers.

Many of the Hashers are local Grenadians and there are also American, French, British, Norwegian, African and Chinese enthusiasts who are attached to the embassies, and tourists who have heard of the legendary Hash and want to experience it for themselves.

Sport and leisure activities are available at many of the resort hotels

Triathlon

The Grenada Triathlon is held in January each year. Competitors from a number of countries enter the swim, cycle and run challenge which starts and finishes at the Grand Anse beach.

The first day is for individuals who swim one kilometre, cycle 25 kilometres and run a five kilometre relay-race.

The Sunday event is for three-person teams, of which one must be a female. It starts with a one kilometre swim in the warm ocean at Grand

OPPOSITE
Hashing in Grenada, a mixture of cross-country and an assault course

OVERLEAF
Spectators supporting their team at the Intercol Sports Day athletics meet, held at Queen's Park, St George's

Anse beach and this is followed by a 25 kilometre cycle run to Point Salines International Airport. The event, which is open to all categories with age group prizes, concludes with a five kilometre relay run along the Airport Road.

As part of the attraction on Sunday, two races are run simultaneously, an open class with no age requirement and one in which the teams ages must add up to at least 100 years.

The Grenada Triathlon committee holds a briefing on the Friday evening before the event and a reception on the Saturday evening of the first event. Many people arrive in Grenada a week before the Triathlon to acclimatise and train and as many stay on a further week to recover (it's not clear from what?). There are special offers in travel and accommodation and for further information contact the tourist board or write or telephone the: Grenada Triathlon Committee, PO BOX 44, St George's, Grenada. Westindies.

Grenada Golf Club

Grenada has one 9-hole golf course, near Grand Anse at Belmont, with a spectacular view of coastline and the areas around St George's. The course is fanned by a calming sea breeze and the fairways are lined with palm trees and ferns. The club house is open to all vistors and has a bar with snacks available. Clubs can be hired, instruction and caddies are available. Plans are under way for the construction of a new 18-hole course on the island.

Grenada Open Golf Tournament

The annual Grenada Open Golf Tournament takes place in February. There are six categories of players: Championship flight (0-8 handicap); first flight (9-15 handicap) second flight (16-24 handicap); Ladies Championship (0-18 handicap); Ladies first flight (19-28 handicap); and Seniors (50 and over).

The first day, practice day and is followed by a welcome reception in the evening at the Golf Club. The tournament proper takes place over a weekend, the first round on Saturday starts at 6.30am, with the second round on Sunday. The presentation of prizes takes place on Sunday evening.

A number of regional and local players participate in the event. Fees for the event includes the practice round on the Friday, lunch on Saturday and Sunday, as well as the reception and cocktail party.

The 9-hole golf course at Belmont, near Grand Anse

Yachting

One sure way to get the most out of a Caribbean holiday or short break is to charter a yacht. In Grenada, Carriacou and Petit Martinique where the sailing is worldclass, it is possible to charter a crewed yacht or 'bareboat'(do it yourself style) for a day or longer.

There is a wide range of options open to visitors interested in sailing. A number of local operators who run regular day trips around the islands and these packages generally include leisurely excursions to nearby harbours and islands with food, drinks and a variety of watersports.

For those who prefer to charter and crew by themselves there is a choice of sail or motor vessels, 50 feet and over. Simply stock up with food and drink and go where you please.

Grenada, Carriacou and Petit Martinique have superb anchorages and marinas and a considerable number of small uninhabited islands providing safe anchorage.

One of the world's leading charter companies has opened a modern full-service marina, at Mount Hartman Bay on Grenada's south coast, where their fleet of 'bareboats' is moored. This marina is also open to visiting yachts. On shore they operate the Secret Harbour Resort, one of Grenada's most luxurious hotel complexes.

At Prickly Bay, Grenada's main yachting centre, there is a choice of charter boats including Seabreeze Yacht Charters. Spice Island Boatyard and Marine Services and a number of yachting and leisure facilities are also located here.

Between St George's Harbour and the Lagoon is the Grenada Yacht Club, a friendly and useful meeting point for visiting vessels. Grenada Yacht Services in St George's Harbour offers sheltered moorings and provides access to shops, food stores and the picturesque Carenage.

Carriacou has several good anchorages on the western shores. Tyrrel Bay in the south is where you will find multi-million dollar yachts moored close to local fishing crafts. Another worthwhile visit is Cassada Bay for scenic views and numerous islands to warrant anchorage.

The most famous spot is Sandy Island, just off the coast of Hillsborough. Ideal for picnics and snorkelling, this tiny island is so beautiful it has attracted advertising companies looking for the perfect Caribbean backdrop for their products. It is a fragile islet and visitors are requested to avoid activities which could damage that environment.

If time is not a problem, then a visit to Hillsborough will prove facinating,

Training yacht off Grenada
Courtesy: Gary-John Norman

and better still a complete tour of Carriacou, where there is lots to see.

At the edge of Hillsborough town there is convenient anchorage and jetty at Silver Beach Hotel where the food is truly excellent and the rum punch 'wicked'. Here there is a friendly well-stocked bar, but remember, Carriacou is Jack Iron rum country!

Grenada Yacht Club

After a visit to the Martinique Yacht Club by Charles McIntyre, Julian Rapier and Gordon Salhab, the three men convened a meeting, in July 1954, to discuss the idea of building a clubhouse in Grenada to provide shower and toilet facilities and a room where visiting and local yacht owners could sit and relax. Twelve people were present at that first meeting, and they became the original founding members of the Grenada Yacht Club.

A lease was secured from the Government for a small portion of land at the back of St George's pier and funds were raised for the initial downpayment on the building. The ground floor provided shower and toilet facilities and a small room for storing sails and other gear. The upper storey was an aluminium prefab building which provided a sitting room, a bar and small library where patrons could relax. A small slipway was also built.

The first Commodore of the Grenada Yacht Club was L O Taylor. The club had several dinghies in the 'mosquito' class, and a mixed fleet of larger sail boats.

The life of the club came to an abrupt end in September 1955 when hurricane "Janet" hit the island. The loss of the clubhouse proved a blessing in disguise, as by then, the executive had realised that the building was too small and car parking facilities inadequate. The government could not renew the lease for the same site as they had plans for port expansion, and it was some years before the committee was able to secure a suitable alternative site. In 1959 the club was granted a lease on the land at the Spout, by the entrance to the Lagoon.

With a plan drawn up by Beresford Wilcox and contributions from all the members, the new building was erected and formally opened over the Whitsun weekend in 1960. The club burgee depicts a local inter-island sailing schooner of those days.

In order to get started, six second-hand 18-foot Tornadoes were purchased from the Barbados Yacht Club. A fleet of 13 GP-14s were also

ABOVE & OVERLEAF
Grenada Sailing Festival
Courtesy: Gary-John Norman

265

brought in as they were ideal for One Design Racing and were already common in the other islands.

In the early years the series were raced in Tornados, GP-14s and Shearwater catamarans brought over from Trinidad. In the mid-1970s, the Mirror dinghy was introduced for the youth sailing programme. In addition, the government purchased 12 lasers which were handed over to the club for their use.

After the mid-1980s, the trend gravitated towards yacht racing and since marinas and hotels were opening in different parts of the island, races were organised which ended in various locations. Some of these races are now part of the club's annual schedule of events, such as the Venezuelan Independence Day Regatta, a two-day race that overnights at The Moorings marina. This event was started a few years ago by Oscar Hernandez, the Venezuelan Consul and an enthusiastic sailor.

Tony Potter, a Trinidadian yachtsman and hotelier, sponsors a Pursuit Race to his hotel, True Blue Inn, where good food and music end the day. Carriacou Regatta starts with a yacht race up to Carriacou for a weekend of local boat races as well as traditional festivities ashore.

The Carl Schuster Memorial Round Grenada Race is a gruelling and exhilarating race which has been run since the 1960s. More recently, Secret Harbour Hotel has organised the increasingly popular Impulse 21 match race in Grand Anse Bay.

Grenada Sailing Festival

The first Grenada Sailing Festival was held in January 1994. It was jointly organised by the Grenada Board of Tourism (GBT) and the Grenada Yacht Club (GYC). The occasion was sponsored by Carib Beer, Coca Cola, Westerhall Plantation Rum, Mount Gay Rum, The Moorings, Ace Hardware and others.

This new week-long annual Sailing Festival consists of competitive races, Junior Sailing races, Sunfish races and a small boat regatta and other challenging events for sailing enthusiasts from around the world.

The first race, beginning at sunrise, is southbound from Bequia which is six miles south of St Vincent. The second race is northbound starting in Trinidad and ending in St George's.

There will be a southern coast series of competitive races ending at different points where food and local drinks will be provided. The success of the inaugural sailing festival helped put Grenada on the world map for

The Lagoon, St George's

OVERLEAF
Carriacou Regatta

268

international sailing in the Caribbean.

The GYC run Junior Sailing Programme is designed to encourage the next generation of sailors to enjoy the sport.

Crew opportunities are available for a fee. Funds raised from the event will be used to purchase new boats for the GYC's Junior Sailing programme.

The week culminates in a Gala Presentation Ball at a leading venue, with prize-giving and live entertainment. On land, barbecues, parties and street festivals accompany the water activities.

The Carriacou Regatta

It is over three decades since the well-known yachtsman Linton J Riggs pioneered the first Carriacou Regatta and the activity has grown to enjoy great significance on the island, where solid seamanship and boat building abound. It has acted as a catalyst to other Caribbean seamen and to building better local boats for seaworthiness and livelihood.

The Carriacou Regatta is a cultural extravaganza, a time when boating skills are challenged, tested and reviewed by boating enthusiasts.

The programme of events is organised by a steering committee, catering for a variety of interests while emphasising the main event of boat racing. And what more evocative sight can the mariners behold than boats under sail, striving for mastery and fame, while battling with the elements.

In addition to boat racing, there are side attractions and games. Food is high on the agenda and the appetising aroma of fried chicken and hot-dogs waft in the breeze. Music, essential to such a festival, plays into the night. The Regatta ends with a salute to prize winners.

Game fishing

In the southern Caribbean, the game-fishing is excellent and a southern circuit is developing with well-organised events in Grenada, Tobago, St Lucia, Martinique and Barbados. There is very little sport-fishing pressure in many of these islands, so the results of an organised tournament can be quite outstanding. The 1992 Tobago event produced large quantities of yellowfin tuna, 223 to be exact, and a 142-pounder caught by a Barbadian angler netted $25,000 for breaking the Trinidad and Tobago sail-fish record.

Grenada has held a well-organised tournament for over 25 years, and though it is just to the north of Tobago, sail-fish are in greater abundance than marlin. A Billfishing tournament is in January and illustrates the

Further information
For more about Grenada's Billfishing Tournament write to P.O. Box 14, St George's, Grenada, WI

Petit Martinique Regatta
Held every year at Easter, competitors from the nearby Grenadines take part in the races

seasonal variations which affect billfishing throughout the Caribbean.

Tournament organisers are fishermen themselves so they schedule their events to hit the peak fishing in their own area.

Grenada's Billfishing Tournament

If you know how to fish and have an hour or two to spend off the Grenada coast, you will soon agree with knowledgeable anglers, who state that Grenada boasts some of the Caribbean's best game fish waters, and that its ideal location at the southern end of the Caribbean islands' chain is a very important contributing factor.

Between November and June, migrating species of sail-fish, white and blue marlin, along with huge schools of yellowfin tuna, converge on Grenada's east and west coasts.

Richard McIntyre (left), International Game Fishing Association and Andrew Bierzynski, Secretary of the Spice Island Billfishing Tournament Committee, with a record 66lb waho

Many years ago, resident American Jim Needham saw the potential of this annual occurrence for Grenada's sport-fishing enthusiasts. In 1964, he organised Grenada's first tournament, which was financed primarily by Needham and his friend Brian Mercer, a wealthy Englishman, who with his now famous 60-foot Hatteras 'Bahari' issued the challenge.

Anglers visited from Trinidad and St Lucia, and competitive sport fishing was born in Grenada's bountiful waters.

The tournament has grown from strength to strength and has attracted international recognition and participation. With such exceptional fishing over the years, the Grenada Billfishing Tournament is regularly featured in all major sport fishing publications.

The Spice Island Billfishing Tournament Committee is supported by the local business sector, and the prize money of over $100,000, is the largest purse for any sport in Grenada.

The tournament attracts participants from Trinidad and Tobago, Barbados, Curacao, St Lucia, Martinique, Turks and Caicos, United States, Canada, UK, Venezuela and local Grenadians.

Billfish competitors land a 313lb mako shark but only win the booby prize!

Billfishing Tournament rules

The rules for the Grenada Billfishing Tournament are those laid down by the International Game Fishing Association IGFA. There are no judges on the boats and a high standard of sportsmanship is required of all participants. In the event of a dispute, the decision of the Tournament Committee is final.

• All types of boats can be used as long as they comply with the 'Coast Guard Regulations for Safety Equipment on Vessels'.

• All fish caught in the Tournament must be caught by registered anglers and all participants in the Tournament do so at there own risk.

• Only blue marlin, white marlin and sail-fish accepted for Tournament points.

• Yellowfin tuna, wahoo and dolphin will also be accepted - but for weight prizes only.

• All fish weighed in the Tournament become the property of the Tournament Committee.

273

Diving

By David Macnaghten, (Dive Grenada)

The underwater scenery in Grenada is every bit as breathtaking as it is above the waves, and just as accessible.

Almost all water-sports, including diving, are based at Grand Anse beach, on the sheltered Leeward side of the island, with most dive sites located within 20 minutes of this landmark.

On the Atlantic side of Grenada the waves are usually rougher and there are frequent and strong currents. There are, however, snorkelling opportunities on the Leeward side of the small islands dotted along the coast.

The best snorkelling sites are based around Molinere and Dragon Bay, both of which are easily reached by boat. A few sites can be reached from the shore, the easiest are the southernmost headland of Morne Rouge Bay and the reef system off Grand Anse.

Unfortunately the innermost reef has been destroyed, so there is a swim of 100-200 feet to reach the better areas, the best of which is directly out from the end building of the Medical School Complex. However it would be safer to take a boat, as it is quite a distance and on cruise ship days there is a lot of small craft activity in the area.

The diving in Grenada is as good as anywhere else in the Caribbean, and, with PADI instructors (Professional Association of Diving Instructors) on the island, anyone can try it as long as they are fairly fit and can swim. A resort course lasts about a day and typically consists of a one-and-a-half hour lecture with pool work, followed by an escorted reef dive.

Within the same 15-20 minute radius of Grand Anse, there are a variety of wrecks, reefs and walls. There are dives for every level of activity with an emphasis on safe, no decompression diving.

Wreck dive sites

There are four main wreck sites which can be visited. The first is the **Bianca C**.

"Sunken treasure, massive sharks, strong currents, and a dangerous dive" are just a few of the many myths about the Bianca C, the cruise liner that sank approximately one mile off the southwest coast of Grenada on the October 24, 1961.

Possibly the largest wreck in the Caribbean, the 600-foot ship, crippled by an explosion, was at anchor for two days, outside St George's while it

Scuba courses can be arranged from most resort hotels. Participants practice in the pool before going to out to sea

Coral reef off Grenada
Courtesy: David Macnaghten

OPPOSITE
Angel fish, off Carriacou
Courtesy: Niki Wiedinger

274

burned. It sank while being towed by HMS Londonderry, in an attempt to beach it out of the shipping lanes.

Sunken treasure? Anything that Bianca C was carrying would have been salvaged in the late 1960s, when the propellers were recovered. The only treasure now remaining is the ship itself.

Though the bell and the captain's wheel have been removed, the contents of the ship are fairly intact, although the internal walls are badly rusted and crumble at a touch. The first-class quarters (top decks), were all impacted on sinking.

While you can sometimes see big fish on the Bianca C, the chances of encountering even a small shark are about one in 150, and even then they only come close enough to see what strange creature has appeared, usually to within 30-50 feet depending on visibility. In fact you are far more likely to encounter hawksbill turtles, eagle rays and schools of deepwater fish such as jacks. There are even one or two large grouper.

However, you always meet barracuda. The larger ones ignore you, but the smaller, younger ones come to investigate before moving on, unless you are wearing a fluorescent orange or yellow bathing costume, then they will follow you around like pets.

Strong currents do occur in the vicinity of the Bianca C, but there are none capable of shifting its 18,427 ton gross mass, and as long as you dive at slack water, there are no currents at all. Sometimes there may be a surface current, but that fades at 50 feet or so, when it encounters the fringing reef.

The Bianca C still sits where it sank, on a level sand plain, the hull split a third of the length from the stem, the fracture line running right down both sides. The top decks suffered most, buckling inward and downward for three to four decks and then to starboard, giving the impression that the ship is listing to one side. Go aft to the stern and you will see it is not.

The Bianca C is not so much a dangerous dive as a deep dive. Once the wreck is found, using landmarks (each dive operator has a personal favourite), a safety line is attached to the anchor line, which is hooked onto the ship.

The top decks lie at 90 feet and most dives proceed around the stern, where you can 'swim' in the pools, visit the wheel-house on the aft deck and peer down at the sandy plain below. Because of the depth, the maximum dive time is 15-17 minutes.

Once everyone is back on the safety line, it is cast off and the slow ascent commences to the surface, where everyone has a different story to

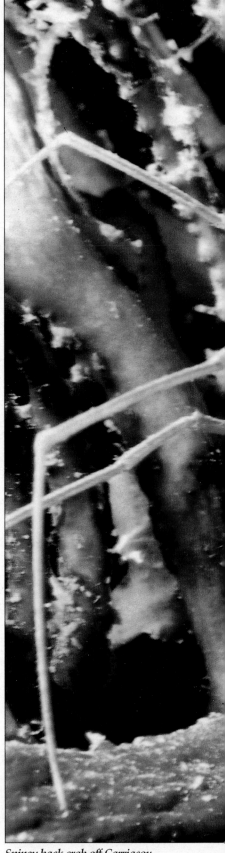

Spiney back crab off Carriacou
Courtesy: Niki Wiedinger

tell, and new myths are invented.

Another wreck, the **Buccaneer**, a 42-foot, two-masted sloop sank 18 years ago. It had been stripped before sinking so now only the superstructure lies on its side in 80 feet of water, making it ideal for photography. Being close to Molinere Reef it is sometimes visited on night dives.

Three Part Wreck - a safe easy wreck dive, even for a novice. The wreck rests at about 40 feet on a sandy seabed, close to a reef and the home to many angel fish and stingrays.

Finally, the **SS Orinoco** lies just off La Sagesse Point. Wrecked on November 1, 1900, on the rocks off the headland, it is in rough water, and only suitable for experienced divers.

Other Grenada dive sites (wall dives)

The wall dive sites are both natural and man-made. The natural walls usually only go as deep as 100 feet before reaching a sandy bottom. The deepest man-made wall goes down to 140 feet. The most popular dives are the **Red Buoy** and the **Grand Mal Canyon**. Red Buoy has a large quantity of Admiralty anchors from a depth of 70 feet. Along the top of the wall there is a profusion of blue vase sponges. Grand Mal Canyon is heavily silted but teeming with marine life.

There are four main natural wall sites - Happy Hill, Halifax Bay, Black Coral Wall and Flamingo Bay.

Happy Hill - within easy snorkelling distance from the shore, this is a natural wall with a quantity of soft corals, gorgonians and sea-whips.

Halifax Bay - an extended wall with canyons and two swim-through caves (barrel and other tube sponges can be found here).

Black Coral Wall - as the name suggests there is a lot of black coral, some as shallow as 40 feet. Close to the wall are the **Mounds** - a series of pinnacles. There is a constantly changing panorama of fish and the occasional tarpon.

Flamingo Bay - a wall diive that runs from the bay to Happy Hill. There are lots of black coral and various schools of fish.

Reef Dives

There are four main reef areas with a variety of dive sites on each of them. Most soft corals and some hard corals are out during the day providing spectacular sights. Visibility is between 60 - 100 feet, unless it rains, when it can drop to around 30 feet.

Lobster off Carriacou
Courtesy: Niki Wiedinger

Bass Reef - stretching from Red Buoy down to Point Salines, it is the largest in the area and the furthest out to sea. It consists mostly of gentle drift dives through vast shoals of creole wrasse and chromis. The top of the reef is about 20-30 feet and the topography changes with the coral.

Grand Mal Reef - is a shallow gently sloping reef garden with schools of goat fish and frequent sightings of large porcupine fish.

Spice Island Reef - is in 20 - 50 feet of water and contains a sloping wall with valleys. There is a sandy area nearby which attracts the reef fish. In each clump of rock there are several small fish of different species, as well as the occasional octopus hiding in holes.

Molinere Reef - is ideal for snorkellors, but for divers there are canyons and valleys that descend 30 - 40 feet with a variety of smaller reef fish, including jacknife and spotted drums. Sea-horses are found in the clusters of soft coral and garden eels abound.

Coral reefs off Grenada
Courtesy: David Macnaghten

Dragon Bay - deep channels of volcanic rock rise from a sandy bottom, 60 feet beneath the reef top. This is a very suitable dive for beginners with the opportunity to see sea-horses and manta rays.

Whibles Reef - A drift dive, for the advanced diver accustomed to dealing with strong currents along the reef, with sand sharks, barracuda and large groupers among the coral heads.

Channel Reef - a shallow reef that drops off to form a deepwater entrance to St George's harbour. Turtles, lobster and a variety of soft corals provide a superb backdrop for a collection of anchors lost by the many ships that visited the port over the years.

For the experienced diver

Areas around the submarine volcano **Kick 'em Jenny** are the furthest sites offshore, and are thought by many to be the best. These dives offer excellent visibility of about 100 feet and are a favourite of the area's divemasters. Rare and plentiful coral and marine life can be seen there. This dive site is often combined with the area around Isle de Ronde in a two-tank dive.

Barracuda among the reefs
Courtesy: David Macnaghten

Carriacou dive sites

Sandy Island - extensive reefs lie just offshore, ranging to a maximum depth of 70 feet. Many fish and turtles populate this area which is also an excellent night dive.

Sister Rocks - just off Point Cistern and Jack Iron Point. A great dive

Dive party at Silver Beach Diving, Silver Beach Hotel, Carriacou

to 100 feet with spectacular walls, large rocks and plenty of barracuda. Because strong currents are often present, this is a dive for experienced divers only.

Pago Das Garden - close to Frigate Island, with an amazing array of corals and abundant marine life. Depths range from 40-80 feet.

Two Sisters of Ronde Island - not to be confused with the Sister Rocks of Point Cistern, this is one of the most spectacular dives in the Grenadines. There are walls and drop-offs descending to 180 feet as well as a mysterious cavern. The depth and strong currents make this a dive for the experienced diver only.

Mabouya Island - this island just off Hillsborough Bay offers a variety of interesting reefs and fish life, including sharks, rays, eels and turtles.

Saline Island - because of currents this is an ideal drift dive providing the opportunity to see extensive reef formations.

A dive party leave Silver Beach jetty and head for Sandy Island, just off Carriacou

General information for the visitor

Briefly about the country

Located in the Eastern Caribbean, Grenada is the southernmost of the Windward Islands, 100 miles north of Venezuela and 158 miles south of Barbados. On the charts it is 12 degrees north of the equator and 61 degrees 40" west longitude. The three-island nation, which includes Carriacou and Petit Martinique, has a land area of 133 square miles. Grenada itself is 12 miles wide and 21 miles long, with the capital city, St George's, and most tourist facilities located on the southwestern tip of the island. It is mountainous and thickly wooded, with streams, rivers and a number of waterfalls. The central mountain range consists of a number of ridges, some of which contain crater basins. The highest point is Mount St Catherine at 2,756ft above sea level. To the north are a chain of tiny islands that lead like stepping stones to Carriacou, Petit Martinique and the Grenadines.

Grenada is an English speaking country with a cosmopolitan population of around 95,000 people. The island is divided into six parishes and there are five main towns with many villages along the coastline and in the hills linked by a well planned road system. St George's is situated in a sheltered bay in the southwestern part of the island.

These islands were inhabited for thousands of years by the Siboneys, Arawaks and Caribs. Christopher Columbus sighted Grenada on his third voyage in 1498. In the ensuing colonisation, these Amerindian races were wiped out. In the colonial wars of the eighteenth century Britain and France traded the island back and forth until 1783 when it came solely under British rule. On February 7 1974 Grenada won Independence.

Grenada is now one of the world's chief suppliers of the "twin crop" of nutmeg and mace, and numerous other spices are grown in lesser quantities. It has come to be known internationally as the "Isle of Spice". Other agricultural products include cocoa, banana, coconut, sugar cane, citrus and a profusion of fruits and vegetables. The main industries are agriculture, commerce, construction, tourism, manufacturing, transportation and communications.

Climate: Annual average temperature - high 80 degrees Fahrenheit, low 70 degrees Fahrenheit. The annual rainfall varies from 50 inches in the low coastal regions to 160 inches in the wet central mountains. Approximate sunrise 06.00 and sunset at 18.00 hours.

Time zone: AST (GMT - 4 hrs, EST + 1 hr).

Currency: Eastern Caribbean Dollar (EC$), valued at EC$ 2.70 to US$1.

Electricity: 230 volts, 50 ac. Some hotels have special outlets providing 110 ac current. Transformers and adapters are generally needed.

Post Offices: Main post office is on the Carenage, St George's. Stamps are on sale at most hotels and shops.

Media: One television station, three radio stations, several weekly newspapers and a number of high quality free tourist guides and magazines.

Medical Facilities: Doctors are on call at most hotels. Diving decompression chamber available. Pharmaceutical services. Air ambulance. 24 hour casualty department. Emergency dental facilities.

Arriving

Airports: Point Salines International Airport, is five miles from St George's, the capital. Taxis/Transport - All fares are fixed by the Grenada Board of Tourism and are quoted in US Dollars. Visitors are recommended to check the price and currency beforehand.

Entry requirements: Passports are not required for US, British & Canadian citizens, provided they have two documents proving citizenship, one with a photograph - a voter's registration card, birth certificate or expired passport - and an onward or return ticket. No visa required by Commonwealth, US, Canada, French and German citizens. Currency restrictions - none. Departure Tax - EC$35.

Airlines: Aereotuy, Air Canada, Air Europe, Aeropostal, Airlines of Carriacou, American Airlines, BWIA, British Airways, Caledonian Airways, Canada 3000, Helenair and LIAT.

Gateways: Baltimore, Frankfurt, London, Miami, Milan, New York, Puerto Rico, Toronto and Zurich. Transfers through Antigua, Barbados & Trinidad.

Cruise Lines: American-Canadian, Carnival, Chandris, Clipper, Costa, Cunard, Epirotiki, Exploration, Exprinter, Hapag Lloyd, Holland America, Home Line, Kloster, NCL, North Star, Ocean Cruise Line, P & O Premier, Regency, Royal Caribbean, Royal Cruise Line, Royal Viking, Salen, Seaburn and Sinbad .

Pet regulations: A permit must be obtained from the Veterinary Office, Ministry of Agriculture, before the pets arrive in Grenada.

Once you are there

Moving around: Driving is on the left hand side of the road. Rentals available include - Cars, scooters, bicycles and four-wheel drive vehicles. Temporary licence/permit requirements (on the strength of a valid foreign or international permit) - A visitor's driving license is required and costs EC$30 for a temporary license and EC$60 for a full year. Taxis are plentiful and willing to tour; they are unmetered, so check fares in advance.

Excursions: Grenada's sister islands of Carriacou and Petit Martinique lie to the north, at the beginning of the Grenadine chain. Lauriston International Airport, Carriacou, is a short hop away by air (twenty minutes) or four hours by ferry. A narrow strip of water separates Petit Martinique and Carriacou and this requires a boat ride. Boats leave the Carenage for Carriacou every morning except Mondays and Thursdays, times vary. Return fare US $12.

Sports: Grenada is a good centre for sailing, not only in its own waters, but in the chain of small Grenadine islands to the north. Spice Island Yacht Charters or Grenada Yacht Services and a number of operators listed here can get you started. For the less ambitious sailors, there are coastal cruises by the Rhum Runner or the Loafer, and plenty of Sailfish, Sunfish and Hobie-cats. The sports fishing is good. The scuba diving is excellent in clear water, with extensive reefs and some interesting wreck sites, including the Caribbean's biggest, the Bianca C., an Italian cruise liner that sank in 1961, and now lying in 120 feet of water. There are a number of health clubs open to tourists.

Marriage requirements: For people wishing to wed in Grenada, the following is required:

Dirk and Bettina fell in love and got married in Grenada. Like hundreds of young couples with hectic schedules, combining a wedding, honeymoon and a holiday of a lifetime is becoming a popular trend. Most hotels cater for weddings. Couples can have a traditional wedding or if they prefer, can have a more casual service.

Grenadians are often treated to the sight of a traditional horse-drawn carriage driving around St George's. This new venture provides a novel view of the city and surrounding districts. It is also ideally suited for weddings.

All documents and papers must be presented in English. If presented in another language, these should be translated into English and certified by a Notary Public.

A certificate of non-marriage must be obtained in your country of residence. This consists of a letter from a clergyman/woman, lawyer, or Registry (on their official letterhead) attesting to the fact that the parties involved have not been married previously. In cases where the parties involved are divorced, the Final Divorce document must be presented.

If a minor is party to the marriage (a person under 21 years of age) a special form must be obtained from the Prime Minister's Office, Botanical Gardens, St George's. This form must be signed by the parents of the party concerned and certified by a Notary Public.

Passports and Birth Certificates must be presented by both parties.

Applicants must be residents on the island for three days before making an application for a Marriage Licence.

The Procedure is as follows: Stamp Duty - purchase EC $25 worth of stamps at a post office (one EC $10 stamp and three EC $5 stamps).

All documents must be shown at the Registrar's Office, Ministry of Health, Carenage, St George's. The marriage licence which costs EC $10 is obtainable from the Treasury Office.

All documents and stamps then go to the Cabinet Secretary at the Prime Minister's Office, Botanical Gardens, St George's. Documents for divorced parties are sent to the Ministry of Legal Affairs by the Cabinet Secretary.

Copies of the Marriage Registration can be obtained at the Court Registry for EC $2.

Allow, at least, two days for the entire procedure. No blood test is required.

Religion/Churches: Anglican/Episcopalin, Bahai, Baptist,

Church of Jesus Christ and Latter Day Saints, First Church of Christ Scientist, Jehovah's Witnesses, Mennonite, Methodist, Islamic, Pentecostal, Presbyterian, Roman Catholic, Salvation Army and Seventh Day Adventist. Information on locations and times of services available at most hotels.

Banks

Banking hours are usually from Monday - Thursday 8.00 am to 2.00 pm and Friday 8.00am to 1.00 pm and 2.30 pm to 5.00pm.

Barclays Bank has three offices in Grenada; at Church and Halifax Streets, St George's Tel: 440 3232 at Grenville, St Andrew Tel: 442 7220 and in Grand Anse, St George Tel: 444 1184. They also have a branch in Hillsborough, Carriacou Tel: 443 7232.

Grenada Bank of Commerce has two branches; at Cross and Halifax Streets, St George's Tel: 440 3521 and in Grand Anse, St George Tel: 444 4919.

Grenada Co-operative Bank has three branches; Church Street, St George's Tel: 440 2111/3549, Fax: 440 6600 at Victoria Street, Grenville, St Andrew Tel: 442 7748, Fax: 442 8400 and at Main Street, Sauteurs, St Patrick Tel: 442 9247, Fax: 442 9888.

Grenada Development Bank has two branches; on Halifax Street, St George's Tel: 440 2382 and at Grenville, St Andrew Tel: 442 6464.

National Commercial Bank of Grenada Limited has six offices; at Halifax and Hillsborough Streets, St George's Tel: 440 3566/8; Grenville, St Andrew Tel: 442 7532; Gouyave, St John Tel: 444 8353; Hillsborough, Carriacou Tel: 443 7289; St David Tel: 444 6355 and Grand Anse, St George Tel: 444 2627.

Scotiabank has two branches; on Halifax Street, St George's Tel: 440 3274 and Grand Anse Shopping Centre, St George Tel: 444 1917.

Sights around the country

Popular sights in St George's

The Carenage is a horse-shoe shaped harbour, surrounded by a road and walkway with a variety of shops, restaurants, vendors and commercial businesses. It provides picturesque views of the capital and is at the centre of most activity in St George's with ocean-going cruise ships, schooners, fishing boats and day-tripper boats constantly on the move.

The Esplanade is located on the bay side of St George's and separated from the Carenage by a high ridge. Access to the Esplanade is through the Sendall Tunnel to the fish and meat markets. Minibuses and taxis provide transportation from here to all parts of the island.

Grenada National Museum. Once an old French army barracks and prison dating back to 1704. The museum includes interesting artefacts from the Arawak and Carib era. There are cultural and historical items offering a glimpse into the nation's past.

The Sendall Tunnel was completed in 1895 and named after Governor Sir Walter Sendall. It is 12 feet high and 350 feet long and it was considered a technological achievement at the time. The tunnel connects the Carenage and the Esplanade.

Fort George, the oldest structure in the country was completed in 1705. There are old tunnels and narrow staircases and the ramparts evoke a feeling of the past. It provides a stunning view of the capital, the Carenage, the harbour, the lagoon and adjoining coastlines and hillsides. Ideal for photography. It is now the headquarters of the Royal Grenada Police Force but is accessible for sightseeing.

Fort Matthew was constructed by the French in 1779 as a siege fort in the battles with the British.

Fort Frederick on Richmond Hill, was built in 1791, and provides a panoramic view of St George's.

The Market Square was established in 1791 and is central to the life of the nation. Today, it provides the visitor with an explosion of fruits, vegetables and an incredible variety of spices and their by-products - jams, jellies, sauces, drinks, curry and ornamental handicrafts. It is also the starting point for parades, political rallies and religious activities. Taxis and minibuses are also stationed here.

The Anglican Church was rebuilt in 1825 on the original site constructed by French Catholics. There are a number of historic plaques and statues.

St Andrew's Presbytery, also known as the Scots' Kirk, was built in 1830 by the Freemasons

St George's Roman Catholic Church was built in 1884 but the tower dates back to 1814.

St George's Methodist Church was built in 1820 and is the oldest original church in St George's.

York House, named after the Duke of York's eighteenth century visit, now houses the Houses of Parliament and the Senate on the top floor, and the Supreme Court on the lower floor. A fine example of Georgian architecture.

The Grenada National Library was established on the Carenage in 1892.

Marryshow House was the home of the 'Father of the Federation' T A Marryshow, the political promoter of one Westindian nation. It is now the local centre of the University of the Westindies and a cultural theatre for plays and shows.

The Queen's Park is used for horse-racing, cricket, football, athletics and all international sports, carnival, pageants, political rallies and other events.

The Botanical Gardens offer fine examples of the island's plant and vegetation life. They were first opened in 1887.

Around Grenada

Bay Gardens, in the suburb of St Paul, these gardens provide a version of a tropical paradise.

Camp Fedon, a flat peak in the central mountain range on the Grand Etang ridge where the rebel Fedon was able to fend off the British attacks for a considerable time.

De La Grenade Industries, a spice processing plant manufactures international award winning products - some with century old secret recipes. Open to tours.

Carib's Leap is at the back of the Roman Catholic Church on the hill in Sauteurs, St Patrick. A chilling cliff drop of over 100 feet, where, in the mid-seventeenth century, the Carib warriors chose to die rather than surrender to the French.

Dougaldston Spice Estate is an historical monument to Grenada's past and where many spices are grown and processed.

Gouyave, set on the west coast, this mainly fishing village has a reputation for its active night life. It is also the setting for the annual Fisherman's Birthday festival.

Grand Etang Lake, is located in an old crater, about 1,740 feet above sea level, within the central mountain range and surrounded by a rainforest.

Grand Etang Forest Centre, is a major attraction close to the Grand Etang Lake. The centre provides information on wildlife, vegetation, forestry, history and culture.

Grenville, on the east coast offers visitors lots of local dishes and drinks. There is a handicraft industry and local products are of the highest quality. It is also known as Rainbow City. Each year there are two weeks of exhibitions, music shows, presentations and celebrations. The Saturday market is filled with fish, fruits, vegetables, spices and freshly baked bread.

Levera National Park, located on the island's north-east coast is a protected area that has a lot to offer both locals and visitors. The Levera Centre gives complete information and is where guides can be arranged to trek to the 'Welcome Stone' for a superb view of the park, coastline and off-shore islands. Here the beaches are protected by inshore reefs and the swimming is safe inside the reef. There is a mangrove swamp and Levera Pond is host to migratory birds all year round.

Lake Antoine, is located north of Grenville along the spectacular coast road, is an extinct volcanic crater is considered a unique geological phenomenon.

La Sagesse Nature Centre, for the nature lover, an ideal site to explore the bird life and the mangrove estuary. There are three beaches with superb coral reefs nearby.

Mount Rich Amerindian Remains in the parish of St Patrick, along the St Patrick river valley at Mount Rich village, there is a large rock with visible petroglyphs. These carvings are almost all that remains of the former way of life of the Amerindians. There is speculation that this huge rock may have been an altar stone.

River Sallee Boiling Springs, located between Lake Antoine and Levera Pond on the northeast coast, these boiling springs are regarded as being of spiritual importance by local people and are believed to possess healing powers. Visitors will find candles lit by those seeking spiritual assistance. There are both clear and sulphurous boiling springs.

River Antoine Rum Distillery, the oldest functioning rum distillery in the Caribbean, has changed little since it was first put into production in the 1800s. A mile down the road from Lake Antoine, this privately-owned distillery uses the original water-driven wheel to crush the sugar cane and the stills are fired up in the traditional way. Sample real rum at one of the treasures of Grenada.

Westerhall Rum Distillery, about twenty minutes from St George's on the southern main road north of Westerhall Bay. This distillery uses modern methods of rum production but many of the artefacts of earlier rum production are on sight and could be used if required.

Waterfalls

Annandale Falls are fifteen minutes from St George's and provide recreational facilities and excellent scenic views.

Concorde Falls, within the Concorde valley are three beautiful waterfalls. Ideal for swimming. The first, Concorde Falls, is accessible by road, the second, Au Coin, and the third, Fontainbleu, are accessible only by foot. At Fontainbleu the water cascades from 65 feet to form a clear water pool.

Marquis Falls, two miles south of Grenville, St Andrew, is the highest waterfall in Grenada. There are plans to improve access and provide visitor facilities.

Seven Sisters Falls is an hour's drive from St George's. You will find the island's most pristine and tranquil falls, with fairly easy access.

Sights in Carriacou

Sandy Island - Marine Park. Surrounded by white sands, this tiny island has the most spectacular coral reef, the home to shoals of variegated tropical fish in clear, blue water. Ideal for picnics, this beutiful island has been used as the backdrop for television and magazine advertisements.

White Island - Marine Park. Virgin reef, beautiful white sand - ideal for picnics, snorkelling, diving and any water sport.

Amerindian Well - Harvey Vale. Only 40 feet from the sea, this source of natural mineral water can do wonders for your health.

Dumfries Historical Site. 200 years of history, experience what life on a plantation was really like.

Paradise Beach. Peaceful, beautiful calm seas - a gem in the Grenadines.

The Botanical Gardens. Displays an interesting selection of exotic, tropical plants and flowers - naturally refreshing.

Canute Calliste Art Gallery. Meet the famous folklore artist and painter in person and experience his work in progress. Calliste

Concorde Falls

has painted as many as 16 works in a single day.

Anglican Rectory Garden. Formerly an old Bousejour Great House, this site has a lot of history and an amazing variety of cactus.

Windward. The home of the old boat building industry. From here you can take a short boat ride to Petit Martinique.

Belair Historical Site. Entwined here are the forces of nature, history and culture.

Ningo Well. The first well ever built on Carriacou.

Anse La Roche Beach. A private and unspoilt beach at the foot of the famous High North Range.

Belair National Park. This is probably the most spectacular view of the northern side of the island. From here you can see Petit Martinique. An array of small fishing boats always decorate the blue-green water.

Oyster Beds. Take the trail from Tyrrel Bay. Then a short boat ride. Observe the oyster growth emerging from the roots of the mangrove. The trail continues to the village of L'Esterre with many scenic views.

Petit Martinique

This dependency of Grenada has a very strong family culture. It also has one of the highest per capita incomes in the Eastern Caribbean. A twenty minute boat trip from Carriacou and worth a visit, especially for its perfect sunsets looking back over Carriacou and the Grenadines.

Annual events

Dates vary from year to year so please check with organisers or tourist board. Grenada Board of Tourism Tel: (809) 440 2001.

JANUARY

New Year's Day (Public Holiday). Consists of Gala Balls and parties at hotels, discos and clubs. Church services held throughout the various parishes to welcome the New Year.

Grenada Sailing Festival. Attracting many overseas competitors and local sailing talent. Grenada Yacht Club Tel: (809) 440 3050.

Grenada Triathlon. Triathlon individual and three-person team races, 25 kilometre Cycle, 1 kilometre Swim and five kilometre Run Race on Day One. A Triathlon Medley Relay on Day Two, comprising a three person team (each with at least one female member) with each team completing a 1.5 kilometre swim, a 40 kilometre cycling race and a 10 kilometre run (Annual Event). Tel: (809) 440 3343. Fax: (809) 440 7088.

Spice Island Billfishing Tournament. This annual event features over EC $100,000 in prizes to be won during three days of competition, including awards for first, second and third place boats. This tournament observes International Game Fishing Association (IGFA) rules. Tel: (809) 440 3327 Fax: (809) 440 4110.

FEBRUARY

Carriacou Carnival Celebrations. Includes male and female disguise shows, Kiddies Carnival, Queen Show, King and Queen of the Band and a street parade. Tel: (809) 443 7948 or (809) 440 2001 (Tourist Board).

Independence Day Celebrations. February 7 (Public Holiday). Grenada, Carriacou and Petit Martinique. Activities include a military parade at Queens Park. Tel: (809) 440 2255.

True Blue "Indigo" Yacht Race/Pursuit Race. Yacht Race ending at True Blue Inn. Tel: (809) 440 3050.

MARCH

St Patrick's Day Fiesta Celebrations. An exposition of local arts and crafts, agricultural produce, food and drinks, together with a Cultural Extravaganza and Mini Street Festival. This grand event is celebrated at Sauteurs in the parish of St Patrick. Tel: (809) 442 7109 or (809) 440 2001 (Tourist Board).

Carl Schuster Memorial Round Grenada Yacht Race. Contact the Grenada Yacht Service for further information. Tel: (809) 440 2508.

Intercol (Intercollege) Sports. Students from Grenada's secondary schools compete in sporting events, at Queen's Park, St George's. Tel: (809) 440 2001 (Tourist Board).

APRIL

Good Friday (Public Holiday).

Easter Dinghy Races. Contact the Grenada Yacht Services for further information. Tel: (809) 440 2508.

Petit Martinique Regatta, Easter weekend.

Easter Monday (Public Holiday).

St Mark's Day Fiesta. Celebrated in the seaside village of Victoria in St Mark. Lots of local craft, agricultural and cultural exhibits as well as food, drinks and music.Tel: (809) 440 2001 (Tourist Board).

MAY

Labour Day (Public Holiday). Workers' celebrations, involving rallies and fetes at prescribed locations.

La Source Grand Anse Race. Yacht Race around the buoys in Grand Anse Bay. Tel: (809) 440 3050.

Whit Monday (Public Holiday). Sporting activities and annual convention of the Methodist Community in Grenada.

JUNE

Corpus Christi (Public Holiday). Religious processions and traditional planting of food crops by Grenadians.

Volley Ball Club Championship. For further information contact the Ministry of Sports. Tel: (809) 440 2734.

Outfitter's International Cup South Coast Yacht Race. Pursuit Race starting and ending on Grenada's south coast. Contact Yacht Services for further information. Tel: (809) 440 2508.

Fisherman's Birthday Celebrations. Involves blessing fishing boats and nets, boat racing, culminating in a mini carnival, with street dancing. The most popular town for the celebration is Gouyave in the parish of St John. Tel: (809) 440 2001 (Tourist Board).

JULY

Venezuela Independence Day Regatta. Two days of racing from St George's Harbour to the south coast and back. Tel: (809) 440 3050.

Carriacou Regatta. Feeder race from St George's to Carriacou Annual Regatta. - Workboat races, cultural shows, street parties, sporting activities, artistic performances and Big Drum Dancing.

AUGUST

CARICOM Day (Public Holiday). Held on the first Monday.

Rainbow City Festival. Popular annual festival in Grenville in the parish of St Andrew. There are displays of local arts and crafts, products of local manufacturers, farmers and livestock. Plenty of food, drinks and music to keep the festival spirit alive. Tel: (809) 440 2001 (Tourist Board).

Grenada Carnival. Held on the second weekend. Pageant, King and Queen of Carnival, steelband and calypso competitions, with a massive last lap "jump-up" on Tuesday. This is Grenada's largest celebration. Tel: (809) 440 2001 (Tourist Board).

OCTOBER

Beach Feast. A fun-filled weekend of beach parties and watersports activities. Tel: (809) 440 2001 (Tourist Board).

Thanksgiving Day (Public Holiday).

NOVEMBER

Match Racing off Grand Anse. Floating headquarters provides the venue for one-on-one racing in fast dinghies. Tel: (809) 440 2001 (Tourist Board).

DECEMBER

Carriacou Parang Festival. Music festival and cultural extravaganza. Tel: (809) 443 7948.

Christmas Day & Boxing Day Festivities. (Public Holidays) Family celebrations and carol singing. Church festivities nationwide.

New Year's Eve. Banquets and celebrations at clubs and hotels.

Midnight Marathon. (New Year's Eve) Half Marathon at Grenville. Tel: (809) 442 6660 or (809) 440 2001 (Tourist Board).

St Patrick's Day Fiesta, celebrated every March in Sauteurs, St Patrick

Accommodation

Hotels, Apartments and Guest Houses in Grenada

Many new hotels, apartments and seaside resorts have been situated close to the magnificent Grand Anse Beach, and on the many inlets and points along the southeast coast.

Bailey's Inn, Springs, PO Box 82, St George's. Tel: (809) 440 2912. Fax: (809) 440 0532. Facilities offered are 14 rooms with private baths and two self-contained apartments. There is a dining room, bar, boutique, bus and car rental, maid service, laundry facilities, ceiling fans. Westindian specialities served daily in the restaurant.

Blue Horizons Cottage Hotel, Grand Anse, PO Box 41, St George's. Tel: (809) 444 4316/4592, Fax: (809) 444 2815. There are 32 rooms. Amenities available are fully equipped kitchenettes with radios, ceiling fans, hair dryers, air-conditioning, colour television and private patios. There are also two bars, car rental, dining room, laundry service, telephone, pool, jacuzzi, water sports and meeting room.

Calabash Hotel, L'Anse aux Epines, PO Box 382, St George's. Tel: (809) 444 4334, (800) 528 5835, Fax: (809) 444 4804. There are 28 suites - eight with private pools and 14 with whirlpools. Other facilities include dining room, bar, air-conditioning, beach, pool, water sports, laundry service, room service, beach bar and conference facility for up to 40 people.

Camerhogne Park Hotel, Grand Anse, PO Box 378, St George's. Tel: (809) 444 4587/4110, Fax: (809) 440 4847. 25 rooms. Facilities are restaurant, bar, maid service, telephone, cable television and island tours. Car rentals can be arranged.

Cannon Ball Apartments, True Blue, St George. Tel: (809) 444 4384, Fax: (809) 444 3641. 14 self-contained, two-bedroom apartments are conveniently located just three miles from the airport and Grand Anse Beach. Each unit features a full kitchenette and television. Facilities include airport transfers, maid service and laundry service.

Cedars Inn, True Blue, PO Box 73, St George's. Tel: (809) 444 4641/1404, Fax: (809) 444 4652. Cedars Inn is a new 20 room hotel which features private balconies, air-conditioning, fully equipped baths, telephone, colour television. There is a restaurant, swimming pool, pool bar, free shuttle to airport. Golf, tennis, sightseeing tours and water sports can be arranged.

Cinnamon Hill and Beach Club, Grand Anse Beach, PO Box 292, St George's. Tel: (809) 444 4301/2/3 or 440 3459, Fax: (809) 444 2874, A Spanish-style village condominium with dining room, cocktail bar, 20 air-conditioned rooms, beach, laundry service, telephone, swimming pool, room service.

Coral Cove Cottages & Apartments, L'Anse aux Epines, PO Box 487, St George's. Tel: (809) 444 4422/4217 or (800) 322 1753, Fax: (809) 444 4718. There are eleven one and two-bedroom Spanish-style cottages and apartments. Amenities beach, pool, tennis court, laundry service and maid/cook.

Coyaba Beach Resort, Grand Anse Beach, PO Box 336, St George's. Tel: (809) 444 4129/4612/4613, Fax: (809) 444 4808. Forty spacious rooms. Each air-conditioned, double-bedroom with a balcony or patio, telephone and television, spacious bath. Facilities include two restaurants, two bars, water sports, cable television, laundry service, outdoor sports and a full range of water activities.

Fairdale Holiday Apartments, L'Anse aux Epines, PO Box 180, St George's. Tel: (809) 444 4579, Fax: (809) 440 4113 (attn. Fairdale). These fully furnished, self-contained apartments come with a full kitchen and spacious balcony. Other facilities include beach, air-conditioning, ceiling fans, cable television, telephone, hair dryers, maid service, laundry service and a gift shop.

The Flamboyant Hotel & Cottages, Grand Anse Beach, PO Box 214, St George's. Tel: (809) 444 4247/1463/1462/1684, Fax: (809) 444 1234, . These 39 tastefully decorated one or two bedroom apartments are air-conditioned. Each suite has a fully equipped kitchen, living room and ceiling fan. All units have cable television, radio, telephone, and a private veranda. Facilities include restaurant, bar, conference room, pool, maid service, laundry service and complimentary snorkelling gear.

Fox Inn, Point Salines, PO Box 205, St George's. Tel: (809) 444 4123/4177 or (800) 322 1753, Fax: (809) 444 4177, Fox Inn offers 16 double rooms and six apartments, fully furnished and air-conditioned. Facilities are dining room, bar, pool, car rental, laundry service, radio, telephone and room service.

Gem Holiday Beach Resort, Morne Rouge Bay, PO Box 58, St George's. Tel: (809) 444 4224/1189/2288, Fax: (809) 444 1189. There are 17 modern, air-conditioned apartment suites with fully equipped kitchenette, sitting room and balcony. Amenities include restaurant, bar, satellite television, telephone, ceiling fans, laundry and maid service.

Grand View Inn, Grand Anse, PO Box 614, St George's. Tel: (809) 444 4984, Fax: (809) 444 2832 (attn. Grand View). The Inn features 20 fully equipped units, complete with tropical gardens, walkways, and a waterfall pool.

Grenada Rainbow City Inn, Grenville, PO Box 23, St Andrew. Tel: (809) 442 7714. There are 15 rooms including three self-contained units. Facilities include private balconies, dining room, cocktail, conference room. Sightseeing arranged on request.

Grenada Renaissance Resort, Grand Anse Beach, PO Box 441, St George's. Tel: (809) 444 4371/5 & 444 4622/5, Fax: (809) 444 4800. This premier two-storey resort offers 186 rooms all elegantly decorated with genuine mahogany furnishings, with each room featuring its own private balcony or patio. All accommodations feature air-conditioning, hair dryers, direct-dial telephone, and colour television. Amenities include a beach-front open-air restaurant, pool-side snack bar, beach bar, and cocktail lounge. There is an array of water sports and outdoor activities.

Hibiscus Hotel, Grand Anse, PO Box 279, St George's. Tel: (809) 444 4233/4008 or (800) 322 1753, Fax: (809) 440 2873. Ten duplex-style cottages. Amenities include a restaurant, dining room, bar, air-conditioning, laundry service, television, pool and telephone.

Holiday Haven Cottages, L'Anse aux Epines, St George. Tel: (809) 440 2606/444 4325/4343. Twelve air-conditioned villas and apartments include a full kitchen, dining and living room, and a large veranda. Amenities are dining room, maid service, cable television and private telephone.

Homestead Guest House, St Peter's Street, Gouyave, St John. Tel: (809) 444 8526. Four single and double rooms, bar and restaurant.

Rex Grenadian Hotel, Point Salines

Accommodation

Horse Shoe Beach Hotel, L'Anse aux Epines, PO Box 174, St George's. Tel: (809) 444 4410/4244, Fax, (809) 444 4844. It consists of 12 villas, all complete with king-sized, canopied beds, air-conditioning, private patio, and fully-equipped kitchen. The new wing has six deluxe units plus four standard rooms furnished in elegant rattan. Also available - dining room, lounge, beach front pool and pool bar, barbecue area. Car rental can be arranged.

Hotel Amanda, Lowther's Lane, PO Box 513, St George's. Tel: (809) 440 2409. There are 14 elegantly decorated rooms.

Lakeside Guest House, Lakeside, Belmont, St George's. Tel: (809) 440 2365. Nine single and double rooms with kitchenette and telephone.

L'Anse aux Epines Cottages, L'Anse aux Epines, PO Box 187, St George's. Tel: (809) 444 4565/4227, Fax: (809) 444 2802. Eleven charming one and two-bedroom cottages and apartments are fully equipped and within an easy walk of a variety of restaurants. Facilities include beach, boating, air-conditioning, television, laundry service, maid/cook and gazebo.

La Sagesse Nature Centre, PO Box 44, St George's. Tel: (809) 444 6458, Fax: (809) 444 6458. The old manor house retains its original grandeur with high ceilings, screened window and fans. Each room has a hot-water bath and kitchenette. Facilities include a restaurant, beach bar, water sports, nature trails, maid and laundry service, telephone and satellite television.

La Source, Pink Gin Beach, Point Salines, PO Box 852, St George's. Tel: (809) 444 2556, Fax: (809) 444 2541. La Source is one of Grenada's all-inclusive resorts. The 100 room complex is set in acres of private land and has its own beach. Included in the rates are airport transfer, accommodation, taxes, all meals, drinks, land and water sports, instructions, and Oasis treatments.

Mace Hotel, Grand Anse, St George. Tel: (809) 444 4788. Fourteen rooms, television, bar and restaurant.

Maffiken Apartments, Grand Anse, PO Box 534, St George's. Tel: (809) 444 4255/4522, Fax: (809) 444 2832. Self-contained apartments, each with a large balcony, maid service, television, laundry, offering comfortable and convenient accommodation.

Mahogany Run, Morne Rouge Bay, PO Box 730, St George's. Tel: (809) 444 3171, Fax: (809) 444 3172. Long leases available. 15 apartments available in three different sizes and styles. Facilities include restaurant, bar, beach club, free use of snorkelling gear, bicycle rental, golf, scuba, laundry service, cellular phone rental, in-room safe. Excursions to island sites are available.

Mamma's Lodge, PO Box 248, St George's. Tel: (809) 440 1459/1623, Fax: (809) 440 7788. Mamma's offer nine rooms with fans, and the dining room specialises in local cuisine. There is also a boutique on the premises.

Mitchell's Guest House, Tyrrel Street, St George's. Tel: (809) 440 2803. Eleven single and double rooms with telephone, television and kitchenette.

Morne Fendue Plantation House, St Patrick. Tel: (809) 442 9330. Three rooms, television, telephone, sports available, cooking facilities and bar.

No Problem Apartment Hotel, True Blue, PO Box 280, St George's. Tel: (809) 444 4634/5, Fax: (809) 444 2803. No Problem has 20 suites, each air-conditioned and contains two twin beds, a complete kitchenette, radio, satellite, television and telephone. There is also a pool and pool bar, laundry service, conference centre,

No Problem Apartment Hotel, True Blue

boutique, mini-mart, free bicycles, free transport to and from airport and Grand Anse Beach and a free welcome drink.

Palm Court Apartment, Grand Anse, PO Box 243, St George's. Tel: (809) 444 4453/4712. Fax: (809) 444 4847. This eight-room guest house is owner-operated and has a restaurant and bar, all within walking distance of Grand Anse beach, shops and entertainment.

Palm Grove Guest House, Grand Anse, PO Box 568, St George's. Tel: (809) 444 4578. This nine-room guest house is owner-operated where visitors can enjoy home-cooked cuisine with refreshing tropical drinks at the bar.

Patnoe Guest House, Gouyave, St John. Tel: (809) 444 8415. Eight two bedroom apartments with bath and kitchenette.

Petit Bacaye, PO Box 655, St George's, Tel/Fax: (809) 443 2902. Self catering in palm fringed cottages. No televisions, newspapers or telephones - intended for pure relaxation.

Rex Grenadian Hotel, Point Salines, PO Box 893, St George's. Tel: (809) 444 3333, Fax: (809) 444 1111. The Rex Grenadian offers a variety of accommodation in its 212 rooms and suites, ranging from residential and premier suites with either beach-front or garden views. Facilities include restaurants, bars, terrace cafe, two beaches, pool, meeting rooms, conference facility, water sports and floodlit tennis courts.

Roydon's Guest House, Grand Anse, St George. Tel: (809) 444 4476. Roydon's has six rooms with private bath, and ceiling fans. Facilities include restaurant and bar serving local cuisine.

RSR Apartments, Springs PO, St George's. Tel: (809) 440 3381. Thirteeen apartments at good rates.

St Ann's Guest House, Paddock, St George. Tel: (809) 440 2717. This family-owned and operated 12 room guest house has a small bar, games room and dinner can be served on request. Breakfast is included in the rates.

Cinnamon Hill and Beach Club, Grand Anse Beach

The All Inclusive resort of La Source, Pink Gin Beach, Point Salines

Accommodation

Calabash Hotel, L'Anse aux Epines

Sam's Inn, Dumfermline, St Andrew. Tel: (809) 442 7853. Features 12 comfortable double rooms with private bath, ceiling fans, and private balcony. Facilities include meals on request, free morning coffee, beaches nearby, television lounge, taxi and laundry service.

Seaside Villa, Morne Rouge, PO Box 159, St George's. Tel: (809) 444 4668. These attractive apartments are designed on a split-level plan and are fully furnished. Accommodation includes three one-bedroom villas and one two-bedroom villa, each with television.

Secret Harbour Hotel, L'Anse aux Epines, PO Box 11, St George's. Tel: (809) 444 4439/4548/4549, Fax: (809) 444 4819. This luxurious 20 room hotel offers complete privacy in air-conditioned suites. Tennis court, pool, and a secluded beach are located on premises. Complimentary water sports. Facilities include dining room, restaurant, bar, laundry service and telephone.

Siesta Hotel, Grand Anse, PO Box 27, St George's. Tel: (809) 444 4645/4646. Fax: (809) 444 4647. The Siesta features 21 suites with kitchenettes, and 16 hotel rooms, all with private patios. Facilities includes air-conditioning, dining room, pool, pool-side juice bar, telephone, fax, cable television, laundry service and maid.

Simeon's Inn, Green Street, St George's. Tel: (809) 440 2537. Nine single and double rooms with telephone and television.

Skyline Guest House, Belmont, St George's. Tel: (809) 444 4461. Six single rooms, kitchenette, bath, telphone and parking.

Solamente Una Vez, L'Anse aux Epines, PO Box 334, St George's, Tel: (809) 463 9506. Beachfront villas, moorings, dining area, dance floor, laundry and maid service.

South Winds Holiday Cottages and Apartments, Grand Anse, PO Box 118, St George's. Tel: (809) 444 4310, Fax: (809) 444 4404. These five two-bedroom cottages and 14 one-bedroom apartments are convenient for banks and shopping. Each has a fully equipped kitchen with telephone service. Facilities include restaurant, air-conditioning, car rental, maid service. Radio and satellite television available.

Spice Island Inn, Grand Anse Beach, PO Box 6, St George's. Tel: (809) 444 4258/4423/4789. Fax: (809) 444 4807. Select from luxurious ocean-front or garden suites with whirlpool or your own private pool suite. All 56 rooms have air-conditioning, ceiling fan, hair-dryer, clock radio and mini-bar. Facilities include: dining room,

beach, laundry, telephone, water sports, tennis, fitness centre, free bicycle, conference centre and weekly entertainment.

Springfield Holiday Cottages, Grand Anse, St George. Tel: (809) 440 2515. Three bedroom cottage with four beds.

Sunset View Apartment Hotel, Grand Anse, PO Box 181, St George's. Tel: (809) 444 4780/4783, Fax: (809) 440 2123 (attn. Sunset). Housekeeping apartments close to Grand Anse Beach.

Tropicana Inn, Lagoon Road, St George's. Tel: (809) 440 1586, Fax: (809) 440 9797. Overlooking the GYS marina with 20 double rooms, ideal for both business traveller and holidaymaker. Facilities include bar, restaurant, lounge, air-conditioning, television, conference room for 60 people, laundry, maid and baby-sitting service.

True Blue Inn, PO Box 308, St George's. Tel: (809) 444 2000, Fax: (809) 444 1247. This consists of three two-bedroom cottages, four one-bedroom apartments with balconies overlooking the sea. Facilities provided are restaurant, bar, pool, swimming in the bay, yachting, dock, air-conditioning, ceiling fans, cable television, maid service and sailing school.

Twelve Degrees North, L'Anse aux Epines, PO Box 241, St George's. Tel: (809) 444 4580, Fax: (809) 440 4580. This is a small elegantly informal resort with tennis court, freshwater pool, and a wide range of water sports. It consists of eight apartments each with own maid/cook and free laundry facilities.

Ursula-Glen Guest House, Belmont, St George's. Tel: (809) 444 4289. Three rooms with kitchenette, bath and parking.

Victoria Hotel, Queen Street, Victoria, St Mark. Tel: (809) 444 9367/8104, Fax: (809) 444 8814. This hotel has 10 spacious rooms, all with ceiling fans, television, and a balcony. Amenities include a restaurant, bar, satellite television and sea view.

The Village Hotel, Grand Anse, St George's. Tel: (809) 444 4097/4098, Fax: (809) 444 4097. The Village Hotel has 12 comfortable, air-conditioned, one and two-bedroom units, each with a convenient fully equipped kitchen and spacious balcony. Facilities include a bar, lounge, air-conditioning, pool, television and games room.

Villamar Holiday Resort, L'Anse aux Epines, PO Box 546, St George's. Tel: (809) 444 4716/1614/1615, Fax: (809) 444 4847. The Villamar has 20 one and two-bedroom deluxe suites, each has a fully equipped kitchenette, air-conditioning, telephone, satellite television and private patio. Available amenities are restaurant, bar, pool, conference facility, arrangements for golf, tennis, sightseeing, and water sports.

Wave Crest Holiday Apartments, PO Box 278, St George's. Tel: (809) 444 4116, Fax: (809) 444 4847. Twenty attractively furnished air-conditioned rooms, managed by owners, with a choice of double bedrooms with bath and veranda or self-catering suites with baths, kitchen, dining/living room, and veranda. Facilities include cable television, reception and breakfast rooms, maid and laundry service, telephone, car rental, parking and baby-sitting on request.

Windward Sands Inn, Grand Anse, PO Box 199, St George's. Tel: (809) 444 4238. This charming informal eight-room inn has a well-stocked bar and dining room, laundry service, telephone. Island tours, self-drive cars, water sports, fishing, golf, and tennis facilities are available.

Yacht's View, Springs, St George's. Tel: (809) 440 3607. Four single and double rooms with telephone, television and patio.

Flamboyant Hotel & Cottages, Grand Anse Beach

Mahogany Run, Morne Rouge

Accommodation

Hotels, Apartments & Guest Houses in Carriacou

Ade's Dream Guest House, Main Street, Hillsborough, Carriacou. Tel: (809) 443 7733/7317. This seven-room guest house is modern, clean, and spacious. It offers maximum comfort, reasonable prices, and is centrally located.

Alexis Luxury Apartment Hotel, Tyrrel Bay, Carriacou. Tel: (809) 443 7179. This 13-room apartment hotel across from the sea offers 10 fully equipped suites with kitchenettes and three single rooms.

Bay View Holiday Apartments, Tyrrel Bay, Carriacou. Tel: (809) 443 7403. These apartments are near the beach at Tyrrel Bay at very attractive prices.

Caribbee Inn At Prospect, Carriacou. Tel: (809) 443 7380, Fax: (809) 443 8142. A small country-house hotel and nature reserve has ten comfortable, en-suite rooms with traditional four-poster beds. Everything is fresh and the Caribbean dishes have a French Creole flavour. Amenities include a restaurant, bar, snorkelling, cycling, hiking and library.

Cassada Bay Resort, Belmont, Carriacou. Tel: (809) 443 7494, Fax: (809) 443 7672. Fourteen units plus a suite perched on a hillside, each unit has air-conditioned double rooms. The dining room serves Westindian and international cuisine. Facilities include open-air bar/dining, maid/laundry service, ceiling fans, day tours, fishing/boat trips to nearby islets, snorkelling, scuba and nature walks.

Down Island Limited, Villa Rental Agents, Carriacou. Tel: (809) 443 8182. A wide selection of private villas and beach cottages for holiday rental.

Hope's Inn, L'Esterre Bay, Carriacou. Tel: (809) 443 7457. This Inn offers six guest rooms with balconies. All rooms feature ceiling fans and the dining room includes a full-service cocktail bar.

Millie's Guest Rooms & Apartments, Hillsborough, Carriacou. Tel: (809) 443 8207/7310. Fax: (809) 443 8207/8107. Fully furnished, ocean view, ceiling fan and modern bath/showers in one, two or three-bedroom apartments.

Peace Haven Guest House, Hillsborough, Carriacou. Tel: (809) 443 7475/8365. Peace Haven is an owner-managed, intimate guest house with six self-catering rooms.

The Sand Guest House, Hillsborough, Carriacou. Tel: (809) 443 7100. This family-owned and managed guest house offers a two-storey house with three double rooms, bath, and fully equipped kitchenette on each floor. No credit cards.

Scraper Holiday Cottages, Tyrrel Bay, Carriacou. Tel: (809) 443 7403. These cottages are comprised of 2 two-bedroom, self-contained cottages with fully equipped kitchens. Near to the beach.

Seaside Fountain Guest House, Harveyvale, Carriacou. Tel: (809) 443 7425. Two rooms, near the beach with dining, telephone, television and laundry service.

Silver Beach Resort, Beausejour Bay, Hillsborough, Tel: (809) 443 7337, Fax: (809) 443 7165. Silver Beach Resort offers 18 units ranging from self-contained apartments with kitchenettes to elegant rooms with private patios. Facilities include water sports, dining room, bar, beach, laundry service and diving shop with full scuba facilities on site.

Cassada Bay Resort, Carriacou

Millie's Guest Rooms & Apartments, Hillsborough, Carriacou

Silver Beach Resort, Carriacou

Eating out

Restaurants in Grenada

Restaurants offer both local and international cuisine such as creole, continental, Chinese, fast food, Westindian, and Italian. There is a ten per cent service charge unless already added to the bill. An eight per cent VAT is also levied on food and beverage charges. Dress code is casual except in the evenings where proper attire is required.

Aquarium Beach Club & Restaurant - International. Tel: 444 1410. Set on a secluded beach at Point Salines, offers fine food and a Sunday barbecue.

Bain's - Westindian/International/Seafood. Tel: 442 7337. Grenville, St Andrew, specialises in local dishes with an excellent view of the surrounding town and harbour.

Beach Side Terrace Restaurant & Bar - Westindian/Continental. Tel: 444 4247/1462. In the Flamboyant Hotel on Grand Anse beach, offers dining in a charming atmosphere with a view of the beach and St George's Harbour.

Bird's Nest - Chinese/Creole. Tel: 444 4264. Located opposite the Grenada Renaissance Resort at Grand Anse, it offers a variety of Chinese dishes including Cantonese and Szechuan.

The Boatyard - Westindian/International. Tel: 444 4662. This charming and secluded restaurant is located in Prickly Bay, L'Anse aux Epines. For yachtsmen, there are docking and marine facilities.

Bobby's Health Stop - Health Food - with two locations on Gore Street and Le Marquis Complex, emphasizes health conscious cuisine.

Camerhogne Park Restaurant, Westindian, Tel: 444 4587. At Morne Rouge, specialises in Grenadian and continental cuisine. Also available is breakfast, tea and pastries.

Canboulay - Westindian/International. Tel: 444 4401. Overlooking Grand Anse Beach and St George's. Using local produce to create favourites such as dabotte, breadfruit vichyssoise and parang poulet.

Cedar's Inn - International/Westindian. Tel: 444 4641/1404. Cedar's Inn can be found at True Blue. Fine dining and friendly service available for breakfast, lunch and dinner. Daily lunch specials are offered, and Friday at pool-side features Happy Hour from 6pm to 7pm, with a barbecue beginning at 6.30pm.

Chef's Castle - Fast Food. Tel: 440 4778/2073. Located on the corner of Gore and Halifax Street , St George's offers take-out service.

Choo Light - Chinese, Tel: 440 2196. L'Anse aux Epines

Cicely's - Westindian/International. Tel: 444 4234. This award-winning restaurant with its reputation for good food and service is located at the Calabash Hotel, L'Anse aux Epines, and overlooks picturesque Prickly Bay.

Coconut Beach - Creole/French. Tel: 444 4644. Featuring French Creole cuisine flavoured with local herbs and spices for a unique experience in an antique house on Grand Anse Beach.

Conch Shell - Westindian/Seafood. Tel: 444 4178. Located at Point Salines, features outdoor patio dining.

Cot Bam - Westindian. Tel: 444 2050. Situated on Grand Anse Beach offers entertainment, local cuisine, and cultural shows.

Coyaba - Westindian/International. Tel: 444 4129. A tropical ambience in Coyaba's open-air Pepperpot and Arawakabana, Grand Anse Beach, featuring distinctive Westindian cuisine.

Delicious Landing - Seafood/Caribbean. Located on the Carenage specializes in fresh seafood and Caribbean dishes.

Deyna's Tasty Foods - Westindian. Tel: 440 6795. Melville Street, St George's provides local tasty treats.

Dr Groom's Cafe & Restaurant - Italian/Westindian. Tel: 444 1979. Near Point Salines International Airport offers authentic Italian and local cuisine with the option of outdoor activities.

Ebony - Westindian. Tel: 442 7311. Victoria Street, Grenville, St Andrew. Offers Westindian-style cooking.

Fish & Chick - Fast food. Tel: 444 4132. Old Sugar Mill Building at Grand Anse, Fish & Chick offers a takeaway service and a dine-in facility for its customers. Credit cards are not accepted.

Floating Bar - Cocktail Bar/Nightspot. Known as the 007, this floating bar is anchored in St George's Harbour off the Carenage and commands a picturesque view of the capital.

Fox Inn Restaurant - Westindian/International. Tel: 444 4123/4177. Situated close to Point Salines International Airport and Grand Anse. The restaurant offers a full international menu and local traditional favourites.

Green Flash Restaurant - International/Middle Eastern. Tel: 444 4645/6. Located in the Siesta Hotel features international cuisine with a Middle Eastern touch, served pool-side under a cabana that overlooks St George's and Grand Anse. Distinctive desserts are specialities of the house.

Grenada Renaissance Resort - Creole/International. Tel: 444 4371/5. Wine and dine in an atmosphere of informal elegance, with a panoramic view of the Caribbean Sea. The Grenada Renaissance offers international and Creole cuisine and specializes in sumptuous buffets.

Hibiscus Hotel - Continental/Creole. Tel: 444 4008/4233. Nestled in tropical setting at Morne Rouge, St George's.

Hole-In-The-Wall - Westindian. Tel: 440 3158. On the Carenage next to Bon Voyage Duty-Free Shop in St George's, serves local Westindian dishes.

Indigo's - Caribbean/International/Seafood. Tel: 444 2000. Situated in the True Blue Inn, Indigo's overlooks a small bay and provides a cool, comfortable, quiet atmosphere for a quick basket lunch or leisurely meals. Open daily for lunch and dinner.

International Cafe - Continental. Tel: 444 3333. At the Rex Grenadian, Point Salines. A la carte menu. Breakfast, lunch and dinner. Reservations required.

Jade Garden - Chinese. Tel: 444 3698 at Mace Hotel, Morne Rouge.

Jefferson's Beach Bar - Westindian. Tel: 444 4334 ext 2010. Sandwiches, snacks, salads, barbecue and light entertainment

Judith's - Westindian. Tel: 440 5732. Gore Street, St George's specializes in authentic local food and drink, including rotis, local soups, seamoss, and fresh tropical juices.

Kentucky Fried Chicken - Fast Food. Tel: 440 3821. Granby Street, St George's, this is one of the many places to get a quick drink or snack while shopping in St George's.

La Belle Creole - Westindian/Continental. Tel: 444 4316/4592. Set among the tropical gardens of Blue Horizons Cottage Hotel at Morne Rouge, La Belle Creole offers gourmet dining.

La Dolce Vita - Italian. Tel: 444 4301/3456. At the Cinnamon Hill Hotel, overlooking Grand Anse Beach and St George's Harbour.

La Sagesse Nature Centre - Seafood/Continental. Tel: 444 6458. This romantic hideaway on a secluded beach is a perfect spot to come for a swim, a hike, or a meal. Featuring excellent seafood cuisine.

Liftoff - Westindian/ International. Tel: 444 4101 ext. 274. Upstairs at Point Salines Airport.

The Little Bakery Coffee House - Westindian. Tel: 444 3623. Offers everything from fresh bread and pastries to full evening meals.

Mamma's - Westindian. Tel: 440 1459. Near to Grenada Yacht Services in St George's. Local food offered and reservations preferred.

Marielle's - Westindian. Tel: 444 4641/1404. Mall 21 at True Blue near the airport and the emphasis is on local food.

Morne Fendue Plantation Great House - Westindian. Tel: 442 9330. This old plantation home offers a unique island experience and great Westindian style cuisine.

Mount Rodney Estate - International. Tel: 442 9420. At Sauteurs, lunch only by reservation.

Nutmeg - Westindian/International. Tel: 440 2539. Is a favourite gathering spot, especially popular with the boat crowd. Centrally located on the Carenage above the Sea Change Book Store, it has a view of the entire harbour. Serving breakfast, lunch and dinner.

Patnoe Enterprises - Ice Cream/Fast Food. Tel: 444 8415. Lower Depradine Street, Gouyave on the west coast overlooking the sea.

Portofino Ristorante Italia - Italian/Pizza. Tel: 440 3986. In the tricoloured building on the Carenage overlooking the harbour, it specializes in Italian cuisine.

The Red Crab - Westindian/International. Tel: 444 4424. In L'Anse aux Epines near the Calabash Hotel, it specializes in local seafood and international cuisine.

Rick's Cafe - Fast Food/Pizza & Ice Cream Parlour. Tel: 444 4597. Grand Anse Shopping Plaza, Rick's specializes in pizzas, hamburgers, subs, ribs, and ice cream.

Roydon's - Continental/Westindian. Tel: 444 4476. Local food and drinks, continental dishes, local soups and curries, served in a charming atmosphere.

Rudolf's - Westindian/International. Tel: 440 2241. Overlooking the Carenage in a relaxed and rustic atmosphere, Rudolf's specializes in fresh seafood prepared with a European and Westindian touch.

Sam's Inn - Creole. Tel: 442 7853/7313. Grenville, St Andrew, serves enticing Grenadian food.

Sand Pebbles - Snack Bar/Westindian. Tel: 440 2688. On the Carenage, this is an ideal spot to stop for a cool drink or ice cream.

Secret Harbour/Mariners - Westindian/International. Tel: 444 4439/4549. Specializing in local foods with an international edge. Mariners at Secret Harbour Hotel in L'Anse aux Epines overlooks Mount Hartman Bay.

South Winds - Westindian/International. Tel: 444 4310/4404. At Grand Anse above South Winds Cottages, provides a scenic view of St George's Harbour. The emphasis is on seafood cuisine.

Spice Island Inn - Westindian/International. Tel: 444 4258/4423. At Grand Anse it offers a fabulous view of St George's. Seafood and exotic island drinks are specialities.

Sur La Mer Restaurant & Aquarius Beach Pavilion - Westindian/International. Tel: 444 4224/1189. For an excellent sunset view and romantic beach-side atmosphere. Seafood is big on the menu.

Tabanca at Journey's End - Cafe/Bistro. Tel: 444 1300. Dine on an open terrace by the sea, with a menu of seafood and other fine dishes. Try their special rum punch and Carib beer on tap.

Traffic Light Bar & Grill - Westindian. Tel: 440 3375. Located in Belmont, St George's, it is a great spot to sample the authentic local cuisine.

Tropicana - Chinese/Westindian. Tel: 440 1586. On the Lagoon Road in comfortable surroundings with a delightful view of the marina. Both local and Chinese cuisine is served. A Westindian special is featured every day.

Villamar Restaurant - Westindian. At L'Anse aux Epines, open from 7.00 am for breakfast, lunch and dinner, with menus that emphasize the variety of local cuisine.

Windward Sands Inn - International. Tel: 444 4238. Dining at the Inn in Grand Anse is well-known among visitors to Grenada.

Restaurants in Carriacou

Al's Snack Bar - Westindian. Tel: 443 7179. Stop by for Al's special cocktail, 'Hurricane David' on Tyrrel Bay, Carriacou.

Ali's Restaurant & Bar - Westindian. Tel: 443 8406. Pull your dinghy on-shore at Ali's and experience fine Westindian food and spectacular Carriacou sunsets right on the beach at L'Esterre Bay.

Callaloo Restaurant & Bar - Westindian/International/Seafood. Tel: 443 8004. This quaint, romantic restaurant and bar on Main Street, Hillsborough, features breezy views of Sandy Island and Hillsborough Bay. Excellent seafood specialities.

Cassada Bay - Westindian/International. Tel: 443 7494. Perched on a hillside overlooking five islands, this open-air dining room specializes in Caribbean and international cuisine.

Kayak - Westindian/Creole. Tel: 443 8446. Lunch at the Kayak features Creole and Spanish dishes.

The Pepperpot - Westindian/Creole. Tel: 443 7380. At the Caribbee Inn at Prospect, a small country-house hotel located at the foot of High North, two miles north of Hillsborough.

Poivre et Sel - French. Tel: 443 8390. Located directly on Tyrrel Bay with beautiful bay views and tropical breezes, Poivre et Sel offers an ever changing menu.

Roof Gardens - Westindian. Tel: 443 7204. Hillsborough, specializes in Westindian cuisine and is known for its friendly service.

Scraper's - Seafood. Tel: 443 7403. Located on the water's edge at Tyrrel Bay. Offers reasonably priced fish dishes and a live band features twice weekly.

Silver Beach Resort - Westindian/Continental. Tel: 443 7337. On the water's edge in Hillsborough, with fabulous views of the Grenadines, this restaurant specializes in Caribbean and continental cuisine with an emphasis on local seafood. Free hook-up to the dinghy dock and pick-up for visiting yachts anchored in Tyrrel Bay.

Talk Of The Town - Westindian. Tel: 443 7118. Main Street, Hillsborough, serving lunch and dinner by reservation only. A full cocktail service is also available.

What's The Scoop/Gramma'a Bakery - Ice Cream Parlour/Bakery. Tel: 443 7256. Corner of Patterson and Main Street, Hillsborough, it is well known for its early morning breakfasts.

Things to do

Nightlife in Grenada

Boatyard Restaurant & Bar - set among coconut palms on L'Anse aux Epines Beach in the marina offers dancing, live steelband and popular disc jockeys on different nights.

Cicely's - at the Calabash Hotel in L'Anse aux Epines, for piano music and steelband.

Coyaba Beach Resort - Grand Anse Beach, provides a barbecue and local band on Tuesday evenings and Saturday nights a barbecue and steelband.

Dynamite Disco - at Limes on Grand Anse every weekend.

Fantazia 2001 - Disco on Morne Rouge Beach offers disc jockey music, local and international artists, and local cabaret.

The Flamboyant Hotel - on beautiful Grand Anse Beach offers crab racing, live steelband, calypso music and show. Happy Hour is 5.00pm to 7.00pm daily.

Island View - at Woburn, St George's, Caribbean music. Late nights Friday and Saturday

Le Sucrier - In the Sugar Mill on the Grand Anse roundabout features appearances by disc jockeys, regional entertainment and live bands.

Marryshow Folk Theatre - Located on H A Blaize Street, St George's, features concerts, plays and special events.

The Grenada Renaissance Resort - Grand Anse. Offers nightly entertainment year round.

Regal Cinema - off Lagoon Road and Paddock, St George's. Showing current movies every evening at 8.30.

Rhum Runner - a 20' x 60' twin-deck catamaran sails Fridays and Saturday evenings from the fire station jetty, St George's.

Rhum Runner II - a 28' x 72' twin-deck catamaran, holds monthly moonlight cruise on the Friday nearest the full moon. The evening includes free unlimited rum punch and all night dancing. Many special trips arranged.

Spice Island Inn - Grand Anse Beach, features dancing and gourmet dining. Wednesday is Grenada Night with authentic Grenadian food and dancing to a live band, Friday's offer a barbecue and steelband, Saturday is Nostalgia Night - dancing and a seafood menu.

The Village Hotel - Grand Anse, offers an evening of live jazz from 8.30 until midnight every Wednesday.

Sports facilities

Golf - The Grenada Golf and Country Club is a 9-hole course located near Grand Anse and open to visitors. There are a wide range of facilities available. Tel: 444 4128.

Tennis - Visitors interested in a few sets of tennis are quite likely to find facilities at their own hotel or can make arrangements with a hotel that has courts. There is also a public tennis facility located at Grand Anse.

Health Clubs

Amada Marga Yoga Centre, Opposite Tanteen Playing field, St George's. Tel: 440 5880.

Body Image Health Club, L'Anse aux Epines. Tel: 444 3254.

The Body Shop, Grand Anse, Tel: 444 4290.

Carriacou Fitness Club, 2nd Avenue, Hillsborough, Carriacou. Tel: 443 8439.

Island Magic Massage Clinic, Grenada Renaissance Hotel, Grand Anse. Tel: 444 3306, after hours: 440 3837.

Shamar, Lucia Street, St George's. Tel: 440 6880.

Water Sports and Dive Shops

Aquarium Beach Club, in addition to offering beach-side dining, provides rental gear for snorkelling on the reef offshore. Tel: 444 1410.

Captain Peters' Water Taxi Service offers daily excursions. Trips to Carriacou, a sunset cruise, and sport fishing charters can also be arranged. Tel: 440 1349.

Dive Grenada, at the Grenada Renaissance Resort. Daily dive trips. The famous wreck Bianca C is a deep dive for experienced divers. Night dives and a selection of PADI (Professional Association of Dive Instructors) courses are available. Windsurfing and sunfish sailing (instruction available). Tel: 444 4371 Ext 638 (Evenings) Tel: 444 5875

Grand Anse Aquatics, at Coyaba Beach resort. PADI courses, snorkelling trips around Grenada, Carriacou and Petit Martinique. Windsurfing and instruction available. Tel: 444 4129

Sail Grenada is a sailing school with classes to suit the individual needs of both adults and children. Uses Laser Olympic-class dinghies. Also available are day charters on a 35ft sailing yacht. Tel: 444 2000, Fax: 444 1247.

Silver Beach Diving, Silver Beach Hotel, modern equipment and an excellent location for day and night dives. Carriacou also offers PADI courses, waterskiing, windsurfing and snorkelling. Tel: 443 7882.

Sky Ride offers safe and exciting parasailing on Grand Anse Beach near the Grenada Renaissance Resort. For this and other activities, Tel: 440 9375.

Snagg's Watersports on Carriacou provides snorkelling trips to secluded Sandy Island, White Islands and Petit Martinque also sunfish rentals and waterskiing. Tel: 443 8293.

Tanki's Watersport Paradise Limited, is located on L'Esterre Bay, Carriacou, and offers scuba, PADI certified instruction, and snorkel trips to Sandy Island. Tel: 443 8406.

World Wide Watersports in Grand Anse has a wide variety of water sports equipment for rent. Sunset cruises, explorations to the Grenadines and the Soca & Calypso Booze Cruise. Tel: 444 1339.

Some of the books, guides and newspapers available at most book shops, hotels and gift shops

Yacht Charters and Sports Fishing

Ambassador 1, a 31ft Chris Craft, offers daily trips to Sandy Island and tours to other islands on request. Make reservations through Fun Tours Tel: 444 3167, Arnold's Tours Tel: 440 0531, Astral Travel Tel: 440 5180, or Windward Islands Travel & Regattas Tel: 444 4732/36.

Alfa is a 40ft Beneteau Oceanis 430 ready to take you on a cruise through the Grenadines, including the Tobago Cays, or simply on a fun-filled day charter from her base in Carriacou. Maximum eight persons. Call Cassada Bay Yacht Charter Tel: 443 7494.

Bezo is a 32ft bowen pirogue ideal for sportsfishing. True Blue Inn Tel: 443 5477.

Carriacou Islander explores the reefs and uninhabited islands around Carriacou. This newly built boat accommodates up to 30 people and is equipped with toilets, freshwater showers, food and beverage bar and an observation panel to view underwater. Contact the hotels' reception desk, travel agents, or book direct through Down Island Limited Tel/Fax: 443 8182. Sunsation Tours Tel: 444 1656. Carriacou Tour & Travel Tel: 443 8238.

Cassada Bay Resort on Carriacou can arrange sailing and speedboat charters for a day or longer. Tel: 443 7494.

Evans Chartering Services offer half-day or full-day deep-sea fishing charter trips on the Xiphias Seeker, a 35ft Bertram Sport Fisherman with an air-conditioned cabin. Sporting fishing charters and trips to Carriacou and other nearby islands can be arranged. Drinks are included on all trips. Tel: 444 4422/4217.

Firefly, an 80ft ketch docked in Carriacou, is available for crewed and provisioned day sails, three-day Grenadines cruises, or longer bareboat sails for which they provide the captain and you provision the boat. For information Tel: 443 8207.

Gaucho, a 50ft Manuel campos-designed classic wooden ketch. Grenadine charters, day charters to Union Island with lunch and snorkelling, and trips to Sandy Island, Petit St Vincent, Petit Martinique. Call Carriacou Boatbuilders Tel; 443 7542.

Havada, 32ft Bowen Pirogue. Deep sea fishing, day trips, snorkelling Tel: 440 2198/3422

Lady Odile, a 42ft sailing yacht available for a day sail or extended cruises from Carriacou. Cassada Bay Resort Tel: 443 7494.

The Moorings' Club Mariner Watersports Centre, at Secret Harbour, offers both half and full day skippered charters, as well as providing rental of small sailboats for qualified sailors. Small sunfish sailboats and windsurfing boards are available at reasonable fees. Waterskiing, snorkelling excursions, and speedboat trips to Hog Island can be arranged. Tel: 444 4439/4549.

Psyche is a sailing yacht that embarks from Grenada Yacht Services on sea adventures and has a fully equipped galley, stereo system, and shower for a comfortable and relaxing cruise. For information, Tel: 440 1353/ 444 4010.

Rhum Runner is a 20' x 60' twin-deck catamaran, and the **Rhum Runner II** is a 28' x 72' twin deck catamaran capable of holding 250 passengers. Both cruise on tours that vary from two and a half to nine hours in duration. For more information, Tel: 440 2198/3422.

Romany, a spacious and comfortable 54ft classic ketch based at Hillsborough Harbour, Carriacou, is available for day charters from 8.00 am to 4.00 pm. Minimum of six and maximum of 15 persons. For reservations or more information, contact Fun Tours at Tel: 444 3167, New Trends Tours Tel: 444 1236, Windwards Islands Travel & Regattas Tel: 444 4732/4736.

Seabreeze Yacht Charters at Spice Island Marine Centre offers daily and weekly charters on sailing or power yachts - either bareboat or skippered and with any of four different provisioning packages. Tel: 444 4924.

Starwind Enterprise has two sailing yachts, Starwind I , a 39ft, and Starwind II , 43ft catering for a maximum of 12 people. Both are available for charters of all kinds. Tel: 440 3678.

Tropix Professional Sport Fishing is available for deep-sea fishing charters around Grenada., Tel: 440 4961/444 1422.

Whistler is a 47ft yacht based at The Boatyard in L'Anse aux Epines, offering day trips and overnight charters. Tel: 440 3075 or 444 4257.

Arriving by yacht

Grenada uses the IALA B (red right returning) rule. Unless you draw more than 10 feet you will not have to pay attention to the two big ship channel buoys outside St George's or use the leading (range) marks.

When approaching from the north, the harbour entrance remains hidden until you reach it. On the left as you enter, you will see Fort George. On the hills above the Lagoon you can see Fort Frederick and the prison.

The main anchorage is in the Lagoon between Grenada Yacht Services (GYS) and the Grenada Yacht Club. Expect depths of 15 to 20 feet in soft gooey mud. The channel into the Lagoon is about 13 feet deep and marked by buoys and stakes. Many people find it confusing, but it is easy if, when entering the harbour, head straight for the right hand (southern) end of the big ship dock, only turning into the channel when you clearly see all the marks lined up.

The customs office is located in the GYS complex. Normal office hours are weekdays 0800-1200, 1300-1600. When you clear in, tell customs which ports you plan to visit.

The Grenada Yacht Club is an inexpensive place to drink beers and watch others run aground as they try to come into the cut. Snacks are available, as are showers, water and a cardphone.

You can take your dinghy from the Lagoon over to town and tie up outside Foodfair. An alternative is to walk to town from the Yacht Club and return by water taxi.

St George's is a busy place with plenty of traffic including colourful buses laden with people and goods, smaller minibuses with loud music, cars, trucks weighed down with building material, and sometimes it seems like they are all honking at once. People will shout "taxi" at you and vendors may offer fruits and spices from baskets.

The Post Office moved near Customs after the old Post Office building burned down in 1990. It is open during lunchtime for the purchase of stamps only, but closed all day Saturday. Most shops are closed Saturday afternoon and almost everything else is closed on Sundays.

Point Salines to Prickly Bay

When sailing between St George's and Point Salines, keep well clear of Long Point Shoal. This may be done by heading west from St George's and waiting till you are on the line between Point Salines and the tanks at Grand Mal before heading for Point Salines. Reverse this procedure when returning.

As you sail around Point Salines and head towards Glover Island, Prickly Point will be the farthest headland that you can see. As you get closer, Prickly Bay is easily identified by all the yachts inside and the handsome houses on the hill. There is plenty of water for most yachts to sail inside Glover Island.

Prickly Bay (Also known as L'Anse aux Epines)

Prickly Bay is a delightful spot. The land is a tapestry of attractive gardens, which form a background of green, speckled with bright flowers. One gets glimpses of lovely homes and all kinds of roofs that peek out, over and through the vegetation. At the head of the bay is a palm fringed beach. One feels very much in the country here, with the sound of birds by day and tree frogs by night, yet St George's is only 15 minutes away by car and the airport and Grand Anse are even closer.

The Moorings Marina at Secret Harbour, Mount Hartman Bay

While Prickly Bay is easy to enter, do not get careless. There is a reef marked by a nondescript buoy in the middle, opposite The Boatyard, which is just deep enough to be difficult to see. Reefs also extend nearly all the way up the eastern shore and one should give the True Blue headland reasonable clearance. Occasionally southerly swells can be uncomfortable, though a stern anchor will do much to restore a sense of calm.

Prickly Bay is a port of entry, Customs is located at The Boatyard. Anchoring is forbidden within 300 feet of the beach as it is reserved for swimmers.

The South Coast (beyond Prickly Bay)

The south coast of Grenada offers beautiful, secluded and protected anchorages. The mass of reefs provide interesting snorkelling. The area should be treated with caution and in places, eyeball navigation is essential. The Porpoises, about half-a-mile off Prickly Point, awash and hard to spot, are as nasty a bunch of rocks you could find to get wrecked on.

Navigation into Mount Harman Bay and Hog Island has been greatly simplified by the new buoys put down and privately maintained by The Moorings. From Prickly Bay, pass about midway between Prickly Point and the Porpoises. Look out for Tara Island, a small coral island about five feet high. Leave Tara to starboard, passing halfway between it and Prickly Point. From here follow the buoyage system into Mount Hartman Bay or Hog Island,

Mount Hartman Bay

Mount Hartman Bay is a deep and well protected harbour. It is a large scenic bay with a modern marina, the luxury Secret Harbour Hotel and a charter base, all operated by The Moorings. This is a great area for dinghy sailing or sail boarding as there is protected water all the way to Hog Island.

(The above are excerpts from: 'Sailors Guide to the Windward Islands' by Chris Doyle published in the 'Grenada Sailing Festival, 1994 Programme'. Doyle is a well known writer whose other books on the area include: 'Cruising Guide to the Leeward Islands', 'The Nature of the Islands' and 'Exploring the Windward Islands'.)

Paradise Beach, Carriacou, with Sandy Island on the horizon, offers superb safe anchorage

Yachting information and services

Shipping

St George's has a natural harbour and is the major port, with berths for two ocean-going vessels, a 250ft schooner pier and a container park. There is a regular service between Grenada and major international ports. Hillsborough in Carriacou and Grenville in Grenada are other ports of entry used mainly by smaller ships. Tyrrel Bay in Carriacou has a 270ft floating jetty and Prickly Bay in Grenada has a dock.

Weather forecasts

A summary of marine weather conditions for Grenada and the Windward Islands is broadcast daily at 10.00am on VHF Channel 6 by Outfitters International Coastal Station. An announcement is made on Channel 16 in advance of the broadcast. During severe weather, warnings are issued as received.

Telecommunications

Grentel provides telecommunications services, including telephone and facsimile. All services are available to the public at the Carenage, St George's and Hillsborough, Carriacou. Major credit cards are accepted at these offices for settlement of international call charges.

Boatphone: (USA amps) for land and marine use is available. Roaming facilities are available to all cellular phone owners with payment by major credit cards. You can use your cellular phone or rent one from Grentel. Boatphone is already installed on many charter yachts.

Home Direct Service: allows credit and telephone charge card holders to call their home country direct.

Credit Card holders: can use their cards to pay for telephone calls from Grenada worldwide.

Payphones: Coin and Card phone services are available at selected locations. All pay phones allow both local and overseas calls to be made. Prepaid cards can be purchased at Grentel offices and at agents located near the card phones. Instructions are displayed in the booth.

On arrival

Arriving yachts should display the yellow 'Q' flag and the courtesy flag of Grenada from the starboard spreader of the main mast.

Customs & Documents

Captains should prepare the following:
* Three crew and/or passenger lists
* Immigration cards for crew or passengers landing
* Ships, stores and health declaration
* A port clearance from last port of call
* ID for crew and passengers, a valid passport or birth certificate etc.

Clearance is provided at the Grenada Yacht Services, St George's and Spice Island Marina, Prickly Bay. There are no port or harbour fees for *practique* during office hours. After hours, the Customs and Immigration officers are entitled to charge overtime.

Customs opening hours are Mon-Thurs: 8.00am to 11.45 am and 1.00pm to 4.00pm. Cashier closes at 11.30am and at 3.30pm. Friday hours extended till 5.00pm.

Anchoring

Yachts shall not anchor anywhere in the Grand Anse Bay area or in the Carenage (Grenada), or by the oyster beds in Harvey Vale (Carriacou). Yachts may not anchor within 200 metres offshore of any other beach in Grenada, Carriacou or Petit Martinique. Visiting yachtsmen should check with customs to see if they need a coastwide clearance (for which there is no charge), to visit the other islands and harbours.

Animals

No importation of animals is permitted without an Import Permit. Proper health documents must be presented. The Government Veterinary Officer must be notified of the port of entry and the expected time of arrival.

Firearms

Must be declared. They will be sealed in a proper locker on board or taken to an official locker on shore to be returned on departure. A receipt will be issued.

Fruit Fly

Grenada is free of the fruit fly pest, unlike most of the surrounding islands and countries. Any organic matter (fruit, vegetables, plants etc) brought into Grenada could carry the pest. All organic matter must be inspected by the pest control officer.

Disposal of Garbage and Sewerage

Organic garbage from overseas produce may not be brought into Grenada. It must be dumped at sea more than 12 nautical miles offshore. If is it ground into small pieces less than 25mm, it may be dumped at sea more than three nautical miles offshore. Non-organic waste may be disposed of ashore in the proper place. There are facilities for disposal ashore at both yacht marinas, the Grenada Yacht Club and at the principal towns and villages. In some cases there is a nominal charge. Do not throw trash into the harbours or anchorages. It is against the litter laws and the trash may be returned to your deck.

Both marinas and the yacht club offer toilet facilities ashore. Marine toilets may not be used within 200 metres of the beaches.

Water, Ice & Fuel

Water is safe to drink. Bottled water is easily available. Ice and fuel is available at Grenada Yacht Services in the Lagoon, Spice Island Marina at Prickly Bay and The Moorings at Mount Hartman Bay. It is against the Port Regulations to pump oil into the water.

Water Skiing

The speed limit within all anchorages is 5mph. Water skiing is strictly regulated. Please consult the Port Authority or your marina management.

Marina Services

Anro Agencies Limited in Grand Anse, offers automotive and marine sales and services. Authorised dealers for Marina outboards. Tel: 440 2044

Grenada Yacht Services Limited, Lagoon Road, provides complete marina facilities, a 230 ton lift, yacht repairs and sales. Tel:

Useful numbers

Sunset at Silver Beach Hotel, Hillsborough, Carriacou

440 2508. Customs and Immigration Tel: 440 3270

McIntyre Bros Limited, at True Blue, are the authorised distributors for Yamaha outboard motors ranging from 2HP to 250HP. Parts and service. Tel: 440 2044

The Moorings Marina, located at the Secret Harbour Resort, provides protected slips, electrical hook-ups, provisions, marina services, complete dockside amenities and more. Tel: 444 4449

Power Tripper, located in L'Anse aux Epines, offers marine repair services. Authorised Mercury dealer. Licensed and certified for Mercury, Yamaha and Johnson. Tel: 444 4106.

Spice Island Marine Services Co. Limited, located at Prickly Bay, offers a full service marina including duty-free chandlery supplies, marine paints/primers, marine sealants, pumps, ropes, a full range of hoses, charts and more. Tel: 444 4342.

Other useful services

Black Rock Medical Clinic, located in the Grand Anse Shopping Centre, provides 24-hour medical, surgical and pharmaceutical services.

Federal Express, provides fast, reliable door-to-door document and package delivery to virtually anywhere in the US and over 170 countries worldwide.

Gleans Garage, agents for Land Rover, Island Cruiser, and Esso oils, as well as Mitsubishi Motors and Hitachi batteries.

Grenada General Insurance, offers all classes of General Insurance including Marine, Hull and Cargo.

Shell Antilles & Guianas, suppliers of gasoline and diesel fuel, motor and marine oils.

Tangie's Laundry, located by Sugar Mill roundabout, offers complete professional cleaning, laundry and pressing services.

Texaco (WI) Limited, providing service and sales of gasoline, diesel and propane gas, motor and marine oils.

Emergencies Services

Police/Fire   Tel: 911
Coast Guard   Tel: 399
Hospitals: General Hospital, St George's   Tel: 440 2051
Princess Alice Hospital, St Andrews   Tel: 442 7251
Princess Royal Hospital, Carriacou   Tel: 443 7400
Ambulance Services: St George's Tel: 434, St Andrew Tel: 724, Carriacou Tel: 774.
Grenada Taxi Association Tel: 444 4925

Other useful numbers

Telephone Service: National Assistance   Tel: 0
International Operator   Tel: 0
Directory Enquiries   Tel: 411
Customer Care Service   Tel: 611
Airlines: Aereotuy Tel: 444 4732/4736, Airlines of Carriacou Tel: 444 4425, BWIA Tel: 440-3818/3819, British Airways/LIAT Tel: 440 2796/2797, Hellenair Grenada Ltd Tel: 444 2266.
Grenada Port Authority Tel: 440 3013/3015/3439/3692
Point Salines International Airport: Customs Tel: 444 4137, Immigration (Arrivals) Tel: 444 4167, Tourist Information Tel: 444 4140

Grenada Tourist Offices worldwide

GRENADA: Board of Tourism, Box 293, St George's. Tel: (809) 440 2279/2001. Fax: 809 440 6637.

CANADA: Grenada Board of Tourism, Suite 820, 439 University Avenue, Toronto, Ontario M5G 1Y8. Tel: 416 595 1339. Fax: 416 595 8278.

GERMANY: Liebigstrasse 8, 60323 Frankfurt/Main, Germany. Tel: 069 726 908. Fax: 069 727 714.

UK: Grenada Board of Tourism, 1 Collingham Gardens, London SW5 0HW England. Tel: 071 370 5164/5. Fax: 071 370 7040.

USA, Suite 900D, 820 2nd Avenue, New York NY 10017. Tel: 212 687 9554/800 927 9554. Fax: 212 573 9731.

Embassies and Consulates

British High Commission, 14 Church Street, St George's. Tel: (809) 440 3536/3222/1250

Embassy of the Republic of China, Archibald Avenue, St George's. Tel: (809) 440 3054

The European Union, Archibald Avenue, St George's. Tel: (809) 440 3561

Honorary Consul of France, 7 Lucas Street, St George's. Tel: (809) 440 2547/444 4967

Consulate of the Cooperative Republic of Guyana, Gore Street, St George's. Tel: (809) 440 2189

Consulate of the Netherlands, Grand Etang Road, St George's. Tel: (809) 440 2031

Swedish Consulate, PO Box 345, St George's. Tel: (809) 440 1832

US Embassy, Point Salines, St George's. Tel: (809) 444 1173/1179

Venezuelan Embassy, Archibald Avenue, St George's. Tel: (809) 440 1721/1722.

Other titles by Hansib Publishing

Country Profiles/Travel

ANTIGUA & BARBUDA - A Little Bit of Paradise (2nd revised edition). This edition explores in a highly informative and sensitively illustrated way, the history of these idyllic islands from the emergence of the Siboney (stone people) 4,000 years ago to the present day democracy, enjoying one of the highest standards of living in the Caribbean. Hardback £25/US $45

DOMINICA - Nature Island Island of the Caribbean. This 320 page book, richly illustrated in full colour, captures the beauty of this Caribbean country and offers a brief account of its sometimes turbulent history and rich culture. Hardback £19.95 /US $40

Sport

INDO-WESTINDIAN CRICKET. By Professor Frank Birbalsingh and Clem Shiwcharan. Two brilliant essays on Westindian cricket by two of the region's leading cultural historians. Hardback £7.95/US $15

100 GREAT WESTINDIAN TEST CRICKETERS. By Bridgette Lawrence with Reg Scarlett. Through the eyes of the leading players of the last 60 years, Bridgette Lawrence traces the rise of Westindian Test cricket from its beginnings at Lord's in 1928 to the triumphs of the last two decades. Hardback £14.95 /US $22

Poetry

COOLIE ODYSSEY. By David Dabydeen. Dabydeen's second collection of poetry probes the experience of the Indian diaspora, the journeying from India to the Caribbean then to Britain, dwelling on the dreams of romance, the impotence of racial encounter and the metamorphosis of language. Paperback £3.95/US $6

GRASSROOTS IN VERSE. An extensive collection of poetry and verse submitted by the readers of the British weekly newspapers *Caribbean Times, Asian Times* and *African Times*. Lively, humorous, provocative and thoughtful - feelings experienced by young and old alike. Paperback £6.95/US $10

Political/Historical

THE OTHER MIDDLE PASSAGE - Journal of a Voyage from Calcutta to Trinidad, 1858. Introduction by Ron Ramdin This book reproduces, in facsimile, the *Journal* of the Captain of the *Salsette*, a ship carrying Indian indentured labourers from Calcutta to Trinidad in 1858. A detailed introductory analysis by Ramdin, puts in context the significance of this document for the better understanding of this little known mass migration. Paperback £3.95/US $6

RASTA AND RESISTANCE - From Marcus Garvey to Walter Rodney. By Dr Horace Campbell. Tracing the cultural, political and spiritual sources of this movement of resistance, highlighting the quest for change among an oppressed people. Paperback £8.95/US $14

THE GREAT MARCUS GARVEY. By Liz Mackie. The biography of one of the great black leaders of the twentieth century, a powerful influence on the development of black pride and black power in America and the Caribbean, and on Pan-Africanism in general. Paperback £4.95/US $7.50

SPEECHES BY ERROL BARROW. Edited by Yussuff Haniff. A collection of speeches made by the late Barbadian Prime Minister, showing Barrow as a true Caribbean man, fighting for the region's independ-

ent identity. This book is now recommended reading in most Barbadian schools. Hardback £10.95/US $17

HOGARTH, WALPOLE AND COMMERCIAL BRITAIN. By Dr David Dabydeen. Dr Dabydeen's first book on William Hogarth was widely acclaimed as a pioneering work on English art and social history. Hardback £15.95/US $24

FORBIDDEN FREEDOM - The Story of British Guiana (Third Edition). By Dr. Cheddi Jagan. A classic document of anti-colonialist and anti-imperialist struggle from one of the veteran freedom leaders of the Third World. This edition includes a new epilogue written by the author after being reinstated to his position as Premier of Guyana. Paperback £5.95/US $9

A NEW SYSTEM OF SLAVERY - The Export of Indian Labour Overseas 1830-1920. By Hugh Tinker. The first comprehensive historical survey of a hitherto neglected and only partially known migration- the export of Indians to supply the labour needed in producing plantation crops all over the world. Paperback £11.99/US $18

INDIA IN THE CARIBBEAN. Edited by Dr David Dabydeen and Dr Brinsley Samaroo. A collection of essays, poems and prose by leading Indo-Caribbean scholars and writers, on East Indian history and culture in the Caribbean. Paperback £8.95. Hardback £11.95/US $18

BENEVOLENT NEUTRALITY - Indian Government Policy and Labour Migration to British Guiana 1854-1884. By Dr Basdeo Mangru. A detailed, scholarly essay on Indian migration, which, for the first time, studies the Indian background of the indentured labourers and explains the economic, political and cultural factors which encouraged migration. Hardback £12.95/US $20

PASSION AND EXILE. By Frank Birbalsingh. A wide ranging collection of essays that offer an illuminating commentary on the literary and social history of the English speaking Caribbean. Paperback £7.95/US $12

A LIGHT IN THE DARK TUNNEL. By Ashton Gibson with Charles Lewis. Described as "an invaluable contribution to race relations", this book responds to the urgency felt by professionals, doctors, social workers and probation officers to understand the needs of the Westindian community and their children. Paperback £4.95/US $7.50

THE UNEQUAL STRUGGLE. By Ashton Gibson with Jocelyn Barrow. A book aimed at examining the reasons behind the poor performers of Westindian children in British schools. Paperback £6.95/US $10

THE IDEOLOGY OF RACISM. By Samuel Kennedy Yeboah. A comprehensive and well-researched study of the history of peoples from the African diaspora, listing outstanding achievements in the fields of arts, science and technology. Paperback £8.95/US $14

PROSPERO'S RETURN? Historical Essays on Race, Culture and British Society. By Paul Rich. In this wide-ranging collection of essays, exploring the nature and meaning of race and racism in British society and the nature of British and English national identity. Paperback £8.95/US $14

Biography

BARRISTER FOR THE DEFENCE. By Rudy Narayan. This book is not so much intended to be critical of the standards of advocacy at the English Bar as to seek to improve the quality of advocacy in the criminal courts. Paperback £6.95/US $10

INSEPARABLE HUMANITY. Inseparable Humanity is an anthology of reflections by one of the world's leading thinkers, Shridath S Ramphal - the former Commonwealth Secretary-General. Hardback £14.95/US $20

Fiction

KING OF THE CARNIVAL AND OTHER STORIES. By Willi Chen. A unique collection of short stories from the Caribbean, capturing the violence, trickery, pathos and racial comedy of Trinidadian society. Paperback £5.95/US $9

THE OPEN PRISON. A novel by Angus Richmond. The story of Angela, a sensitive and disturbed child, growing up on the estate of her white guardian in British Guiana, is slowly and painfully awakened to a society in turmoil, in which both black and white are struggling to reassert their roles during the First World War. Paperback £4.95/US $7.50

Critique

THE WEB OF TRADITION: USES OF ALLUSION IN V.S. NAIPAUL'S FICTION. By Dr John Thieme. An exciting study of one of the Caribbean's major and most controversial novelists, V.S. Naipaul, who has won several of the world's literary prizes including the Booker Prize. Paperback £6.95/US $10

Music

THE REGGAE FILES. By Gordon C. A collection of interviews with reggae superstars from Jamaica and Britain who speak about the influence of Jamaican politics, Rastafarian ideas and the black British experience on the creation of their music. Paperback £6.95/US $10

General

THE BOOK OF COMMON SENSE. Compiled by Neil Prendergast. A collection of proverbs and quotations, old and new, bringing to the reader sections on humour, wisdom, life, love marriage, etc. and drawing on the writings of 'many wise people'. Paperback 6.95/US $10

ENQUIRIES:

UNITED KINGDOM
Hansib Publishing Limited, Third Floor, Tower House, 141-149 Fonthill Road, London N4 3HF. Tel: 071-281 1191, Fax: 071-263 9656.

CARIBBEAN
Hansib Publishing (Caribbean) Limited, P O Box 2773, St John's, Antigua, Westindies.

UNITED STATES
Hansib Publishing (USA), 17498 Tuscan Avenue, Granada Hills, California CA 91344.

CANADA
Hansib Publishing (Canada), 22 Gaslight Crescent, Scarborough, Ontario M1C 3S8.